The Oxford Book of
FRENCH-CANADIAN
SHORT STORIES

The Oxford Book of
FRENCH-CANADIAN
SHORT STORIES

Introduced by
MARIE-CLAIRE BLAIS

Edited by
RICHARD TELEKY

Toronto Oxford New York
OXFORD UNIVERSITY PRESS
1983

Canadian Cataloguing in Publication Data
Main entry under title:
The Oxford book of French-Canadian short stories

ISBN 0-19-540298-7

1. Short stories, Canadian (French) — Translations into English. *
2. Short stories, English — Translations from French. I. Teleky, Richard

PS8321.093   1983   C843'.01'08   C83-098961-7
PR9197.32.093   1983

THE PUBLISHER IS GRATEFUL TO
MISS ISABEL McLAUGHLIN
FOR HER GENEROUS SUPPORT OF THIS PROJECT

OXFORD is a trademark of Oxford University Press
Introduction © Marie-Claire Blais 1983
Selection © Oxford University Press Canada 1983
1 2 3 4 — 6 5 4 3
Printed in Canada by
John Deyell Company

Contents

Acknowledgements

HUBERT AQUIN. 'Back on April Eleventh' appeared originally as 'De retour, le 11 avril' in *Points de fuite* (1971). Reprinted by permission of Andrée Yanacopaulo. GÉRARD BESSETTE. 'The Mustard Plaster'. Reprinted by permission of Gérard Bessette. MARIE-CLAIRE BLAIS. 'An Act of Pity' appeared originally as 'Un acte de pitié'. Printed in translation by permission of Marie-Claire Blais and Louise Myette, Literary Agent. ROCH CARRIER. 'What Language Do Bears Speak?' by Roch Carrier, from *The Hockey Sweater and Other Stories*, translated by Sheila Fischman (Toronto: House of Anansi Press, 1979). Reprinted by permission. LOUIS DANTIN. 'You're Coughing?' appeared originally as 'Tu tousses?' in *La Vie en rêve* (1930). JACQUES FERRON. 'Mélie and the Bull' by Jacques Ferron, from *Tales from the Uncertain Country*, translated by Betty Bednarski (Toronto: House of Anansi Press, 1972). Reprinted by permission. ALAIN GRANDBOIS. 'May Blossom' appeared originally as 'Fleur-de-mai' in *Avant le chaos* (1964). Printed in translation by permission of Éditions Hurtubise HMH Ltée. ANNE HÉBERT. 'The Torrent' from *The Torrent* (Montreal, 1973) translated by Gwendolyn Moore. Reprinted by permission of Harvest House Ltd. CLAUDE JASMIN. 'Lulu the Tailor' appeared originally as 'Lulu le tailleur' in *Les Coeurs empaillés* (Éditions Parti-Pris, 1967). NAIM KATTAN. 'The Neighbour' from *The Neighbour and Other Stories* by Naim Kattan, used by permission of The Canadian Publishers, McClelland and Stewart Limited, Toronto. ALBERT LABERGE. 'The Patient' appeared originally as 'La Malade' in *Visages de la vie et de la mort* (1936). Printed in translation by permission of Pierre Laberge. PAMPHILE LEMAY. 'Blood and Gold' from *French Canadian Prose Masters: The Nineteenth Century* (Montreal, 1978) edited by Yves Brunelle. Reprinted by permission of Harvest House Ltd. ROGER LEMELIN. 'The Stations of the Cross' reprinted by permission of Roger Lemelin, Mary Finch, and Sybil Hutchison, Literary Agent. LOUISE MAHEUX-FORCIER. 'The Carnation' appeared originally as 'L'Oeillet' in *En toutes lettres* (1980). Printed in translation by permission of Éditions Pierre Tisseyre. ANTONINE MAILLET. 'Two Saints' appeared originally as 'Les Sargaillounes' in *Par derrière chez mon père* (Éditions Leméac Inc., 1972). CLAIRE MARTIN. 'The Gift' appeared originally as 'Le Talent' in *Avec ou sans amour* (1969). Printed in translation by permission of Éditions Pierre Tisseyre. RINGUET. 'The Heritage' from *The Tamarack Review* (1958). GABRIELLE ROY. 'Ely! Ely! Ely!' © Gabrielle Roy. First published in French in *Liberté* (Montreal, no. 123, mai-juin 1979); translated into English by M.G. Hesse and published in *Canadian Fiction Magazine* (Toronto, no. 34/35, 1980). Reprinted by permission of François Ricard, Literary Agent. YVES THÉRIAULT. 'The Whale' appeared originally as 'La Baleine' in *La Femme Anna et autre contes* (1981) by Yves Thériault. Reprinted in translation by permission of VLB Éditeur Inc., Montreal. MICHEL TREMBLAY. 'The Devil and the Mushroom' from *Stories for Late Night Drinkers* (Intermedia Press Limited, 1977), translated by Michael Bullock. Published originally in French by Éditions du Jour. Reprinted by permission of Intermedia Press Limited and John C. Goodwin et Associés for Michel Tremblay.

Introduction

Reading the earliest storytellers in this volume, we may be surprised to discover how wide the gap has become between their preoccupations and those of today's writers. They take us back to our past, yet any nostalgia we may feel for their unparalleled vitality of language is not unmixed with irritation as we remember the outrageous censorship they had to submit to, and the narrowness that was a product of their social and cultural milieu. We can sense how religion and duty subdued the thought of Philippe Aubert de Gaspé in 'Rose Latulipe', a tale of Shrove-Tuesday festivities among family and friends that is blighted by the appearance of the devil who, embodying sensuality and corruption, casts a shadow over the scene of innocent folly. A similar obsession with good and evil dominates 'Blood and Gold', Pamphile LeMay's horror story about greed, which accurately depicts human foibles. Louis Fréchette ('Tom Cariboo') romps through this clerical darkness with rebellious enthusiasm and an ironic style, poking fun at moralizing. Lively and cheerful, he uses wonderfully lyrical language, and celebrates the pleasures of the land with imagery sometimes bordering on the Rabelaisian.

With Louis Dantin ('You're Coughing?') and Albert Laberge ('The Patient'), we enter a more refined and literary world, one already influenced by both the French novelists of the period and middle-class gentility. In 'You're Coughing?', the young narrator has a chance encounter with an

Armenian immigrant girl ('As for her station in life, I guessed that she was from the working-classes, though of a fine stock well above the ordinary'), and his decision not to pursue the acquaintance, for fear of being disappointed, contains an element of racial intolerance. Dantin, Laberge, and Ringuet ('The Heritage') like to portray scenes of country life, examining its harshness in language that often sparkles. For these writers the battle against hardship is a long heroic story. Painful episodes such as the killing of an old dog, or a drought that sweeps over the countryside, are powerfully evoked. 'And now a long dry spell came down on the earth. The sky was constant and cruel in its splendour. Every evening a giant sun crashed down upon a horizon in flames that foretold another killing day to follow'—this passage by Ringuet brings to mind Faulkner's spellbinding dried-out landscapes, the torpor of men and beasts under a scorching summer sun.

The great poet Alain Grandbois breaks free of this stagnant atmosphere by exploring the rest of the world—Europe, Africa, India, China are the settings for his poetic interior probings. 'May Blossom', a moving portrait of a young Chinese girl (a portrait that would be purer still without the author's dream of her conversion to Christianity) is one of his charming glimpses into exoticism, recalling Conrad's islanders and mysterious sea voyages: 'The captain and I were stretched out on the upper deck. The evening was drenched in sublime sweetness. A russet moon, ringed with northern lights, swayed lazily in the rigging. Every so often a large junk crossed over our bows, her sail like the underside of a giant bat's wing, and we could see naked men gathered round a fire on the after-deck, still and glistening as if cast in bronze.' The whole world is out there; the route map available to those who can read and write. Burning with curiosity, many French-Canadian writers are keen to travel across their own vast country, offering us universal understanding, as Gabrielle Roy does in 'Ely! Ely! Ely!': 'How happy I was, going ahead, as receptive to the unknown of our country as to the whole future that was still possible for the world.' This is a lovely analytic story blown through with a wind from the wide-open spaces and the invitation—typical of her work—to serene contemplation.

Although the stories of Claire Martin, Louise Maheux-Forcier, and Antonine Maillet represent all too briefly their well-known major works, 'The Gift', 'The Carnation', and 'Two Saints' still show us the craft and discipline of these authors, whose books—free of the modesty that can be disastrous for a writer—are so fierce and daring. Let us especially remember the courage of Claire Martin, forerunner of many others, who in 1962 published *Dans un gant de fer*, in which she overcame the prejudices of our trade (so often, as in other areas, a trade for men alone), bursting forth with a flash of violence and a cry of independence. In 'The Carnation' Louise Maheux-Forcier associates the fragility of a flower—enjoyed one evening by a woman who has few illusions left—with the end of life. The sensitivity of the writing in this story, the rapture over a simple flower, do they not remind us of that moment in Katherine Mansfield's 'The Garden-party' when a young soul, filled with the intensity of life, suddenly opens onto the realization that to-morrow the flower, the garden, and the festive sounds will be no more?

Yves Thériault and Roger Lemelin are the most vigorous of writers—wise men who enjoy satirizing the faults and vices of their people. They openly attack the poor, the middle-class, artists, all walks of life, and nothing fazes them. Reliable observers of their time, they have been prophets and silent educators for generations of writers and poets. They have a passion for the whole complex of feelings that makes us human (Thériault, for example, encompasses a wealth of ethnic experience in his work, as Gabrielle Roy has done, with her characters from all corners of the world), and that passion becomes our own, awakening and also disquieting us. The zest of Jacques Ferron ('Mélie and the Bull') shows a pleasing kinship to that of Louis Fréchette—both take pride in enriching their writing with new words and expressions, serious or playful, as they see fit. Roch Carrier and Claude Jasmin also observe the rites of language. Tending to deal with solitary destinies (a child in 'What Language Do Bears Speak?', a homosexual in 'Lulu the Tailor'), they are interested in the linguistic and sexual differences that create such awful gaps between people—though one may regret the shadow of reticence, nationalist or moral, that silently intrudes on the objectivity of these stories. One must read *La Guerre, Yes Sir!* by Roch Carrier, and the recent and varied works of Claude Jasmin, in order to understand these writers in all their true complexity and exuberance. Unfortunately it is with sorrow that we read 'Back on April Eleventh' by Hubert Aquin, aware that we have lost a great witness to our way of life, a visionary and a rebel whose life was consumed by the writer's passion he analysed so well. The death that broke off his Dostoievskian dialogue was a grave loss to our literature.

Naim Kattan and Gérard Bessette seem to me to be the most intimate writers in this volume, unafraid to probe, gently or harshly, into the most personal aspects of life, challenging our indifference, exposing our racism. The exile among us, even in our families, is an important theme to Bessette; the exile is like an indictment in the work of Kattan, but is lifted by a song of joy, for Kattan, like Bessette, glorifies the spirit of the man of the future, whether improved, transformed, or simply capable of change. 'The Torrent', by Anne Hébert, amazes us by its youthfulness and the strength of its passion. We recognize the writing of a poet and feel the flow of a torrent that is sustained right up to *Les Cormorans,* a violent outburst reminiscent of works written thirty years earlier, as are the characters in their refusal to submit (the child to its mother in the story, a seminarian to his God in the novel), preferring the calm of infinite solitude: 'I am leaning out as far as possible. I want to see down into the gulf, as far down as I can. I want to lose myself in my own adventure. My sole and fearful wealth.' In these lines the breath of a great poet transports us (as in Virginia Woolf's *The Waves*, which also contains a torrent) with writing that whirls towards the edge of death.

The last writer in this collection, Michel Tremblay, is familiar to English-speaking readers as a dramatist, poet, and novelist. His work seems to reflect all the diversity of our authors: the urge towards self-expression that we see in 'The Torrent'; the desire of our earlier writers to understand their people; and the anguish of contemporary artists in the face of atomic terror. In 'The Devil and the Mushroom', where we see the mushroom on the wall, as yet only a shadow that vaguely disturbs all who notice it, we understand our authors' passion to write and to be read. The more peaceful times that once greeted writers no longer exist, and Tremblay's pacifist tale has a special resonance for us today, signalling that writers, here and abroad, are working in a state of anxiety shared by all. From now on, they cannot rest.

It is only just to end this introduction by mentioning some fine writers, not included in this book, who still await a wider audience in English Canada: Victor-Lévy Beaulieu, Dominique Blondeau, Monique Bosco, Nicole Brossard, Marcel Dubé, Réjean Ducharme, Madeleine Gagnon, André Langevin, Michèle Mailhot, André Major, Jovette Marchessault, and Hélène Ouvrard. Perhaps this anthology will help to create that audience.

Montreal, May 1983   MARIE-CLAIRE BLAIS

Editor's Preface

Presenting translations of some of the finest short stories to appear in French Canada since the early nineteenth century, this anthology includes stories from Québec, Acadia, francophone Ottawa, and the Prairies. All but one are formal short stories: chapters from novels have been excluded. This has meant that several prominent contemporary fiction writers —Réjean Ducharme and Nicole Brossard, to mention only two—do not appear.

French Canada's best short stories have both reflected the major trends of Québécois fiction in general and extended its subject matter and stylistic range. The first writers seized upon familiar legends, escaping imaginatively into folk-tale fantasy. Although this is not the place for detailed literary history, it is important to recall that until the 1920s Québécois writers had to struggle with the distrust of fiction that plagued their society. Many French classics were listed on the Index of Forbidden Books and not available in Québec; but some writers were still able to gain access to them, and to read the pioneering short stories of Flaubert and de Maupassant. (Albert Laberge, who wrote Canada's first realistic novel, *La Scouine,* 1918, and is represented here by 'The Patient', was expelled from his college in Montreal after he confessed to the 'sin' of reading the French naturalists.) This situation resulted in a body of writing that would be approved and read: moralistic fiction idealizing the rural past and present.

With a gradual loosening of the authority of the Church, writers began to treat subjects they had previously avoided, daring to criticize their society. Then the political edge of literature—critical and potentially subversive of any status quo—made itself keenly felt in Québec, where, as Jacques Ferron has written, 'le pays sans nos contes retourne à la confusion.'

This anthology begins with one devil and ends with another. Our opening story, 'Rose Latulipe', originally appeared in chapter five of the novel *L'Influence d'un livre* (1837) by Aubert de Gaspé the younger. Early as it is, this self-contained tale displays most of the elements commonly associated with Québécois writing—religious concerns, gothicism, a surreal atmosphere—and a crisp narrative that reminds us of the oral tradition, and its clever plot devices, at the source of all story-telling. Between Aubert de Gaspé's devil, and the very modern one of Michel Tremblay, are some classic stories of French Canada. No representative anthology would be complete without Ringuet's 'The Heritage', Anne Hébert's 'The Torrent', Roger Lemelin's 'The Stations of the Cross', and Hubert Aquin's 'Back on April Eleventh'. There are also stories of religious torment and doubt (sometimes considered, especially outside Québec, to be the dominant mode of Québécois writing), such as Marie-Claire Blais's 'An Act of Pity'. The humour of the oral tradition is central to Louis Fréchette's model campfire yarn, 'Tom Cariboo', written at the turn of the century, and also informs Jacques Ferron's contemporary 'Mélie and the Bull', where one almost expects the calf to settle down for a chat with his mistress, like the talking beasts in old fables. There are some surprises here in the work of less-familiar writers: Louis Dantin's 'You're Coughing?', an ironic yet tender account of romantic self-deception; Albert Laberge's acidic story 'The Patient', with its wicked but wise final line; 'May Blossom' by Alain Grandbois, whose world-weary elegance is an unusual strain in French-Canadian fiction; and Louise Maheux-Forcier's 'The Carnation', a brilliant piece of legerdemain.

In compiling this anthology I have kept in mind that the stories will not be read in their original language but as re-creations by translators, whose work is another art in itself. French-Canadian writers have found many able translators, and this volume contains some of the most prominent: Betty Bednarski, Alan Brown, Michael Bullock, Sheila Fischman, and Philip Stratford. Many other fine translators—Yves Brunelle, Mary Finch, M.G. Hesse, Sally Livingston, Judith Madley, Gwendolyn Moore, Anthony Robinow, Patricia Sillers, and Morna Scott Stoddard—are also represented. Twelve of the twenty-two stories appear in existing translations, including Louis Fréchette's own translation of his story 'Tom Cariboo'. However, eight have been translated for the first time ('You're Coughing?', 'The Patient', 'May Blossom', 'The Gift', 'The Whale', 'Two Saints', 'Lulu the Tailor', and 'An Act of Pity'), and two others are offered in new translations ('Rose Latulipe' and 'The Carnation').

Toronto, May 1983   RICHARD TELEKY

The Oxford Book of
FRENCH-CANADIAN
SHORT STORIES

PHILIPPE AUBERT DE GASPÉ

Rose Latulipe

There once was a man named Latulipe who had a daughter he doted on. And a pretty girl she was, the dark-haired Rose Latulipe, though a bit wayward, not to say reckless. She had a sweetheart named Gabriel Lepard who was the apple of her eye; yet they say that she could be fickle when somebody else came along.

She loved parties, so one Shrove Tuesday more than fifty people had come to the Latulipes'. Contrary to her usual custom, the coquettish Rose had kept faithful company with her suitor all evening long. Naturally enough: they were to be married at Easter. It must have been about eleven o'clock when all of a sudden, in the midst of a cotillion, a carriage was heard stopping outside the door. Several people ran to the windows, but the weather was so bad they had to bang on the frames to knock the snow off before they could see the new arrival.

'Must be someone important, eh Jean?' exclaimed one. 'Look at that black horse—his eyes are blazing! Devil take me if he doesn't jump the roof.' As this discussion was going on, the gentleman entered the house and asked the master's permission to rest there for a while.

'We would be honoured,' Latulipe said. 'Please, take off your things and we'll unharness your horse.' The stranger firmly declined on the grounds that he was in a hurry and would only stay for half an hour. But he did take off his

1

splendid raccoon coat, to reveal a black velvet costume trimmed all over with braid. He kept his gloves in his hand and asked permission to keep his hat on as well, complaining that he had a headache.

'Monsieur will take a shot of brandy?' asked Latulipe, handing him a glass. As he swallowed, the stranger made a diabolical face (a wicked one, at any rate), for Latulipe, being short of bottles, had emptied the holy water out of the one he was holding and refilled it with spirits. He was handsome, this stranger, but very dark, with something shifty about his eyes. Going over to Rose, he took her hands and said: 'I hope you will be mine this evening, pretty maid, and that we will always dance together.'

'Yes, of course,' said Rose, speaking softly and casting a timid glance at poor Lepard, who bit his lip so hard it began to bleed.

The stranger stayed by Rose for the rest of the evening, and poor Gabriel was left to scowl in the corner, playing an unhappy second fiddle.

In a little room that looked out on the dancers, a saintly old woman sat on a chest at the end of a bed, praying fervently; in one hand she held a rosary, while with the other she beat her breast. Suddenly she stopped and signalled to Rose that she wanted to speak to her.

'Listen, my girl,' she said. 'It isn't right for you to leave Gabriel, your own fiancé, for that gentleman. And there is something else wrong here; every time I say the holy names of Jesus and Mary, he throws me a furious glare. Did you see how he looked at us just now? His eyes were blazing with anger.'

'Go on, auntie,' said Rose. 'Tell your beads and let worldly people enjoy themselves.'

'What was that old dotard saying to you?' asked the stranger.

'Pooh!' said Rose, 'you know how old people are always preaching to the young.'

Midnight struck and the master of the house wanted to stop the dancing, observing that it was hardly proper to dance on Ash Wednesday.

'One more dance,' said the stranger.

'Oh yes, please, Papa!' said Rose; and the dance went on.

'Pretty Rose,' said the stranger, 'you promised me you would be mine all night; why shouldn't you be mine forever?'

'You mustn't say such things, sir. It's not right for you to make fun of a poor farmer's daughter,' replied Rose.

'I swear to you,' said the stranger, 'nothing could be more serious than what I am proposing. Only say yes, and nothing can ever part us.'

'But sir . . .' and she glanced at poor Lepard.

'I understand,' said the stranger with disdain. 'You love this Gabriel fellow? In that case let us discuss it no further.'

'Oh, yes! I love him . . . I loved him . . . but oh! fine gentlemen like you always flatter girls so, I can't trust what you say.'

'What!' exclaimed the stranger. 'You believe me capable of deceiving you, pretty Rose? I swear by all I hold most sacred . . . by . . .'

'Oh no, don't swear; I believe you,' the poor girl said. 'But what if my father will not consent?'

'Your father!' said the stranger with a sarcastic smile. 'Say you are mine, and I will take care of the rest.'

'Well, then . . . yes,' she answered.

'Give me your hand,' he said, 'to seal your promise.'

No sooner had the ill-starred Rose given him her hand than she pulled it back with a little cry of pain, for she had felt a sting. Turning pale as death, she feigned a sudden illness and left the dance.

At that moment two young horse-dealers entered, looking frightened, and drew Latulipe aside:

'We've just been outside looking at that gentleman's horse, and you wouldn't believe it—all the snow around him has melted and he's standing on the bare ground.'

Latulipe confirmed their report for himself and was all the more horrified, for having noticed his daughter's sudden pallor a few moments before, he had gotten her to half-confess what had happened between her and the stranger. Dismay spread quickly through the crowd; the guests began whispering, and only Latulipe's entreaties prevented them from leaving.

Apparently indifferent to what was going on around him, the stranger continued courting Rose. Presenting her with a magnificent necklace of gold and pearls, he laughed and said: 'Take off your glass necklace, pretty Rose, and put on this one of pearls, for my sake.' But hanging from the glass necklace was a little cross, and the girl refused to take it off.

Meanwhile, at the parish rectory, another scene was taking place. Since nine o'clock in the evening the aged curé had been on his knees praying to God, begging Him to pardon the sins his parishioners were committing as they spent the night of Shrove Tuesday in dissipation. Still praying fervently, the saintly old man had fallen asleep, and had been deep in slumber for an hour when suddenly he awoke and ran to his servant, crying: 'Ambroise! My good Ambroise! Get up and harness my mare! Quickly, in God's name, hurry! I'll give you a month's wages, two months', six!'

'What is it, sir?' cried Ambroise, who knew the charitable curé's zeal. 'Is someone in danger of dying?'

'Dying!' answered the curé. 'Far worse, my dear Ambroise! A soul is in danger of losing its eternal salvation. Hurry, quickly, harness up!'

Five minutes later the curé was on the road to Latulipe's, travelling with incredible speed in spite of the dreadful weather, for Saint Rose was clearing the path.

The curé arrived just in time. The stranger had broken the string of the necklace and was just about to seize poor Rose when, quick as lightning, the curé forestalled him by placing his stole around her neck. Clasping her to his breast, where that morning he had received his God, he thundered: 'Wretch! What are you doing here among Christian folk?'

All present had fallen to their knees at this terrible spectacle, weeping to see their venerable pastor, who had always seemed so timid and frail, now strong and courageous, face to face with the enemy of God and men.

Rolling his bloodshot eyes, Lucifer replied: 'I do not recognize as Christians those who, in contempt of your religion, dance, drink, and revel away the days your cursed precepts have devoted to penitence. Besides, this young woman has given herself to me. The blood that flowed from her hand is the seal that binds her to me forever.'

'Satan, begone!' cried the curé, striking him in the face with his stole and pronouncing in Latin words no one else could understand. At once the devil vanished with a frightful noise, leaving behind a smell of sulphur that nearly suffocated the company.

With the hapless Rose, who had fainted, still in his arms, the good curé fell to his knees in an ardent prayer to which all responded with renewed sighs and lamentations.

'Where is he?' the poor girl cried when she regained her senses. The answer came from all sides: 'He has disappeared.'

'O father! Father, don't leave me!' cried Rose, falling at the good pastor's feet. 'Take me with you! Only you can protect me . . . I gave myself to him . . . I'm afraid he'll come back . . . A convent! A convent!'

'Poor lamb, you were lost, and now you repent,' answered the reverend pastor. 'Come with me. I will watch over you and surround you with holy relics, and if your vocation is sincere, as I have no doubt it is after this terrible trial, you will renounce this world that has been so baneful to you.'

Five years after these events, the bell of the Convent of * * * was ringing, as it had been for two days, announcing that a nun only three years in her calling had gone to meet her heavenly bridegroom. Early in the morning, a crowd of curious spectators had gathered in the church to attend her funeral. While all the rest watched with the idle frivolity of worldly people, three were broken-hearted: an aged priest who knelt in the sanctuary, praying fervently; an old man in the nave who was sobbing, bemoaning the death of his only daughter; and a young man dressed in mourning, there to say his last farewell to the one who had been his betrothed: the unfortunate Rose Latulipe.

Translated by Sally Livingston

PAMPHILE LEMAY

Blood and Gold

One night I was telling the story of the haunted house to some neighbours: *bonhomme* Chénard, old man Blais, old man Letellier, *père* Ducap, and others. They found it entertaining, but they seemed to suspect my veracity as a historian somewhat, and took turns throwing gibes at me that made everybody laugh. This needled me, but I would not let them see that it did. I can dissemble like a politician.

However, *père* Ducap suddenly became very pensive. He seemed not to be hearing anything any more. When I finished, he got up, and slowly, with a deep voice vibrating with emotion, he said: 'I know what happened in that house on the mill road. I know what spectre haunts it and what crime brought upon it God's curse.'

He stopped for a moment. We were all very surprised, because he had never mentioned these things before. Usually one hastens to say what one knows. There are even some who talk about things they don't know anything about. He must have had a good reason to hold his tongue.

'I did not believe,' he went on, 'either in the fantastic owl or in the expansive ghost of that hovel. The laughs and groans of the dead have never prevented me from sleeping. But if what has just been told is true, then I can only assent.'

'I swear it's true,' I asserted coolly.

He seemed to ponder a while longer, then he added:

'It's always hard to speak ill of others, particularly of your own family.'

'What's this?' several said, astonished, 'you're making fun of us. You're not of the cursed man's family!'

'Yes, I'm of that cursed man's family, only by marriage. But that's still too close,' he admitted.

Then, as if strengthened by this avowal, he went on:

'Well, it's not my fault, it's fate. The chaff mixes in with the grain, thistles grow among flowers. When it comes down to a matter of soul and conscience, virtue and vice, God does the sorting, and He does it well.'

We asked him to tell us more . . . to tell all. We are men of honour and we can keep a secret when we must.

'Not tonight. Tomorrow,' he answered. 'I have to collect my thoughts. Right now several things are confused in my memory; then too, I'm not sure it's right to awaken bad memories and to relate the lives of those who did not fear God.'

The next day, right after supper, we were all seated in our armchairs, some in the shadows, others within the pale circle of light near the table where a glass lamp burned palely. We were talking about spectres, phantoms and ghosts, while awaiting the old neighbour who was going to tell us about the inhabitants of the haunted house. He was late. Perhaps he had decided not to talk any more. His secret would die with him. The stove roared with a fire of red spruce.

Then we heard the snow crunching under heavy feet at the door. It was he, the old man. He came in and we exchanged the usual greetings. He hung his cap and his grey-cloth overcoat on the iron hook, he warmed his chilly hands at the stove, and sat near the table in the light. As we wanted not to lose a single expression on the old man's earnest face, we were very attentive. A Latinist would say:

> *Conticuere omnes, intentique ora tenebant;*
> *Inde toro pater Aeneas sic orsus ab alto.*

You remember the first lines of the second book of the *Aeneid*?

But there was no hapless queen among us, swooning with love; there were only good housewives of the neighbourhood, well shielded from the storms of the heart by the care of children, prayers and the seventy-five years of the new Aeneas.

Père Ducap coughed three times, leaned back in his chair, and spoke:

'The cursed man was my uncle!'

'Your uncle?' we all exclaimed, shocked.

My father and he married sisters, two fairly pretty and comely young ladies, it was said, but of very different temperament. My mother was pleasant and kind, the other, hard and miserly. One is always cruel when one loves money.

The two weddings took place the same morning in the church of Sainte-Anne-de-Beaupré. My mother's family came from Sainte-Anne. My father was from Île d'Orléans, Sorcerers' Island, as they used to call it.

My uncle Michel Babylas had no relatives around here. He said he came from overseas. He even claimed to be directly descended from the High Priest Hanan, who mocked Jesus. He was jesting, of course; he could not show his papers. But what he could have done, though, was to crucify the sweet Saviour of the world.

He was short, dark-skinned, very lively, and a great talker. He was a pedlar, and he rambled through our parishes, his shoddy goods on his back. It was on one of those business trips that he met Miss Lucie Dupincourt, my mother's sister.

The young lady was proud to be noticed, and responded to the stranger's attentions. She was a foolhardy girl who declined the friendship of a good farm boy, her neighbour, under the pretext that he lacked elegance and could not express himself with ease.

The Babylas couple had only one son. To everybody else he was a child like any other, but to them he was a prodigy.

They found him beautiful, well made, crackling with wit, certainly too smart to live long in our poor world, as if only fools could live to have white hair. Yet, it is true that he died young, but not from too much intelligence.

He had his share of it, which he probably wasted on foolish things, as many others do. Still, he did not appear to be given to dissipation, and he seemed naturally good. A wholesome fruit on an already sick tree. But he too was to be worm-eaten, as the family tree, by the worm of ambition. He wanted to be talked about, and for that he needed money. According to the world, money is the beginning of wisdom and the pedestal for all the grandeurs of a day.

Then as now in our countryside you needed to work a long time to fill a purse with silver coins. He got tired of waiting. He kissed his mother, shook hands with his father, and went off. The mother shed a tear and the father smiled.

'Don't forget us,' she said, 'and come back soon.'

'Go and make money,' the father enjoined him. 'Money is a powerful lever that pries all wills open, a magical oil that lubricates all gears, an irrefutable argument, a veil that hides flaws, a lens that magnifies virtues. Poor, you are nothing; poorer, you become contemptible; very poor, you are a blockhead. Rich, you get consideration and respect; richer, you have all the wit and talent you can buy; very rich, you possess all the genius a human mind can muster . . . and you can swoon sniffing the incense of flattery.

'All the foolish and starving writers will put their servile pens at your service, and all the rhymesters in search of a theme will sing your glory. And the more you pay for publicity, the more publicity will add feathers to your cap. Go!'

And he was on the road that leads everywhere.

At nightfall, Babylas and his wife would sit by the fireplace and pensively look at the cat-like undulation of the flame that consumed the resinous vine-shoots, and they seemed to take pleasure in the mournful solitude of their home. They would speak in monosyllables, either through laziness of mind or whim of voice. They understood each other or scorned each other.

Taking long puffs, he smoked a pungent tobacco; chin drooping on her large bosom, she made her knitting-needles fly. Then, in their egoism, they jealously looked into the fire, and stretched their chilly limbs toward it.

There was sadness in the depths of their souls. There was also envy, because they were annoyed at other people's happiness; they never said anything good about anybody, and they never thought of doing charitable deeds.

There was even hatred. They would have liked to see poverty assail their neighbours' door and misfortunes poison their existence.

Sometimes, however, bitterness melted away suddenly and they smiled. They would speak of wealth, outline seductive plans, and promise themselves a rich old age.

They were not liked in the parish. Babylas flaunted his contempt for all that was respected. He never went to church. He said that the confessional is an obstruction where a man's freedom is wrecked and a woman's love is shattered; that priests ply an easy and lucrative trade; that superstition is in full swing in our country; that there is only one sensible religion, the belief in a waggish God who laughs at our fancies . . . In short, a heap of nonsense, which no one even bothered refuting. People shrugged their shoulders and turned away. . . .

The little pedlar became isolated. Friends and neighbours even stopped visiting him, because of his nasty behaviour. He was a blackguard. His wife allowed herself to be corrupted. She had loved him at first. When it is pure, love gives strength and courage; when it is evil, it inspires singular cowardice and extreme cruelty.

She saw her first suitor again, the one whom she had refused to marry out of foolish vanity. He was married and seemed happy. She used all the wiles that restless flesh can inspire—memories shrewdly recalled, conversations carried on too long, sighs hardly stifled, looks full of fire—and he was won over.

Babylas discovered the affair, which outraged him. And, one morning, his rival was found dead by the side of the road. No one had witnessed the crime, but everybody knew who the guilty party was.

Life became unbearable for the notorious couple, so the adulterous wife and the murderous husband moved.

It was at that time that a stone house was built in the woods near the mill, at Lotbinière. You are familiar with its remains, but not with its history.

In those days there were neither ships nor railroads, and travellers were taken from one town to another by carriage, on rocky or rutted roads.

Then as now the straightest road is the shortest, and the shortest is the most advantageous: it affords economy of time, of horses, and of money. So, from Saint-Croix to Gentilly, the straight line cuts off superb headlands, which jut out in the Saint Lawrence like a fringe of rocks and capes, crowned with woods and flourishing villages: Platon, Lotbinière and Sainte-Emmélie, Cap Charles, Cap-à-la-Roche and Saint-Jean des-Chaillons, Cap Levrard and Saint-Pierre-les-Bacquets. Usually travellers followed a straight line that went through the woods near the mill, in the second line of Lotbinière.

In the wilderness, on the edge of a beautiful river, the spot was not inappropriate for an inn, and men and beasts gladly rested there.

Babylas' inn was well patronized. One could sleep there peacefully in the scented air of the forest; eat plentifully of partridge and rabbit served with sauces Brillat-Savarin never even dreamed of, and drink good old Jamaica rum, which often stirred up our fathers' spirits. However, from time to time, strange rumours spread about the place, and its reputation declined. Travellers no longer dared sleep there. Going by, some might stop, have a drink, eat a bite, but then they would hasten to move on.

But Babylas was rich. He had run his business with success for ten years. Never bothered by scruples, he had not been particular about his choice of means. Few expenses, no Sunday clothes, no horse, a cow which fed on the forest plants and roadside grass, hens, small game, venison, there was actually no need for depredation to make his pile. His savings could have snow-balled.

One day news got around that he had been robbed. No one felt sorry for him. He could never understand how anyone could have found his well-hidden money. Had he been betrayed? Only his wife knew of the hiding-place, and she too seemed grieved. Sometimes very strange things go on in the heart of a woman who has once gone astray.

However, not all his hard-earned dollars had disappeared. He had split them into two bundles, and had buried them in different places. He never put all his eggs in one basket. He became irritable and saturnine. He started to watch his wife carefully. Since she occasionally went to the mill to buy flour, he went too.

One evening in October he went to chat with the miller. There was not a star in the sky and the river ran dark on its rocky bed between the high banks.

The mill-stones were turning with a monotonous rumble, grinding the wheat made golden by the light of a lamp. White flour dust was rising to the darkened ceiling. The whole room seemed filled with a very light fog which left no dampness anywhere, but which covered everything as if with a thin layer of flower pollen. In the darkness that shrouded the road and the mill, the sky and the shoreline,

there could be heard the endless clamour of the river flowing over the dam.

Suddenly the iron-shod hooves of a horse rang out on the
little bridge. A vehicle was going by. The miller said:

'They're travellers, because those who are on their way
to get the priest or the doctor always greet me as they go by.
If they don't come in, they call and I go out.'

'Well, then, good-night. I'm going home,' Babylas said.
'The cat must be near the hole when the mouse comes out!'
And he went out.

'It's hellishly dark,' he grumbled.

'A good night for a crime,' the miller replied, laughing.

Babylas could hear the rattle of the carriage a short distance away, and he hurried, knowing the road well. When
he got near the hill, he heard a rough voice yelling:

'Where's that damn inn road? It's so dark everywhere.'

He started to run, yelling in turn:

'Wait, gentlemen, I'll take you there.'

The carriage stopped. Babylas took the horse's bridle and
led it to the door of his house.

'I'm bringing you a traveller, Monsieur Babylas,' the coachman said as he stepped down.

'Thanks a lot, Monsieur Spenard, and come often.'

'Not on nights like this . . . But this gentleman was in a
hurry, so I had to come along. I'm glad he is here safe and
sound, but I'm going back.'

Babylas took his guest in and gave him the best room.
Then he went out again looking for Spenard who was already getting into his carriage.

'Does he come from far away?' he asked.

'I don't think so,' the coachman answered; 'he doesn't
have much luggage.'

'Is he a salesman?'

'I have no idea. Maybe he is an angler . . . He doesn't
talk much.'

'He told you where he's going, at least?'

'He doesn't know . . . He seems to be looking for something . . . He only inquired about the price and quality of the farms around here. He also asked if there was some pretty little house for sale in our village. There isn't any. If he wants to go on further, as is likely, you'll find him a carriage, won't you? A good one because he doesn't like to be tossed about like a parcel . . . I can't take him any further because I have to drive Monsieur Baby to Trois-Rivières tomorrow morning. Good-night!'

He plunged into the gloom.

The traveller, a young man about twenty-five years old, dropped into a sofa, and head in hands, seemed absorbed in serious thought.

He had a rough manner. Weariness, perhaps, or vexation, or disappointment; one couldn't tell. Yet he was not unhandsome, with his frizzy hair, his piercing eyes, his weather-beaten cheeks, his thick moustache.

Madame Babylas came in. He gave a start and got up to greet her. She asked him if he wanted a cup of tea; it would take only a minute to boil the water. He declined, pleading fatigue and the need to sleep.

She led him to a clean, white-washed room behind the drawing-room. She was leaving, but he called her back, to entrust a round and very heavy leather pouch to her.

'Take good care of this,' he enjoined her, 'it's my whole fortune.'

The woman's eyes sparkled and she smiled oddly.

'Good care, yes,' she replied. 'You can sleep soundly.'

When she went into the kitchen, Babylas was waiting for her by the table. He took the pouch and felt its weight.

'What could be in there,' he said, 'it's so heavy?'

Then he added sarcastically:

'Is the gentleman a lead salesman?'

Madame Babylas answered that it was probably money,

since he had asked her to take particular care of it, that it was his fortune.

'A fortune! A fortune in that!' Babylas went on, choking with the desire to see, to feel, to . . .

'We could always look,' the woman suggested. 'There's no harm in that.'

'Harm? No, there isn't . . . A fortune! You don't often see that, all at once, at a glance . . . Let's let him go to sleep. He seems tired . . . He is very tired. He said so.'

They threw dry kindling into the fire, and brisk flames shot out, filling the humble room with a soft, floating light. They put out the candle. Why have a candle burning? Useless expense. Wood costs nothing in the forest; you can have a good fire in the hearth without scruple.

He must have been asleep by now. He had been in bed for at least an hour. In fact, he was asleep. He was sleeping calmly, in full confidence, and a blissful smile had wiped the roughness off his face.

The hideous couple came closer to the hearth where the resinous wood was still blazing.

The pouch was locked. They were getting impatient.

'We can't very well break the lock,' the woman said.

'Yet we have to see,' the man answered.

They sat down side by side, facing the fire, and their anxious and evil faces turned the colour of blood.

Babylas suggested that they go through the pockets in the clothes.

'We have to be careful and not wake the guest up,' the woman warned.

He went off, tiptoeing on bare feet and without a light. Ten minutes later he came back, all smiles, displaying a small key which he devoutly held between thumb and index finger. He placed the key in the lock, sacrilegiously simulating the priest proffering the blessed host at Communion. A log split explosively in the hearth and sparks flew in the faces of the wretches.

The little bag opened, and the two vile creatures uttered a cry of surprise out of throats taut with fear and pleasure. They bent over the treasure, then looked at each other speechless and almost trembling. They were afraid of being caught. If the traveller should waken . . . if he had heard their badly stifled cry! But no, it wasn't possible; he was sleeping soundly in his good feather bed, and the door was closed.

They sank their hands into the open pouch and shook the coins out of the bills. How wonderful it all sounded, how good it felt to the touch!

'Let's count the coins,' Babylas proposed.

They came closer together as if to sustain each other in the impending battle. They took out the bills.

Disillusion! About fifty ones!

There were more which they spread feverishly.

That was better: fives, tens, fifties, hundreds.

Real dazzlement! And those ringing pieces that had earlier seemed white in the half-light were now tawny in the light of the fireplace! Gold! It's gold!

On the table they had pulled near the hearth the piles were rising like altar candles.

What a dream! What delight!

Overjoyed, the two friends stepped back from time to time to take in all this sparkling fortune.

There were ten thousand dollars.

Each counted them ten times, and there were always ten thousand dollars, never less. They could not take their eyes off them.

'Still we have to put it all back in the pouch,' she sighed.

'Yes, yes, no doubt, but there's no hurry. He is sleeping blissfully. He should never wake up,' he answered.

'Never wake up,' she repeated like a fading echo.

'Ten thousand dollars, woman, that's heaven on earth, and one should enter heaven when the door is opened.'

She agreed, saying that a bird in hand is better than any number of them in the bush.

He went on in a woeful tone:

'Ah! if only we hadn't been robbed! . . . Maybe this is our money being returned . . . There are compensations. And then, must we lose forever all we worked so hard to earn?'

He was seeking an excuse for the crime of which the idea was beginning to take form in his mind. She then said in a plaintive voice and sighing:

'No, we must not let ourselves be tempted . . . Sometimes temptation is strong and the flesh is weak . . . It's true we should take things where we find them . . . But that money . . .'

He cut in abruptly:

'Money belongs to everybody . . . no more to him than to anyone else . . . I was robbed, good enough; I rob another; that's still good enough. Tough on the one who gets caught. He pays for everybody. Victory to the strong and clever. The big ones eat the little ones . . . The main thing is to succeed. Success justifies everything.'

The temptation was becoming overpowering, and they were offering little resistance. They were blinding themselves. Even the good don't resist the force of certain suggestions for long. One's energy is soon worn down when one is fighting oneself, and man is so much in need of happiness that he often sacrifices a lasting but delayed bliss for a fateful and passing gratification.

'What are you going to do, Babylas?' the woman asked somewhat excitedly.

'Keep the gold!' he answered coldly.

She retorted that the man would not let himself be robbed like that . . . that he would lodge a complaint, and it would perhaps be difficult to get out of it.

'He won't lodge a complaint, not with our magistrate at least . . . We'll extend his sleep . . . If we're ever asked we'll say he left on foot early in the morning . . . We're not obliged to watch over our travellers . . . nor to escort them . . . It'll be all right!'

They put the gold and the bills back into the pouch and made for the stranger's room. He carried a hammer, she a dripping candle. When they reached the door, he asked:

'Do you want to be wakened early?'

He was doing this to ascertain whether the young man was asleep. The young man answered sleepily:

'No; I'm tired, let me sleep.'

He turned over on his bed. They were startled when they heard him speak.

'Come along,' Madame Babylas whispered. And she pulled her man by the sleeve.

When they were by the fire again, she said that they could take a bit of the gold without his noticing it. 'He can think what he wants if he notices it . . . No one will ever find anything . . . There are hiding-places in the woods.'

'Hiding-places in the woods,' the husband muttered suspiciously. 'Don't talk about those.'

'He must not be killed,' she went on; 'I'm afraid of blood . . . And then that young man must have a mother . . . his poor mother! . . . No, let's not kill him . . . stay here!'

'Fool!'

'I'm going to wake him up.'

'And I'll put him to sleep!'

He shook the hammer at her. She pleaded:

'I'll steal everything . . . I'll run away with the gold. You can say that I'm the most wretched of women, your shame . . . that you've turned me out . . . anything! . . . But to shed the blood of that young man who trusted us, and sleeps now perhaps dreaming of his mother . . . of his mother who waits for him tearfully and anxiously. Oh! no, never!'

'Fine, woman,' he answered. 'Let's go to bed like two dumb creatures, and let's not touch a copper of that fortune that stares us in the face . . . we whom the world has ruined and robbed . . . Come on!'

They went to their bedroom. The fire in the hearth was dying out and darkness was invading the house. They feigned sleep, each keeping an eye on the other. Images of gold danced before their eyes in the night. The darkness was magnificently lit up . . . The precious dollars were swirling like gleaming dust. Bewitching and extravagant visions rose delightfully, then a feeling of fear like a cold breeze dispelled them. But they kept coming back, and the will was weakening. Madame Babylas finally said to herself, dazed with covetousness:

'If only he looked after this by himself . . . He should think about it . . . Why should we both get involved?'

And she pretended to sleep soundly.

The mysterious waves that sometimes travel lightning-fast from one person to another, carrying an intimate thought or a strange message, hovered around their brows and mingled their criminal thoughts.

He got up noiselessly, slowly, lit a lamp, then covered it with a cloth to conceal the light. Then he picked up his hammer and once again went to the traveller's room. He stopped at the foot of the bed. The stranger was asleep. He could tell by his calm and regular breathing.

He let a bit of light shine and he could see the happy face of the rich man whom fate had put before him. He hesitated a moment, even shaded the light again. But in the dark he again saw the pieces of gold glistening, and he felt dizzy . . .

The blow was horrible and the young man's death instantaneous. He pulled the corpse into the woods, then he quietly came back to bed. His wife was still snoring. He knew that such deep sleep was not natural, but he never let on.

Rising in the morning he said he would waken the traveller. She smiled queerly. He rushed back yelling:

'Gone! he's gone! The room is empty . . . How strange!
. . . And the pouch,' he added ironically, 'maybe he left it?'

'It's there,' the woman answered, pointing to the cupboard between the two windows of her room.

'We're rich! What luck!' Babylas shrieked, raising his
hands to the sky.

'But surely he'll come back,' she said, to appear not to
know what had happened.

'Never! set your mind at ease.'

And she was undisturbed.

He went back to his victim, dragged him to the river, tied
stones to his feet and neck, and dropped him in fifteen feet
of water.

Sometime later they went to the village to buy clothes.

As he measured out material for a dress, the merchant
asked them if it was true that their son had returned.

They didn't answer—they were too surprised to be able
to answer—and they looked at each other stupidly. The
merchant, thinking they had not heard him, asked again:

'Your son has come back?'

'Our son!' they answered breathlessly.

The merchant went on: 'He's been gone ten years, hasn't
he? You told me that one day . . . He was fifteen then?'

'Yes, fifteen,' Babylas muttered.

'And he's come back. What a joy it must be for you.'

'Come back? how? . . . No, he hasn't come back.'

Babylas's wife was shaking and extremely pale.

The merchant added: 'It's old man Spenard, from Saint-
Pierre, who gave me the news. He even told me that it was
his son who drove him to your place, last week . . . It seems
he brought a lot of money back with him.'

'Our child!' the wretched woman shrieked, and fell heavily
to the floor.

Although they tried to revive her, she seemed not to want

to live or think. She came to, but fainted again, several times.

'It's the excitement, the surprise,' said Babylas, who was also panic-stricken.

He was about to give himself away when the merchant asked him if his son might have come without divulging his identity. He seized that anchor-sheet:

'No, he didn't reveal his identity! . . . No! But why? We would have been so happy to press him in our arms! . . . We hadn't seen him for ten years! He left a child and came back a man! . . . We didn't know him! . . . God tries us severely! . . . But maybe he'll come back again unexpectedly . . .'

The unhappy mother finally came out of her swoon and asked to leave, saying tearfully that she was sick, that she would die.

They went off, leaving the merchant very perplexed. There weren't many people around then; people didn't visit one another much, and rumours died quickly. Yet there were conjectures about the Babylases. But the police were indulgent and criminals escaped easily.

There were bitter reproaches, dreadful threats, mortal hatred between the evil couple. They accused each other, and each vowed to kill the other. They were tempted to admit all out of revenge. But the sight of the treasure that was still shining in the pouch gradually softened the bitterness of their words and of their remorse. The quarrels became less frequent.

However unnatural a mother may be, there always remains at the bottom of her heart a breath of sacred love that she alone can know, and her efforts to forget fully the blessed joy of motherhood are always bootless. The more she wallows in evil to stifle the voice of nature, the more the invincible voice shouts at her:

'You are a mother! you are a mother! you are a mother!'

Less than two years after the murder of the young traveller, her son, Madame Babylas died. No one could understand the illness that carried her away. It was remorse. She had seen the priest.

Babylas lived several more years, alone in his bloodied inn. He claimed to be poor, but no one believed him, and people avoided his door like the gate of hell. More even.

One morning in January, it was noted that there were no tracks on the path to his house, although it had not snowed for several days. He was thought to be sick. He could not be left to die like this without confession. His soul had cost Jesus Christ dearly. Neighbours opened the door. It was Gagnon, Lépine and Rivard. They found him dead before the fireless hearth.

'*Requiescat in pace*,' old man Gagnon said.

The house shook to its foundations, and a terrible and mysterious voice answered:

'*Non est pax impiis!*'

Translated by Yves Brunelle

LOUIS FRÉCHETTE

Tom Cariboo

'*Cric*, *crac*, girls and boys! *Parlons*, *parlee*, *parlow*! The whole thing if you want to know, pass the spittoon to Fiddle Joe; *sacatabi*, *sac-à-tabac*, all who are deaf will please draw back.'

It is hardly necessary to mention that the narrator who thus commenced his speech was Fiddle Joe himself, my friend Fiddle Joe, presiding over a *veillée de contes* (a story-telling party), on Christmas Eve, at the blacksmith's, old Jean Bilodeau.

Poor old Bilodeau, it is over fifty years now since I heard the sound of his anvil, and I fancy I can see him yet, sitting in the light, with his elbows on his knees, and the shank of his short pipe tightly held between his three remaining teeth.

Fiddle Joe was a queer kind of a fellow, very interesting and very popular, who had spent his youth in the shanties, and was very fond of relating his travelling adventures in the *pays d'en haut*, the timber lands of the Ottawa, the Gatineau and the Saint Maurice.

That day he happened to have a fit of inspiration.

He had been *compère* in the morning, which meant he had stood as godfather to a new-born child; and, as the accessories of the ceremony had brought a slight breeze into the sails of his natural eloquence, his stories went on marvellously.

All camp and forest incidents of course: fights, casualties, fishings extraordinary, miraculous hunting exploits, visions,

24

sorcery, feats of all kinds; he had a collection to suit every taste.

'Do tell us a Christmas story, Joe, if you know one, to fill up time until we leave for church,' cried a girl by the name of Phémie Boisvert.

And Fiddle Joe, who prided himself on knowing what was due to the fair sex, had responded by the characteristic formula as above. Then, after having moistened his throat with a finger deep of Jamaica, and lighted his pipe at the candle, with one of those long cedar splinters which were used by our country folk before, and even after the invention of phosphorus matches, he opened his narrative in the following terms:

This is to tell you, my friends, that, on that year, we had gone rafting above Bytown, at the elbow of a small river called La Galeuse, a funny name but which is of no importance to what I am going to relate.

We were fifteen in our camp: beginning with the boss, and ending with the choreboy.

Nearly all were good men, not quarrelsome, not given to cuss words—of course I don't speak of a little innocent swearing here and there to keep things going—and not drunkards—with the exception of one, I must acknowledge —a tough one indeed.

As for this fellow, boys, he was not exactly what may be called a drunkard: when he happened to come face to face with a demijohn, or when his lips met those of flask or bottle, he was no longer a man, he was a regular funnel.

He came from somewhere back of Three Rivers.

His real name was Thomas Baribeau; but as our foreman, who was Irish, had always some difficulty over this French name, we had nicknamed him 'TOM CARIBOO'.

Thomas Baribeau—Tom Cariboo—it sounded pretty much

the same, as you see. At all events, it was the fellow's *nom de guerre*, and the boss had caught it as easily as though it had been a name freshly imported from Cork.

Anyhow, to speak in polite terms, Tom Cariboo, or Thomas Baribeau, as you wish, had a galvanized-iron throat of the first quality, and he was, moreover, a patented ruffian; but something out of the common, to give the Devil his due.

When I think of all I have heard him say against God, the Blessed Virgin, the good angels, the saints of Heaven and all the Holy Trinity taken together, I still feel a shiver down my back.

Oh! the worthless swagger, what a scamp he was!

He swore, he lied, he cursed his father and mother five or six times a day, he never said a word of prayer; in short, I don't hesitate to say that his miserable carcass, with his soul into the bargain, was not worth, with due respect to the company, the wag of a dog's tail. That's my opinion.

There were not a few in our crowd who swore to having seen him on four paws, at night, in the fields, roving about in the shape of some devilish *loup-garou*.

As for me, my friends, I saw the brute on all fours several times, but, take my word, he was neither playing the *loup-garou*, nor anything so respectable, I assure you: he was too beastly drunk for that.

Anyhow, I must tell you that, for some time, I was one of those who thought if the rascal practised any sorcery at all, he had a preference for the *chasse-galerie*; for, one night, Titoine Pelchat, one of our road-cutters, had spied him coming down a big tree, when the pagan had told him: 'Toine, curse my soul! if you ever mention a word of this to anybody, I'll rip you cold, that's all!'

Of course, Titoine had not failed to tell everybody in the shanty, but in the greatest confidence.

If you don't know what the *chasse-galerie* is, my friends, I am the man to post you fine on the matter, for the *chasse-galerie* I can boast of having seen with my own eyes.

Yes, I, Fiddle Joe, one Sunday afternoon, 'twixt mass and vespers, in full daylight, I saw the infernal machine pass in the air, right in front of the church of Saint Jean Deschaillons, on my soul and conscience, as clear as I see you now.

It was something like a canoe, which travelled, rapidly as an arrow, at about five hundred feet above the earth, manned by a dozen reprobates in red flannel shirts, paddling like damnation, with Satan standing in the stern, steering straight forward in the direction of Three Rivers.

We could even hear them sing in chorus with all sorts of devilish voices:

*V'la l'bon vent! v'là l'joli vent!**

But I may say there are many who don't require such a display to practise *chasse-galerie.*

The regular scalawags like Tom Cariboo, have only to climb up a tree, and launch themselves on a branch, or stick, or anything else, and the Devil drives them on.

Thus they travel thousands of miles in a single night to concoct God knows what kind of jugglery, in some infernal recess where honest people wouldn't set foot for a fortune.

At all events, if Tom Cariboo did not practise *chasse-galerie,* when he used to steal out alone at night, peeping about to

*AUTHOR'S NOTE: The origin of this *chasse-galerie* legend can be traced to the Middle Ages. In France and Germany, they had what was called the Black Huntsman. It was a fantastic coursing which rode in the air with wild clamour and desperate speed, through the darkness of the night. In French Canada, by a curious phenomenon of mirage observed in some circumstance similar to that related by Fiddle Joe, a mounted canoe was seen flying through the air, and the same was naturally substituted for the Black Huntsman, who went also, in some Province of France, by the name of *Chasse-galerie.* It was supposed that the lumbermen—who, by the way, did not enjoy a very enviable reputation—managed through some devilish process, to travel in this way to save fatigue and shorten the distance.

see if anybody watched him, it was certainly not to go to confession, for, to the astonishment of our gang, although there was not a drop of liquor in the whole shanty, the black-guard smelt, every morning, like an old whisky-cask.

Where did he get the stuff?

It was in the latter part of December, and Christmas was drawing near, when another gang working for the same firm, about fifteen miles higher up on the Galeuse, sent word that if we wanted to attend midnight mass, we had only to join them, for a missionary on his way down from the Nipissing would be there to celebrate it.

'By Jove!' we said, 'it is seldom enough that we see an Infant-Jesus in the shanties, let us go!'

We are not angels in the lumber camps, you know that, boys. Even when we don't plague all the saints in the calendar and scandalize the *Bon Dieu* from morning till night like Tom Cariboo, one can't reasonably pass six months in the woods and six months on the rafts every year, without getting a little 'off' on his duties.

But there must be a limit to rascality. Although one may not wear out his knees in the church, or play *mistigri* every night with the beadle, he likes to remember at times, do you see, that a good Canadian boy has something else than the soul of a dog in the mould of his waistcoat, so to speak.

Consequently the trip was soon decided upon, and every-thing carefully stowed for the occasion.

It was brilliant moonlight; the snow was fine for a tramp; we could start after supper, be there in time for mass, and back again for breakfast in the morning, in case we could not spend the night over there.

'You shall go by yourselves, you confounded fools!' cried Tom Cariboo, with a string of blasphemies, almost splitting his knuckles with a blow of his fist on the shanty table.

As you may well imagine, none of us thought of kneeling down to coax the ruffian. The absence of such a parishioner could not spoil the ceremony, and there was no need of his sweet breathing voice to intone the sacred hymns.

'Well, if you don't wish to go,' said the foreman, 'do as you please, my dear fellow. You'll stay here to watch the fire. And since you don't care about seeing God, I hope you won't see the Devil, while we are away.'

Well then, boys, off we go, with belts tight around the waists, snow-shoes well fastened at the toes of our moccasins, each with his little bag of eatables on his shoulder, and a twist of tobacco right behind his teeth.

As we had only to follow the frozen bed of the river, the road was a trifle of course; and we marched on, singing '*La Boulangère*', on the fine, levelled, white snow, under a sky as transparent as crystal, without a crevice or jolting to hamper our progress.

All I can say, my friends, is that merry parties of that kind are far between in shanty life.

'Pon my word, I fancied we could hear the old church bell pealing: 'Come on! come on!' as in the good old times; and more than once, bless my soul! I couldn't help turning round and looking back to see if we were not followed by some of the fine little Canadian trotters of home, with manes floating in the wind, and a row of merry bells ringing at their martingales.

That's what sharpens the wit of a country boy, I tell you. And you ought to have seen Fiddle Joe paddling his canoe that night!

I suppose it is useless to tell you that our midnight mass was not as brilliant as an archbishop's ceremony.

The vestments of the priest were not exactly what may be called imposing; there was no danger of being blinded by the glare of the altar decoration; the singers' windpipes were not oiled like a nightingale's throat, and the acolytes would doubtless have showed a more natural gait with shoulder under a canthook than a censer at arm's length.

You may add, besides, that there wasn't even the shadow of an Infant-Jesus; which, as you all know, is no small drawback to a Christmas performance.

To tell the truth, the good old man Job himself couldn't have been more poorly fitted to say his daily mass.

But no matter, there are lots of church services with music and gilded ornaments which are not worth the one we had that night, my friends, take Fiddle Joe's word for it!

It reminded us of old times, do you see, of the old parish, of the old home, of the old mother, and all that.

Good gracious me! you all know that Fiddle Joe is no squinny nor crying baby; well, I had never done passing my quid from one cheek to the other to control my emotion.

But that's enough about this part; let us see what had happened to Tom Cariboo during our absence.

I need not tell you that, after the mass was over, we returned to our camp by the same way, so that it was full daylight when we reached the shanty.

At first, we were greatly surprised not to see a single thread of smoke rising from the chimney; but we were still more astonished when we found the door wide open, the stove without an ember, and not a trace of Tom Cariboo.

As true as I live, our first thought was that the Devil had carried him away. A worthless chap like him, do you see . . .

But, after all, that was no reason for not looking for him.

Hard enough it was to look for him, for not a bit of snow had fallen for several days, and the consequence was there were thousands of foot-prints around the shanty and even in the surrounding woods, all so well crossed and mixed up together, that it was impossible to make out anything of them.

Fortunately the boss had a very smart dog: *Polisson*, as we used to call him for a pet name.

'Search, Polisson!' said we.

And off goes Polisson searching out right and left, his

nose in the snow, wagging his tail, while the rest of us followed on with a double-barrelled gun loaded with bullets, and which I carried myself.

A good gun in a shanty is like the petticoat of a woman in a family. Remember that, my friends.

We had not been two minutes peeping through the branches, when our dog suddenly stood still in his tracks, trembling like a leaf. 'Pon my word, if he had not been ashamed I think the scamp would have made a right about for the house.

As for me, I threw up my gun and stepped forward.

You'll never imagine, my friends, what I saw right in front of me, on the slope of a ravine where the wood was thicker and the snow heavier than elsewhere . . .

It wasn't funny at all, I tell you. Or rather, it would have been very funny, if it hadn't been so fearful.

Just fancy that our Tom Cariboo was roosted in the fork of a big wild cherry tree, pale as a winding-sheet, his eyes starting out of their sockets, at the muzzle of a she-bear who clung to the trunk about two feet below him.

Thunder! Fiddle Joe is not a man to skedaddle when called upon to face a squall, you all know that; well, this terrible sight made my blood whirl up from my toes to the nape of my neck.

'This is the time not to miss your aim, my poor Fiddle Joe,' said I to myself. 'Point blank! or God save your soul!'

Shifting was no use: bing! bang! . . . I aimed and shot both barrels at once, my two bullets striking the beast right between the shoulders.

She gave a growl, stretched her paws, swung for a moment, and then fell headlong with her back broken.

It was high time. My gun was still smoking, when I saw another mass tumbling down from the tree.

It was Tom Cariboo, who spread himself fainting and sprawling right across the dying she-bear. He was terribly torn by her claws, which had struck him more than once, and his hair . . . Well, now, try and guess, my friends . . . His hair had all turned white!

Yes, as white as snow. Fear had turned his hair white in a single night, as true as I intend to take *un p'tit coup* by and by, with the grace of God, and the permission of Uncle Bilodeau, who shan't lose anything by it.

Yes, honestly, the rascal had suddenly grown so old, that some of us would not believe it was the same man.

We hurriedly made a kind of hand-barrow with branches, and we laid the poor fellow on it, cautiously handling that portion of his body which had been damaged by the bear's claws; and so carried him back to the shanty half dead, and frozen nearly as hard as a piece of Bologna sausage.

After which, it was the bear we had to drag to the camp.

But here's the fun of it.

You may call me a liar if you wish; it wasn't credible, but the infernal beast seemed to have inherited poor Tom's most characteristic quality, and was smelling of rum like a seasoned cask, so much so that Titoine Pelchat said it gave him a mind to lick the animal.

But it was no miracle.

You know, my friends—if you don't, Fiddle Joe will tell you—that the bears don't spend their winters working hard as we do, poor lumbermen building rafts for the spring.

So far are they from working, that they haven't even the energy to eat.

At the first frosts of Autumn, they dig a hole between the roots of a tree, and lie there for the winter, buried alive in the snow which the animal's breath melts from the inside, so as to form a kind of oven where they spend the whole season, half asleep like marmots, and licking their paws for a living.

Our own, that is Tom Cariboo's bear, had chosen the roots of that particular cherry tree to shelter himself, while Tom had chosen a forked branch in the same . . . You'll know what for in a moment.

Only, as you remember that the ground was on a slope, Tom Cariboo—which was quite natural—gained his branch from the upper side of the declivity; and the she-bear—which was natural also—had dug her hole from the lower side, where the roots were not so deeply buried in the sod.

This accounts for these two savages having lived neighbours and almost partners, without having ever met; each of them being under the impression that he had the exclusive possession of the premises for himself.

You will probably ask what business Tom Cariboo had in the fork of that tree.

Well, in that fork there was a hole, and in that hole our drunkard had hidden a jar of high-wines which he had smuggled into the camp, we never exactly knew how. I suppose he had made us tow it under water behind one of our canoes, at the end of a string.

At all events, he had it; and almost every night he would sneak out and climb the tree to fill his flask.

It was from that nest of his that Titoine Pelchat had seen him coming down, that time we spoke of the *chasse-galerie*; and that was why, every morning, one could have set the scoundrel on fire, merely by passing a live coal under his nose.

Well, then, after we had left for the midnight mass, Tom Cariboo had gone to fill his flask out of the hidden demijohn.

On a merry day like Christmas, of course, the flask was soon emptied, although there was only one drunkard to treat; and Tom returned to his cupboard to renew his stock.

Unfortunately, if the flask was empty, it was not the case with its master; on the contrary, its master was too full.

The demijohn, carelessly handled and uncorked, overflowed on the other side of the cherry tree, right on the muzzle of the she-bear.

At first, the animal had naturally licked her chops, sniffing; and then, finding that this kind of rain had a peculiar taste and smell, she had opened her eyes. Her eyes open, the whisky had flowed into them.

High-wines, friends! it's no use asking if the beast awoke for good.

On hearing her howls, Tom Cariboo began to descend the tree, but not a bit! Stop, boy! The bear, having also heard a noise, had walked around the tree, and before the poor devil was half-way down, she had clapped a destroying paw on the most prominent part of the descending intruder.

But the monster was too torpid to do more; and, while our heathen was climbing back up the tree, bleeding and terrified, she remained clinging to the bark, without being able to follow further up.

That's what had happened. You see, that if the bear smelt of whisky, it was no miracle.

Poor Tom Cariboo! between ourselves, it took three long weeks to repair his damages.

Never could we convince the repentant drunkard that it was not Satan who had appeared to him, and who had thus lacerated his . . . feelings.

You ought to have seen him, begging even the dog's pardon for all his oaths and all his nightly sprees.

He couldn't sit down, of course; and so had to kneel.

It was his punishment for having refused to do so on Christmas Eve.

And lifting his glass to his lips, Fiddle Joe added:

'*Cric, crac!* . . . *Sacatabi sac-à-tabac*! ... Here's to your luck, old Jack!'

Translated by the author

LOUIS DANTIN

You're Coughing?

My friend Sigourdin had invited me to his country place for the weekend and I had accepted, even though I had a touch of bronchitis. I took my seat in the Vaudreuil train a little ahead of departure time. A train trip is always a kind of adventure for me, a plunge into the unknown. The moment I land in the coach the air seems fresher, more vital; I feel rejuvenated, my curiosity revives. I throw off the stale every-day routine, the roar of the factories, the confinement of my room, the boring sidewalks and uninteresting faces; I also leave behind the part of myself associated with these things. Just for a day I strike out, free and easy, into another life, knowing that its end is sure—a little like death—and that the unexpected lies in wait for me along the way in the form of incidents and discoveries. I enter with almost solemn tread through the steel archway of the coach, with its decorative frescos and lamps. I love the long rows of seats, reminiscent of drawing-rooms and foreign hotels; the feel of the plush as I sink onto it; and the gilt luggage rack on which I place my bit of baggage. All this luxury seems made expressly for me and I revel in it with all the self-satisfaction of a man of property. Each traveller is a companion, hand-picked and observed with childlike attention: from their faces and mannerisms I tease out deductions about their inner lives that would earn the admiration of Sherlock Holmes. Every pretty woman is the unsuspecting subject of a silent interrogation and a veiled flirtation. The coach is a world unto itself, as strange and varied as the normal one, and it, too, carries me towards my destiny.

So I settled in, prepared to indulge these studies of human nature. Two labourers took the seats next to me and I detected in their features signs of a week's work ended and a long-awaited return to their kids and their pipes. They were almost certainly carpenters: their jackets showed traces of sawdust and one of them had a bandaged thumb, the mark of an unlucky hammer blow. Behind them, a well-dressed man was ogling and sniffing a magnificent melon that protruded from a wicker basket; one of those canteloupes ripened under southern suns and embossed with delicate lace-work, their rinds evenly grooved as if to mark out generous portions in advance, that are the glory of Westmount's market-gardeners; I pictured tomorrow's table laid with fine linen and silver and, forming a circle around the regal melon enthroned on a china platter, the family, expectant and rapt as if for a solemn ritual. A couple stood framed in the doorway of the coach: the woman, full-figured and tall, her manner confident, clutched to her bosom a woolly ball that turned out to be a Pekinese; the diminutive husband, loaded down with parcels and packages, wore the air of total resignation that only long-standing obedience can confer.

As time passed other characters crowded in, specimens of all shapes and sizes from every walk of life, and my divided attention reduced me to viewing them as a mere group, a throng murmuring and swaying in the coach, which now began to feel like a steam bath.

The seat ahead of me had remained vacant. Soon a young woman slipped silently into it. Since she had come from be-hind and now presented only her back to me, all I could see was the pleasing curve of her shoulders, the half-concealed nape of her neck, revealing a brunette, and a coil of thick dark hair. Though her dress was simple and made of a plain fabric, I noticed the unusual colours and exotic design of the silk scarf that gave a certain flair to her costume. As soon as she was seated the conductor's voice rang out, listing the various stops; a few puffing latecomers hurried in, and the train moved out amid a clanking of metal. We had left behind us the last of the shabby streets and factory soot; the countryside was now beginning to turn green, though traces of the city remained in the scores of suburban houses and squared-off gardens. Every so often the grey ribbon of the canal made an appearance, almost level with its shallow banks. Seized with a vague torpor, I watched the fields, the shrubs and bushes, the rows of vegetables racing away from the train, jostling each other as if fleeing from the giant strides of the telegraph poles.

Just then I felt a little tickle in my throat; it was my bronchitis. By no means severe, it pestered me just enough to keep me from forgetting it altogether. I had a momentary fit of dry coughing, quite unobtrusive since it was drowned out by the surrounding racket. Still, when it was over I thought I noticed that the lady in front of me had stiffened and cocked her ear.

The other travellers had made themselves comfortable and the coach had acquired a homey aspect. Three or four giggling little girls were running up and down the aisle, catching at the sides of the seats and at each other's skirts. One young man was completely absorbed in the latest sports news. The large, full-figured woman sat fanning herself, while the little man with the long-suffering air, crammed into his quarter of a seat, held the Pekinese horror.

We were approaching Lachine and could already feel the cool breeze from the river. It may have been the slight tang in the air that set off my second coughing fit. Then, to my surprise, I saw the young woman in front turn to face me, staring at me with her two great flashing black eyes. At the same time I noticed that her face had a foreign sort of beauty:

an exquisite oval, a pretty mouth, an olive complexion that was pale except for the cheeks, which were tinted by two circles the shade of ripe pomegranates. But the eyes were especially remarkable, with their large orbs, dark pupils, and bright sparkle. All her features bespoke a foreigner; Italian perhaps, or Greek, or possibly from the south of France. She seemed young to me, in that less-than-blooming, but more vivacious manner of young women between twenty-five and thirty. As for her station in life, I guessed that she was from the working-classes, though of a fine stock well above the ordinary.

In her deliberate gaze, which lasted only a second, she had met my eyes without reserve or surprise. I read into her look a rather earnest intensity and, perhaps, a silent question. She had then sedately resumed her former attitude; and the train rolled along as before, past the whirling tree-tops and deep embankments.

It is always flattering to be stared at by a pair of beautiful eyes, even if there is no rhyme or reason to it. I relished for a moment the image of those dark, flashing eyes. But then the ear-splitting cries of a baby that would not be pacified diverted my attention and I fell to commiserating with the martyrdom of mothers of small children. We had just passed the cottages of Dorval when a new irritation warned that the bronchitis had not finished with me. The little cough started up again. Outrageous! At that moment my foreign neighbour turned her pretty face towards me and wrapped me in a thoughtful gaze, more pointed and intense than before; then, slowly, as if loath to do so, she turned away, showing me only the down of her neck and the slope of her shoulders.

This time I was consumed with curiosity. Who was this woman? Why had she looked at me three times with that strange expression? Was she, despite her respectable appearance, on the lookout for some intrigue? Had she perhaps heard in my modest little cough some sort of disguised appeal? And yet she had not smiled. Her huge eyes, meeting mine, had seemed sad. In any case, she fascinated me and I began to attribute the most romantic plots to her, and to wish I had a pretext for getting her to explain herself. Even the merest flirtation from those eyes would have been far from disagreeable. For a second I had the childish idea of faking a cough, just to see what would happen. But I did not have long to resist this unworthy impulse: fate intervened. As we were passing the outskirts of Valois and just beginning to catch sight of the broad shimmering surface of Lac Saint-Louis, I felt the first stirring in my larynx; then came the inevitable tickle.

Slowly my neighbour turned to me, quite boldly fixing me with those eyes like black diamonds, and with a catch in her voice, said:

'You're coughing?'

'Just a little, ma'am,' I replied, rather dumbfounded. 'I hope you will excuse me.'

She was silent for a moment, continuing to scrutinize me. Then she asked:

'Have you been coughing like that for very long?'

'Oh, a week or so; it's most annoying in company.'

She shook her head as if I had not understood.

'Come and sit beside me,' she said.

I went. With downcast eyes she murmured, in a voice full of solicitude, 'Be careful. These coughs are nasty. You think it's nothing, and then . . . you must look after yourself. Stay out of draughts, and drink milk before you go to bed.'

Incredible! I was floating through a dream. Quite at a loss, I stammered, 'That's good advice. I'm very grateful.'

'It hurts me to hear someone cough. Where are you going?'

'To Île Perrot, to visit a friend.'

'I'm going to Vaudreuil to see my brother.'

'And spend Sunday on the water?'

'Oh, no! In the nursing home. My brother is ill—very ill.'

Her breast heaved with a deep sigh. She went on:

'Have you any family hereabouts?'

'No, unfortunately. I'm all alone—just as if I'd dropped out of the sky. And there are times, you know . . .'

'What do you do for a living?'

'Several things, ma'am. Mostly I'm an artist. But I also operate a saw in a box factory, and at night I write stories and play the organ in a movie theatre.'

'So you have some education then?'

'Yes. Many different kinds,' I had the nerve to reply.

'My brother would have been a doctor, if he hadn't got this illness. He was in his final year at Laval.'

She became lost in thoughts of her brother. I began to see how important this brother was to her.

'You expect to see him though?'

'We don't know. Sometimes he gets his strength back, but then he starts coughing more than ever. That's what it is—this terrible consumption. He's only twenty-three! He used to be so strong—he was wonderful—but this winter he caught a cold after a party and since then, nothing seems to help. It breaks our hearts to see him like this. My father was so proud of him, he would have done anything for him. We've tried our best to take care of him; we sent him to Vaudreuil for the fresh air, and I visit every week. But this cough is so frightening; we're terrified.'

There was now real terror in her eyes and voice.

'That's why I don't like to hear you coughing.'

Thus the whole mystery was cleared up. Plainly, this woman was a hundred miles from plotting any kind of doubtful venture; it was obvious that she had stared at me and pitied me without regard for propriety; that her words had sprung from honest human sympathy. Tormented by her brother's battle with death, she had imagined that I was threatened with the same danger; irresistible compassion had driven her to warn me, to comfort her unknown brother. She may even have given in a little to her own need to talk about her troubles, to find a bit of consolation. Ashamed of my earlier suspicions, I began to despise the shallow speculations they had given rise to. A different feeling came over me; I was moved by this astonishing encounter, grateful for her pure spirit of charity. And so, out of respect for this woman who treated me with such sisterly warmth, I abandoned the reserve that etiquette prescribes for conversations with strangers.

'I understand now why you spoke to me. You're very kind. Tell me, what is your nationality?'

'I'm Armenian.'

'And your name?'

'Ritza Hadjian. Have you never seen that name on Notre Dame Street—over my father's dry-goods store?'

'But you speak French so well. Where did you learn it?'

'In my own country at first, and then in Montréal, from the nuns.'

Armenian! The word instantly transported me to a thousand places; to ancient biblical lands, inhabited by a people as old as the world. It seemed to evoke in me an oriental strain that I might have possessed in some remote existence. My seat in the train, the whole vulgar coach had vanished. I was in the plains of Armenia, refreshed by its springs, lulled by its whispering palm trees. I had come across this woman walking along a path that for five thousand years had been trodden by herdsmen. On her head she carried a vessel filled with oil, or wine; on her feet were sandals. Close by in a little vale, under a tent made of goatskins, her brother lay helplessly writhing in the throes of some mysterious malady. His ancient father, downcast and brooding, kept a vigil over him. As she approached she began to weep at the sight of me, fastening upon me her enormous black eyes and saying,

'You're coughing?' And this unspoiled sympathy offered to a wandering stranger had in it something of the innocence and spontaneity of Eden.

'Are you married?' I asked.

'No. I live with my father.'

'Why haven't you married? You're so pretty and such pleasant company.'

'Yes,' she said, 'but you see the responsibility I have. I did have a friend at the time my brother took sick, but he wouldn't wait for me.'

'How unfeeling!' I couldn't help exclaiming. 'Another man would have seen your worth and loved you for it.'

At that moment a glance out the window told me we had reached the open countryside near Sainte-Anne-du-Bout-de-l'Île. It whisked me back to reality. In a few minutes we would reach Île Perrot. My dream of the Orient was coming to a close almost before it had begun. Now this sisterly stranger, brought to me by a trick of fate, would disappear forever. And this sympathy, born of a chance encounter, was about to dissolve, again at the mercy of chance. Ritza Hadjian was going to a brother more dear to her; her face, so fine and thoughtful, the black velvet of her eyes, her warm gentle voice would now fade for me into the distance of things past.

I can't say why, but I felt a cruel constriction in my heart, rather like the despair one might feel at losing a last hope of support; my voice trembled and faltered as I bent towards her and murmured close to her ear:

'I'll be leaving soon. But I thank you. I thank you more than you could possibly understand. Without knowing it you are the only person who has ever cared whether I suffered, either in body or in spirit. In an instant you've given me more kindness, compassion, true love, than I've ever had in my life. I will never forget your name, your face, or your words. I hope your brother will recover and I wish you happiness.'

The train was slowing down. 'Île Perrot! Île Perrot!' cried the brakeman. I got up. She extended her hand and pressed mine warmly. Then she plunged into my eyes one last time a look from her deep dark ones (oh! so filled with human compassion, so brimming with instinctive womanly tenderness!), and turned aside as if to hide some strong feeling:

'Take good care of yourself,' she said. 'I am your friend for life. I will pray for you.'

A week later I happened to be walking down Notre Dame Street. For no apparent reason I was deep in a black depression. And then, as I walked, I recalled my travelling companion and took a notion to look for the place she had vaguely described to me. I began to examine the signs on the shops on either side of the street, hunting for the unusual name she had given. It wasn't long before I made out two words displayed along the length of one of the buildings across the street: EPHREM HADJIAN; and, in smaller letters: Armenian Imports, Fabrics, and Smallwares. The shop looked substantial enough, its show-windows crammed with all sorts of merchandise; draperies, linens, jewelled boxes, and an assortment of gaudy clothing. It occurred to me that part of this enterprise must have been to furnish our pedlars' nomadic push-carts with florid neckties, embroidered tablecloths, and other trinkets. To all appearances the business was a considerable one and its proprietor likely well-to-do. Above the store was a private dwelling, obviously well kept, its windows draped with discreet curtains.

I said to myself, 'This is where they live. During the day she may be found tending the counter. If I were to give the door a push I would discover her old father, with his white patriarchal beard, and she would be at his side, with her intense eyes, those compassionate eyes that would recognize me and smile.'

I hesitated for a long time, my heart racing. I walked back and forth in front of the shop, taking inventory of the show-window and glancing up to watch for a sign of life behind the curtains. But in the end I thought, 'Why spoil something exquisite by probing too deeply? Better to keep the delicate, flower-like charm of this lovely memory in my heart.'

Already, just from being near the place, I felt less alone. My depressed spirits had been soothed by a gentle balm. I left, saying a secret adieu to Ritza, my Armenian sister, who might, perhaps, have heard it.

But as I strolled away I began to relive the scene in the Vaudreuil train, and then to dream of a world where each heart would be linked to every other; where sympathy would circulate like the air and radiate like sunshine; where all that dwells in the heart would rise to the lips, freed from the artificial barriers of etiquette; where one might freely go up to the passerby who seemed to be in pain; the red-eyed woman; the gaunt-cheeked old man, and say, 'Are you suffering?' Where one could share in other people's joy, crying out to the laughing couple, even though their names were unknown, 'Hey there! Here's to the lovers!' Or to the beautiful stranger that one chances to pass, 'You're gorgeous! I admire you!' To the carpenter, carefully moulding his lintel, 'What a skilful artist you are!' And all this would well up and burst forth from innocent brotherly souls, and it would become a part of etiquette and tact, and would be dignified, appropriate, and prescribed.

Translated by Patricia Sillers

ALBERT LABERGE

The Patient

About a week before Christmas Caroline Bardas, who had been ailing for some time, became so ill she had to take to her bed. Her husband Anthime Bardas, a farmer who had spent his life working other people's land, went to fetch their daughter to look after her; Zéphirine was in service with Monsieur Lauzon, a landowner in the village.

Madame Lauzon was not pleased, and she let her maid know it: 'Well, that's a fine way to behave! Leaving me on my own for the holidays, with company coming and all that cooking to do. Just like that, at the busiest time, you want to up and go!'

'I didn't pick the time, ma'am, things happen that way. It's no holiday.'

'Don't stay away too long, in any case. I need you here,' declared Madame Lauzon.

Which was to say, let the old cow kick the bucket and get it over with fast.

Zéphirine climbed into the sledge with her father and left for the farm, to keep house and look after the patient.

The girl found her mother greatly changed, and very weak. True, she was sixty-one, and had seen her share of hard times: more hard times than roast chicken, as she used to say.

The old woman was getting sicker every day.

'We can't let her die without seeing the doctor,' said farmer

Bardas the day after Christmas; sunk down in the bed, his wife was already beginning to look like a corpse.

And he went to fetch the doctor.

Short, stout, grey-haired Dr Casimir examined the patient briefly. He looked discouraged. Always the same story: calling him in at the last minute, when it was too late to do anything.

'She's done for,' he said as he went out. 'She won't last two days.'

All the same, one should never despair. So he gave the dying woman a spoonful of the medicine he'd brought with him, left the bottle on the dresser, and recommended that the patient be given a dose of it every three hours.

'The doctor says she's done for,' said Zéphirine to her father. 'And I can't do everything myself. Délima's got to come home and help me.'

So farmer Bardas went to the village to fetch his second daughter, who worked at Mailloux's tavern. And that was another story.

'You must be crazy,' declared the owner, a former policeman who had bought himself a beer parlour. 'Take my waitress away just when I need her the most? We make a lot of money in the holidays, but we have to serve the people. How long would you be gone?' he asked the girl.

'Not very long, that's for sure. The doctor says she won't last two days.'

'All right,' he conceded. 'If that's how it is, go.'

On the way Délima wondered if she'd find her mother alive. If she were dead, she could be back at the tavern for New Year's; that wouldn't be too bad.

But old Caroline was still breathing. Sallow, wrinkled, toothless, nothing but skin and bones, she lay limp as a rag in the old bed under a cheap patchwork quilt. Yes, she was still alive; but she didn't seem to recognize her daughter.

'It won't be long and that's a fact,' said the latter. 'Bet she's gone by tomorrow morning.'

'You know what, Zéphirine,' remarked Délima after dinner, when the two of them were doing the dishes, 'I bet Ma doesn't have a proper dress.'

'No, she doesn't; it must be five years at least since she's had anything new.'

'Well, we'll have to find something to bury her in. She can't go in that worn-out old skirt. And we can't very well borrow anything, can we? If you and me put in a buck each and Paul and Ti-Fred both put in one, we'll have four. We should be able to get a decent dress for that.'

In fact, Paul and Ti-Fred, who worked in the village, had heard their mother was dying, and they came to see her that night.

Délima told them about the dress.

'I haven't got a buck to put in,' said Paul. 'Haven't got enough for myself. Don't ask me for any money.'

'Deal me out,' said Ti-Fred, who usually spent his evening playing cards in the back of the barber shop.

Délima was furious: 'So it's up to the daughters to dress their mother, is that it?'

'You don't have to dress anyone but yourself,' retorted Paul.

And that was the end of the discussion.

Later that evening, Zéphirine remembered the medicine the doctor had left.

She poured a spoonful and tried to get her mother to swallow it. The brownish liquid stained her lower lip and dribbled down her chin. Then the old woman turned her head to the side, made a face, and spat out the rest onto the quilt.

'She doesn't want any medicine,' she told her sister. 'Oh well, if she's going to die anyway she can do it without medicine.'

'That's right,' agreed Délima. 'So we'd better hurry up and get her a dress, even if Paul and Ti-Fred are too cheap to help out. I'll go to the village and buy one tomorrow morning after breakfast. We'll pay for it between the two of us.'

'No choice,' concluded her sister regretfully.

The next day as farmer Bardas was finishing his tea Délima spoke to him: 'Pa, go and harness up the horse. We have to go to the village and buy a dress for Ma to be buried in.'

An hour later, father and daughter were on their way in the sledge.

While they were gone there was a knock at the door. It was the doctor, stopping by on his way back from visiting another patient.

'The old lady's not dead yet?' he asked as he came in.

'Not yet, but it won't be long now,' answered Zéphirine.

Dr Casimir put his black leather bag, otter-skin hat, and raccoon coat on a chair, then went into mother Bardas's room.

The old face on the dirty pillow was still the same: thin, grey, wrinkled, toothless.

'Have you been giving her the medicine, as I told you to?' he asked the daughter who had followed him to the bedside.

'She doesn't want to take it,' answered Zéphirine. 'She just spits it out all over the covers.'

Sternly the doctor turned to her: 'Look here, my girl. It isn't a question of whether she wants it or not. This is no joke: it's serious. Your mother's life is at stake. You come and get me to see a patient, I prescribe medicine, and then you can't be bothered to give it to her. If that's how you feel it's not worth my trouble. Now go and bring me my bag, on the chair.'

Taking the old woman's hand, he felt for her pulse. Then he leaned over and, putting his ear to her chest, listened to the faint heartbeat.

Zéphirine returned with the bag. He opened it and took out a black case from which he drew a long needle. Lifting the patient's sleeve to expose the limp, faded flesh of the wasted arm, he plunged his needle into the lifeless skin. Then he wiped off the steel point, put it back in its case, and went into the kitchen, where he lit his meerschaum pipe and smoked for a while in silence.

'And where is your father?' he asked finally.

'In the village.'

'Bring me the medicine I left you,' he said to the girl. He poured out a spoonful and got the patient to swallow it. She looked at him for a moment, her eyes expressionless, then muttered a few unintelligible words.

'You see, she's perking up already after that injection I gave her just now. She looked like a corpse when I came in. Now, you make her take the medicine every three hours, the way I told you. Then at least if she does die it won't be your fault.'

And putting on his raccoon coat and otter-skin hat, Dr Casimir left.

Délima and her father returned from the village a couple of hours later.

'I bought a black dress and a pair of shoes,' she announced as she opened the long box. 'The dress cost three bucks.' Unfolding it, she held it up against herself and stretched out her arms to show her sister. 'And the shoes were a buck twenty-five. We won't have to be ashamed if Ma's buried in this outfit. All the same, I'd rather have bought a hat; they had some nice ones at Robillard's. I sure hope I'm back at work for New Year's.'

'You're not the only one,' complained Zéphirine. 'I could've got myself some nice silk stockings with that money.'

They went to see the old woman. As they entered the room, she laboriously turned her head in their direction.

'You'd think she was getting better,' remarked Délima.

'The doctor came this afternoon and gave her a shot; it's perked her up. I guess it's time for her medicine.'

With that, Zéphirine poured out a dose of the syrup and got the patient to swallow it.

The day passed.

That evening, Paul and Ti-Fred arrived at the house half-drunk. Farmer Bardas gave them a good tongue-lashing, but his sons were thick-skinned.

'Come on, it's the holidays,' answered Ti-Fred. 'When someone buys you a drink you can't turn it down.'

'It's no time to go drinking when your mother's dying,' Bardas said sternly.

'It won't kill her,' Paul answered back. 'Anyway, you're only young once, eh Pa?'

The two days predicted by Dr Casimir had now passed, and still old Caroline hadn't died. The next day she took her medicine again and even recognized her husband and daughters. Another three long days went by without any change. Délima was in a foul mood, and as she was drying the dishes after dinner she happened to drop a plate on the floor. It made her feel better. How much longer was this going to drag on? Her father had been pretty quick to come and take her away from the tavern!

Then it was the first of January. The patient saw the new year in despite what the doctor had said.

Dr Casimir came every afternoon.

'I'll give her another injection, to stimulate her,' he said on his New Year's visit.

Together the shots and medicine achieved miracles. Now the old woman was talking and breathing easily, her heart was working without too much strain, and she was resting comfortably in her bed under the colourful quilt.

'Tomorrow, give her some soup for lunch,' the doctor ordered. 'Kill a hen and make a good strong chicken broth, and put some rice in it. I'll come myself and watch her eat it.'

So farmer Bardas took a chicken and wrung its neck, and

Zéphirine made the soup. Dr Casimir arrived at the appointed hour.

'Now,' he said, 'you feed it to her.'

He himself lifted old Caroline's head, took the pillow from father Bardas, and placed it behind her shoulders. Then Zéphirine dipped into the bowl and began slowly spoon-feeding the patient, just the way her mother had done so many times in the past, when she herself was a baby.

'That's enough for today, but you can give her some more tomorrow. Well, it looks to me as if your mother's in the clear. All she needs now is lots of care, and she'll be back on her feet in no time.' In the tone of a man well-satisfied with his work, the doctor added: 'She'll live another ten years yet, you'll see.'

Smiling cheerfully, the doctor left the house.

Zéphirine and Délima stood in the kitchen and looked at one another in dismay. So mother was on the mend; all that time and money gone for nothing. She was so close to dying—why not just get it over with? To think of the old lady with a new dress and shoes, while the girls do without!

'It's a pain in the neck,' said Zéphirine. 'Now we have to waste more time looking after her! After the money she's cost us, all we get from her is more trouble.'

'We've missed out on our wages and our New Year's presents—everything,' added Délima resentfully. 'And now here we are saddled with her for another ten years.'

'It's all the doctor's fault,' Zéphirine declared bitterly.

'That's right,' Délima realized. 'Well, the bastard can wait for his pay!'

Translated by Sally Livingston

RINGUET

The Heritage

The man stopped for a minute at the crossroads in obvious embarrassment. He had to make a choice: to go right ahead along the highway and eventually get lost in the bush that was shimmering on the horizon in the heat of the day, or to turn to the left along the dusty road that wound around several hillocks where the land had been cleared and seemed to come to an end at the foot of a slope, crowned by a tuft of pine-trees sleeping in the sun. There was also, on the right hand guarding the crossroads, a low house behind a row of maples, with one wall blistered all over with gaudy advertisements.

The man chose to climb the slope where there was welcome shade under the network of branches. He took it on an angle with a heavy tired lope; passing over the carpet of pine-needles, he came to a sandy rise beyond which the ground fell away.

His new suit and bright-coloured shirt revealed a good carriage and square shoulders. Outlined against the sky they looked a little like a strong wooden yoke made to carry burdens. He had set his pack down on the ground.

Under his eyes the landscape unfolded; perhaps in front of him was the very land he was looking for. Now that he had stopped, the shadow and the cool spring wind brought some relief, for the climb had made the sudden heat almost unbearable.

The land lay before him in long undulating folds. It fell away in a sharp descent; then after a few small valleys it took a plunge into a deep gorge, and up again on the other side; beyond, fold after fold, mounting and green, it rose until the last hill was too high for him to see over. He would have had to go far to the right to do that.

At the crossroads, down below, a cock in the barnyard began to sing out at the top of his voice, a triumphant song of satisfied love, a resounding song that poured his joy over his whole world, the earth, the sunlight, the spring day. For a moment it filled the wide countryside, then stopped, as if astonished at having accomplished nothing. For peace returned at once, unconquered, majestic, and final. The rustle in the branches, in the light breath that touched only the very tops of the pines, right up in the sky, seemed but a part of this silence.

On the veranda of the house a woman in a smock appeared for a moment; then almost at once she was joined by a man. Shading their eyes, they watched the man standing up on the little hill, filling the landscape with his unaccustomed presence. Then they disappeared.

Moving along the rise a little, the traveller noticed something: a grey bridge crossing the gorge. The river was certainly there. He picked up his pack and went down the hill. Before entering the store, he hesitated for a while; then, shrugging his shoulders, he pushed the door open. The woman in the smock slipped behind the greasy counter where a few candies and packets of chewing tobacco were offered for sale in a glass case.

'Can you tell me if the property of the late Baptiste Langelier is anywhere near here?'

'What?'

'They told me that the land belonging to the late Baptiste Langelier was somewhere around here.'

'Oh. Baptiste Langelier's land.'

'Ya, Baptiste Langelier's land.'

He had repeated what they said mechanically, like a man used to the ways of these simple folk.

'Well,' she continued, 'it's Baptiste Langelier's land you want to know about?'

He did not reply.

The woman disappeared behind a blanket heavy with dust hanging like a curtain over a doorway. After a minute a man came out. He looked at the stranger with an inquiring air.

The latter repeated again without any trace of impatience:

'I want to know where Baptiste Langelier's land is.'

'Baptiste Langelier? But he's dead. He's been dead some time.'

'Yes, I know. But his land?'

'All right, I'll tell you. Take the road on the left at the bottom of the hill. It's quite easy to find. It's the third place after the fork in the road.'

'Fine. Thanks very much.'

When he was away down the road, the man and the woman were still at the window behind the curtain.

'Perhaps it's really him,' said the woman.

'Looks like it is,' replied the man.

It was him all right.

When old Baptiste Langelier died suddenly, in February, everyone had been wondering who would inherit his property, for he was a bachelor and had no relatives, as far as they knew, either in the township or farther afield. For some time no one had heard a word. Then somebody from Saint-Alphonse turned up who had seen the heir; and the news came that there actually was an heir, a city fellow called Langelier too. A cousin, perhaps.

Better than that! Little by little the story came out: this new fellow was the old man's son, sure enough. But the old man had never been married, they whispered. The son of a woman Baptiste had married twenty-five years before, other people stated quite definitely. They even went into details: she was a Montréal woman, and he had only lived with her a few weeks while he was working on munitions in 1916. The only fact that everyone agreed on was that the child had been brought up by the nuns as if he were an orphan or a bastard.

Whatever was the truth of it, Albert Langelier moved in. He took possession of the house; he had the key. He took possession of the farm-buildings, sure of himself, as owner of the property. He took possession of the farm as if he did not understand anything about it at all, with a hesitating, uncertain air. And the very first day he flung open all the windows, even in the parlour.

For a few days the neighbours were worried and friendly. After all! Seeing that the house was empty, they had made a point of going and having a look at it at night, and if old Langelier had returned he would have had to look a long time for a number of things that were certainly not in their usual places.

For some time the Vadenais never dared to use their tobacco cutter, and Ma Caron, the woman in the corner house, kept the big soap-kettle hidden in the cellar.

Another neighbour, Langlois, arrived with a broad grin, bringing back the manure-spreader; he had been keeping it in his barn in case it should get stolen.

In the same way an old horse came back, also two cows and a pig which thoughtful souls had sheltered so that they would not die of cold and hunger. That had cost them something in feed. The newcomer frowned, but he never argued; he paid up. It seemed a bit queer to him.

As for the chickens, they must have been eaten by foxes for nobody could tell what had become of them.

At Grands-Pins the land is poor and no good for ordinary

farming, so for a long time it was almost abandoned. It was only when they began to plant tobacco that people came and settled there, people as poor as the land itself. In hardship and poverty at first, and then a little more easily, tobacco-growing will keep families alive even at Grands-Pins.

Old Langelier had been one of the first to try it. As he was no longer young and expected only a few years of peace as the reward of his toil, he had not had to spend a great deal. He had built quite a good dryer, the usual square building with two ovens heated from outside. He contented himself with a few thousand seedlings which he had grown from seed indoors on his old iron stove during the dead days of February. But when the time came to set them out he had paid a neighbour's boy or a passing labourer for a few days' work. He did the same in the busy cutting season.

He was proud of his tobacco, a strain he had preserved for years. Jealously he collected his seeds. Like everyone else, he covered seven or eight plants and let them come to maturity tied up in paper bags. But he had his own ideas. For instance he would never gather the seeds when there was an east wind.

In the kitchen Albert Langelier found the long boxes for the seedlings, but they were all dead. There was nothing left but dusty powdered earth, dead earth, with a few withered threads—all that was left of the old man's famous strain.

Winter had rusted the stove, and around it were lying a lot of empty cans; he gave them a kick and brought in his own cans, full ones.

Coming in at the back door, the usual entrance, you went through the kitchen into a sort of parlour with nothing in it but two horse-hair chairs that were losing their stuffing and a rickety sideboard. An old calendar on the wall still showed the February page, the one the old man had been unable to tear off.

Of the two bedrooms upstairs, Albert chose the smaller

where it was not so dark. The old man must have slept there, for on the bed there was a crumpled sheet and, dragging on the floor in the dust, a dirty blanket. The newcomer thought he might feel more at home in this room where evidently someone had lived before him.

Absent-mindedly he rummaged through the furniture, opening the dresser drawers one by one. A big pine cupboard occupied all one wall. He glanced in it: a broken glass, a crust of mouldy bread, and under the cobwebs in the corner, an old number of the People's Almanac. There was a bit of rag too with which he wiped the shelves before stowing his gear away. Then he saw sticking out of a crack a piece of paper. He took it out and began to read it. It was a fragment of a letter:

'. . . *at Montréal, I couldn't see you. I was staying with friends. But I would have liked to, because I needed to see you. I should have listened to you and done like Violette, instead of going off like that. But if you will keep your promise, it'll be all right. I have been to the Sisters to see . . .'*

The letter was torn here:

'*not too bad. But I managed to buy . . .'*

'*pants, and a cap . . .'*

'*make sense . . .'*

He looked at the back, but the damp had made the ink run and he could not make out the words.

Sitting on the foot of the bed with the letter in his hands he read it again and began to wonder. Was it talking about him, of the child he had been, the poor child, shut up in an orphanage, the only place he could remember from his childhood?

He could not recall ever having seen his mother; and the Sisters had made a point of telling him that she had made no provision for him, that the convent got nothing from any-one to pay for his keep.

He glanced at the paper again, then threw it on the ground

in the bachelor's careless way. But no, he must not do that, for this was his house. His house. He slipped the paper into his shirt-pocket.

What was the good of wondering? Why call up ghosts from the past when he would never even know their faces? Just before, he had instinctively looked for some photograph on the parlour walls that might show him his father's features. From this father he had received only two gifts, but they were remarkable ones: first life itself, but a life that no one welcomed. As soon as he had realized this, it had hurt him, hurt him so much that he had never started a life of his own, a real life, the product of his own hands, faltering at first perhaps, but gaining confidence and going ahead. The second gift was this unexpected heritage. At first he had refused to believe in it, so convinced was he of his own incurable bad luck. He heard of it in the middle of the off-season when he was out of work, waiting for the ice to go out and navigation to start so that he could go back to his job as a longshoreman. Every year was the same: he would earn big wages in the summer but spend them all as he got them; every fall would find him gazing out at the last liner going down the river before the freeze-up, and all he would have in his pocket would be his last week's pay.

When he inherited eight hundred dollars in a lump sum in the month of March, he thought he was a rich man; he had also been left a farm somewhere, at Grands-Pins, away at the back of beyond. That was the silly part of it. He would certainly never see that farm.

In a day or two he had gone through a hundred dollars and never regretted it. It was a wonderful noisy celebration, and the memory of it would last him the rest of his life. Then a friend offered him a chance to go in with him and another man in a bootlegging venture where all they needed was a bit of capital to buy their raw materials. After that there would be big money to burn. A piece of cake!

The very minute they began to make a bit, the police came down on them and their distiller was caught in the act.

Then Albert thought of the farm at Grands-Pins. It was so far off. Nobody would ever find him there, at the world's end. He would take refuge there from the police.

All he had to do was to live, to earn his living, like everyone else. That should not be so difficult; and since these country folk made a go of it, surely he could do as much, a bright town boy like him. 'Nobody's fool,' they called him. In this way his father, whom he had never known, had become a sort of Providence to him, intervening in the nick of time, to be regarded henceforward with almost religious gratitude.

Also he still felt he was well-off.

Of his inheritance he had nearly three hundred dollars left, which he had not had time to gamble away or squander. He had never had so much money all at once; he often touched his belt where his little roll of bills made a comforting lump.

His confidence failed him, however, in these unfamiliar fields. There was something sly about the land that muffled his footsteps; something mysterious in the bush that shrouded the river; something disturbing in the space all around that seemed to leave him isolated. To regain confidence, he endeavoured to work his land, the most tangible part of his property.

He bought seedlings from the neighbours and listened to their lengthy explanations with the expression of a man who knows more than he seems to. On the third day he was out in the fields with the horse harnessed up when he glanced back towards the house and saw someone looking in his direction. For a moment his heart was in his mouth. But no, it was all right; it was only a woman. A woman?

'Hi!' she called.

'Hi!' he replied.

He stopped the horse and climbed up towards the house

while the woman came slowly down to meet him. She waited, leaning on the fence.

'Good day. I'm Butch.'

'Good day.'

'I came to tell you that when the old man was alive I used to clean up for him every morning.'

'Oh.'

'Ya, I did up the house for him. Swept the place, washed the dishes, did the washing. He used to give me two dollars a month.'

'All right.'

Puzzled, Albert looked at Butch.

For him there were only two varieties: tarts and good women. The first class wore silk stockings and lipstick and advertised their curves; you could pick them up; they knew the answers and could laugh and chatter and join in a rowdy good time on pay-days. But good women were devoted to their homes, their children, their housekeeping, their husbands; they only went out on Sundays, to church; they never drank liquor.

This was a very simple classification. But the girl in front of him did not fall into either class. She had the youth and the smiling face of the first class, and her figure was slimmer than country folk like to see as a rule. But her lips were unpainted, and looked pale; her hair was left as nature made it and her legs were covered with common cotton stockings.

'Who did you say you were?'

'I told you. I'm Butch.'

'Butch what?'

She looked at him in surprise. Wasn't Butch enough?

'I live at the Vaillancourts', the third house down there, the green house.'

'Then Vaillancourt is your—'

'No. He's no relation. They took me in when I was little.'

'Your parents, where did they come from?'

'My parents?'

She shrugged her shoulders in astonishment. It was so long since anyone had asked her such a question.

'I just live with the Vaillancourts. My name's Saint-Ange. Marie Saint-Ange. But they all call me Butch.'

'All right. Now listen, Marie. If you'll do the same for me as you did for the old man, I'll give you your two dollars a month. Perhaps more. You don't look too bad. You know your work.'

'Sure I do.'

'And then maybe you know something about tobacco.'

He was really teasing her, but she replied quite seriously: 'Sure I know all about tobacco. It's all that we grow hereabouts. I always help, especially at planting time.'

She had evidently not understood his insinuation. After all, he told himself, she's only a country girl.

He had been there a week when he had a visit from an agent selling farm-machinery, a big man with glasses. He seemed dull on first acquaintance, but he was actually a very keen business man.

He was used to dealing with country folk and had adapted himself to their ways. He spoke their language and understood their doubts. He would never have tried to dazzle them with a line that would only have made them suspicious. He was particularly careful never to mention money until the last moment, after he had examined—or pretended to examine— the land, the machinery, the tobacco seedlings.

But this time he knew he had a different sort of customer to deal with. Above all he had smelled out a very rare thing: cash in the hand; and rarer still, cash ready to change hands.

Together they had checked what remained of Baptiste's gear: the old manure-spreader and an old-fashioned planter.

'It's unbelievable,' repeated the agent. 'It's unbelievable that old Langelier could have grown such good tobacco with old stuff like that, just a lot of old junk. The whole lot's hardly worth anything. Every year when I came in this direction I used to call and see him. He was a fine old fellow, a real good old Canadian type—but old-fashioned, you know, very old-fashioned. I was sorry for him.'

'Sure thing. You were sorry you couldn't sell him.'

'Well, after all, that's my job. But there was something else.'

He looked mysterious, and stared around as if every plant had grown ears. Yet the highway was deserted; the only living things in all the countryside were the busy black starlings over the fields; the air was full of the strange heaviness that comes in spring from the pregnant earth and acts like a tonic on the farmer's muscles.

'Sure, there was something else. Do you know that the people here were always jealous of old Langelier?'

'Jealous? Why would they be? He never did anybody any harm, I shouldn't think.'

'Lord no. But I was going to tell you. Old Langelier's tobacco, his own tobacco, was not ordinary stuff. I've been around tobacco-farms for twenty years and I've seen a lot of tobacco, good and not so good: big red and little red and little blue; comstock and cannelle. But never tobacco like old Langelier's . . .'

He gave a whistle between his dingy teeth.

'He got a good price for it?' asked Albert.

'My boy, you've hit the nail on the head. If the old man had wanted, he could have been rich in a few years, but he wouldn't change his ways. He stuck with his old machinery. You should have seen his cutter, for example. It tore up the plants, it was just a crime. It just spoiled them for sale. But he did leave you something, didn't he? Something good . . . ?'

He lowered his voice to a thrilling whisper.

'. . . the seed . . . of his own tobacco.'

By now they had come to the end of the field where the slope fell sharply away among the wild raspberry-bushes and the tiger-lilies by the stream until it came right down to the river.

'If you want to make some money, and I mean *big* money, you've got to have good tools. You know that. You come from the city. The big manufacturers are the ones who've got the best tools, the newest machines, aren't they? Whatever they cost they save you money, if only in saving time—they pay for themselves.'

In short he talked Albert into buying all he needed in modern machinery. The terms were easy: a hundred dollars cash and the balance later.

The seedlings were coming along well. On the agent's advice, and because he was handy with tools, he had made a hotbed. He spent happy days there in the warm spring sun, and felt himself unfolding like the tender shoots of his seedlings. He marvelled at them as they grew, as he watched the tiny green dots swelling, scarcely able to believe that they would turn into leaves, broad leaves spreading like a generous hand.

Sometimes when he was up on the hillside mending his fences along the slope by the black fir-trees, he would raise his head and see a big dark cloud on the horizon. Then he would rush home to the hotbed and lift the frame to give the seedlings air, terrified that they might be stifling before the storm.

He was still a city man and there were some things he could not get over. One was his continual astonishment when faced by nature's little tricks both beneficial and dangerous: the obstinate warfare of the weeds; the storms, where the drumroll of the thunder drowned out the voice of the wind; the hail, whose sharp crackle he learned to dislike when he realized the danger it could be to future harvests. The other thing that was new to him was his conception of the immensity of the land where his shadow covered only an infinitely small part, even when the setting sun lengthened it and made it a flat black giant on the ground.

He had kept the city man's habit of late rising. Of course

he was up by six o'clock, but every time it was a new sensation to find himself about at such an hour, and especially to feel so free, so full of vigour and get-up-and-go. On the other hand he was always astonished to see his neighbours already at work before him in the soft clear light of the morning.

About nine o'clock Butch would come along. He was eager for company so he used to watch for her coming and go up to the house as soon as she went in.

'Say, Marie, have you seen my spade?'

She would jump when she heard the name she had almost forgotten, which he insisted on using.

'Now don't tell me you've forgotten something else. In any case, since you're here, d'ya want me to make you some coffee? Did you have any breakfast?'

'I had something this morning.'

'All right. You come back in a minute or two and I'll give you something hot.'

She began to suspect that all this forgetfulness was really inspired by hunger. What surprised her even more was that he was so well-behaved, not bold at all. She started every time he appeared, imagining that she would feel two arms around her waist and have to put up a little self-defence. After all, the old fellow had been bad enough! But no. Monsieur Albert, as she still called him to the great amusement of the neighbours, had something else on his mind. He scarcely even called to her to say 'Good-night' when his day's work was over and he was sitting on the veranda, smoking his pipe and playing with his dog. For he had adopted a dog. And what a dog!

He had found it one morning at the door, panting, filthy, full of fleas. And simply reeking of skunk as a final touch. Where had he come from? Probably from a long way off. It was easy to reconstruct the 'tragedy'. He must have chased one of these evil-smelling creatures and met the usual defence.

One jet and the dog had fled away like a crazy thing, suffocating, seeking to rid himself of the intolerable stink clinging to his coat; rolling in the mud, dashing into the water, and never escaping from the shameful smell.

Albert had to chase him away, the odour was so appalling. The poor beast took refuge in the ravine, by the stream, spending hours in a pool trying to get clean and always returning to the house. So in the end they fed him, and at last accepted him.

The man, who had never had anything to do with animals, got on with this one, which seemed so strange to him that he tried to explain it to Butch, the only person he ever had a chance to talk to.

'The country's funny, all the same. Yes, it's queer how people can change.'

'Sure, you can't be the same on the land as you are in the city.'

'You said it. Who ever would have thought I'd have a dog. And he's not even a good-looking one.'

'That's true. He's not very good-looking.'

'No, he's not. But all the same, he's not dumb. In the evening, when I sit and have a smoke on the veranda, I talk to him. People need somebody to talk to.'

Butch was busy hanging out the washing which she had just finished bleaching; filling the line that stretched between the back shed and a young willow-tree, bending over the old basket to pick up the clothes, then holding them at arm's length like a flag while she put in the clothes-pins she took from her apron pocket.

She was standing with the sun behind her, outlining her silhouette on the white sheet and making a halo of her hair stirring in the wind—a somewhat indiscreet sun, revealing her slender legs in her flimsy skirts.

Albert watched her for a minute, a wisecrack on his lips,

but all he said was: 'Yes sir. I talk to my dog. I tell him about the city and I talk about myself, too. I wouldn't say he understands me, but he looks as if he does.'

'It must be lonely sometimes, though, even now you've got him.'

'Sometimes, but I'm getting used to it.'

'It's no life for a man, alone on a farm like that.' But she said that without any intention.

'Well, I'm not sure if I'll stay on the land. If things go all right I guess I'll wait a bit and sell it when the time comes.'

'Sell your land? Well, I suppose there are some people nowadays who would sell their land.'

However, he was beginning to adapt himself to his strange new life. He found his greatest satisfaction in proving to these country folk that a city fellow could farm. After all, he had got the salesman to explain his machinery, and he remembered all he had said. On the few occasions when he had gone visiting he had listened to every word about the land or tobacco-growing or the next job to be done on the farm.

What gave him most pleasure was the very irregularity of his life. Sometimes he had a holiday because of the rain; sometimes he was forced to work from early morning until late at night, especially at transplanting time. Then it really was tough.

He had hired one man, also Butch, for he knew she was strong and could stick at it; in fact she was one of the very few women in the district who could plant all day long with the men.

He spent three anxious days in the driver's seat with his back up against the water-tank warmed by the sun. Behind him, on two little seats, level with the earth, Jeremy Beland and Butch sat holding the boxes of seedlings on their knees. The blades in front would open up the furrow; they would set out a seedling, and hold it barely a second; there would be a mouthful of water for it from the tank, and then the blades behind would cover the furrow. They had to work fast and it was a back-breaking job. But in this way they planted twelve hundred seedlings the first day, fourteen hundred the second, and six hundred the third day before the rain came.

It had all been done so quickly. Yet he had felt strangely awkward. He had to keep his eyes on the horses so as to guide them straight ahead with the two planting behind. They were all keen workers and did not have much to say, but from the beginning, Jeremy let fall a few teasing remarks in his coarse but friendly way, and Butch had retorted without the slightest shyness.

Then the sun climbed high in the sky, stupefying them with its burning breath. Their actions became mechanical. From time to time the planters stole a mouthful of water intended for the seedlings and drank it from the palm of the hand with the sticky earth still clinging to it.

They took time off at midday after their lunch down by the river, which under the crushing noonday heat looked like a stream of molten tin. Albert suggested bathing, and the other man, who had at first refused, surprised at such an idea or perhaps intending to make up to Butch, finally followed him down to the waterside. They slipped into the stream among the reeds, and the glassy light shone on their hard, tough, masculine bodies. As for Butch, she was sleeping soundly.

But when the last day came, before the storm broke, it became very oppressive. They felt it blowing up and hurried with the planting. The sky was so heavy that the drops of sweat fell like rain in the furrow. And, doubtless spurred on by the electricity in the air, Jeremy started teasing the girl again and touching her knees whenever her hands were occupied.

In front of them Albert's back became strangely stiff and tense.

Several days later he noticed a cut on Butch's forehead.

'Say, Marie, have you been in a fight?'

She went on working without a word.

'I bet you've been celebrating. What on earth's that?'

'It's nothing,' she said in a quiet grey voice. He felt that something queer was going on.

'Did you fall over something?'

This time she turned and looked straight at him with her big heavy eyes.

'No, I didn't fall down. It was Jean-Jacques that did this to me.'

'Jean-Jacques?'

'Sure. One of the Vaillancourt boys, the one who's about sixteen.'

'What got into him? Is he crazy?'

'We were wrestling around.'

'Tell me about it.'

He insisted, more to keep up a conversation than out of curiosity. It came to him every now and then: he had need of human contact; he was tired of being eternally alone with nature's chilly silence.

'So you were wrestling around,' he repeated. 'I think your Jean-Jacques is an up-and-coming young fellow. You seem to like your boy-friends young.'

'He's not my boy-friend. He's a bad lot. He chucked a cup at my head. He could have killed me.'

'What had you been doing to him?'

'He started it. I wouldn't let him kiss me in the milk-house yesterday, so he said some awful things to me. I never did anyone any harm. I don't want anything, except to be left alone. To get his own back he said I had let the calf out into the tobacco on purpose. And when I said it was him who let it out, and that somebody else had seen him do it, he started pushing me around. And he called me names.'

'What did he call you?'

She had never talked about herself like this; she had learned to keep her troubles to herself, throwing them one by one into a great heap in some dark corner of her memory, so dark that they could not be seen or felt very often. Now Albert's questions opened up a window on this dark corner, and the whole heap of her troubles came into full view, welling up in her eyes and burning in her heart.

'What did he say to you, Marie?'

'He called me such names. Said I was no good, that I didn't have any parents.'

'Oh. What did you say?'

'I never said anything.'

They stopped talking. Marie turned to the stove where the peas were cooking for the soup. But he heard her give a little whimper now and then. At this moment the dog woke up, stretched, and yawned, showing his bright pink tongue, his black palate, and his gleaming white teeth.

'Come here, Patira.'

'Why do you call him Patira?'

'Why? I'll tell you, Marie. It's a name I saw in a book.'

'You've been reading a book?'

'Yes. I found it on a bench somewhere. There was an unlucky fellow in it, like me. He was called Patira. He was always in trouble. That dog, when I found him, was all alone; no father or mother. So I called him Patira.'

'But this Patira's different. He's lucky enough now!'

'Maybe. What do you think, fellow? Not bad just now, is it? If only it lasts. But if you're anything like me, you'll have no luck at all.'

Marie looked at him and felt something stirring within her, something warm and gentle, a feeling of brotherhood. She patted the dog's head, and said: 'Good dog.'

And now a long dry spell came down upon the earth. The sky was constant and cruel in its splendour. Every evening a giant sun crashed down upon a horizon in flames that foretold another killing day to follow.

All day long thousands of crickets made one single shrill clamour that never stopped; it began in the morning and was never hushed until late at night, under the soft naked light of the stars. The heat, beating on the fields, bore down with all its enormous, invisible weight to crush the man's feeble harvest.

At first the streams went on running, with their careless, happy song, trusting that rain would soon come and fill up the rocky bed. Then their morning music grew fainter, until it was nothing but a murmur. Where there had been shallow pools, there were only scabrous patches that showed more cracks every day.

At first the tobacco had flourished in the burning heat; the roots went deeper and deeper and still found the water in the subsoil. Then the heat dug into the sandy ground, drying it up a little more every day. The seedlings struggled, sending out their tiny rootlets, seeking the moisture that they felt was there. Soon there was nothing to find, nothing but a hard-baked crust crumbling gradually to dust.

Then the stems weakened, and the leaves; their green had gone and their edges were curling. Every day they drooped a little more, weary, desperate, dying.

At first the country folk had waited; then they fought back. Out in the fields at daybreak they filled their buckets at the river, and measured out a mouthful of water for each plant that vanished at once as if poured through a sieve. But the sun rose high in the sky and got ahead of them. No sooner had the water touched the soil than it straightway evaporated and rushed up towards the sun. The whole family kept at it in a feverish burst of speed; then, when high noon was unmistakably triumphant, the farmer would stand still in the middle of his field, raising his sweaty brow to the copper sky, scanning the weather, looking for the smallest breath of wind that might turn to the south-east.

Sometimes the very air seemed thick, saturated with the moisture that the thirsty earth was craving; it steamed like a cauldron. One cloud appeared on the horizon, vague and small at first, but soon swallowing up the blue. Then the farmers came out of their houses, men, women, and children, gazing towards the promised storm, watching it spreading its wings like some great bird in the sky, hoping it would alight on them and on their harvest. The rain-clouds would stream out on the horizon, but alas elsewhere, always elsewhere. At the last minute would come the saving rain, just when the dying earth expected no reprieve, a real downpour, but never at Grands-Pins—away over at Saint-Sulpice where the land was not so poor and not in such desperate need.

Albert gave up and enjoyed the pleasures of idleness. At first, like the rest, he had tried to save his crop, hauling to his fields under the hammer-blows of the sun the water that the heavens refused, but later he abandoned the effort. The neighbours had six, eight, ten in family; he was alone.

More than that, he was disillusioned, filled with a calm, definite distaste born of his inability to do anything at all. Now he began to realize that nature was not simple, but a book he could not read.

At first he had innocently imagined that a bright boy from the city could win out without any difficulty if these *habitants* could get ahead. All he knew of them was their calm and rather stupid-looking faces. Now he saw that the man of the fields must know more things, and more difficult things, than the man of the factory; and that he must also know how to be much more patient, more ingenious, more responsible.

Then insidiously there arose in the township a wicked wind; and over the minds of its inhabitants another sort of wind, in its effects like the one that tore up the weakened seedlings where their withered roots could not keep them anchored in the soil.

Albert had told some of them that he had never had any luck; others disliked him—distant cousins of old Baptiste who had hoped to inherit; two especially who had almost had the land staked out or bought for next to nothing.

They decided that Albert was a Jonah. The long drought was his fault. Where had he come from? And that absurd belief in magic, never far below the surface in the country, that sleeps in the dark ravines and the secret woods and the suspicious hearts of men, appeared, as always in time of disaster. They had prayed with no result. They had sung the special service against drought, they had paid for one mass after another, with no result. There must be something standing in the way since such remedies had proved useless. And despair turned man into what he was long ago, in the distant ages: a scared and spiteful animal, ready to run and hide or to bite.

The fiendish beauty of the sky seemed to have withered all joy in their hearts. Usually simple, kindly folk, quick to joking rather than anger, they felt their spirits growing heavier with each storm that hung over their fields and never broke.

At first they showed their feelings merely by an awkward, suspicious attitude. Albert, who did not know these people, felt more and more a stranger in their midst. They still said 'Good-morning' to him when they met on the roads, but if he turned round after passing a group of farmers, he found they were staring at him and whispering.

It was Butch who explained it to him.

One morning she never turned up. When he came back from the fields where he had been languidly trying to minister to his dying plants, he found neither the girl nor the coffee that she always had waiting for him at that time of day.

She did not appear until the next day, when she served his meal in a brooding silence.

'I don't think I can come back any more, Monsieur Albert,' she said.

'Why not, Marie?'

'I just can't come.'

'You're not sick, are you?'

'No, I'm not sick.'

'Well then . . . ?'

She began washing the dishes with her back to him; he could see only her shoulders bending over the dish-pan and the big yellow bun of her hair and the golden down on the back of her neck. He forgot himself for a moment, just looking at her. He had been alone so long. Then he came back to the present, to the immediate problem.

'Why don't you want to come back? Don't I pay you enough?'

'It's not that. It gives me a bit of money . . . it's all I get, for the Vaillancourts don't give me any. I just work for my board and lodging.'

'Then what is it?'

This time she turned round, her eyes misty. He scarcely recognized her face, and for the first time he realized, now that the brightness was gone, how bright and lovely her smile had been.

'They're bad people, Monsieur Albert. Bad people, I tell you. They say . . . they say—'

'What do they say?'

'They say you're unlucky, that you've brought your bad luck with you into the parish. They say . . . they say it won't rain until you've gone away.'

'So that's it. Yes . . .'

Through the open door Patira came in and lay down at his master's feet. Albert bent down and patted him mechanically:

'Good dog. Good dog.'

'Then the Vaillancourts say I had no business coming here.'

Outside the terrifying song of triumph from the crickets

was announcing another day of heat, another day of defeat.

'There's not much sense to that,' replied Albert. Then he laughed, but it was a laugh on the surface, like a ripple on a bottomless lake.

'I know I've never been lucky. But Marie, it doesn't make sense, does it?'

Butch hesitated; she started fussing with her washrag so as not to look at him in the face. 'I don't know. Really, I don't know. But all the same, there's something queer about weather like this. Nobody's ever seen anything like it. You never know.'

It went on for a few days more. The neighbours began stripping the plants that still survived—hard work, where all day long you are bent over, picking off the useless shoots that prevent the good leaves from growing and spreading out.

But when Albert went looking for helpers, he found none. Some replied that they had jobs already; others just looked at him, and when he did not leave they turned their backs on him.

Then he had a letter from the salesman telling him a payment would have to be made on the machines he had bought. Yet when he had signed, he had understood that he would not have to pay until after the harvest, after the crops had been sold, after he had collected his money, any time at all.

One evening, another evening when the air was like a sticky bitter paste, he felt that the end had come. He went down across the field where the yellowing stems stood in lines like withered offerings on tiny tombs. He went straight on down without looking where he was going, trampling the tobacco that rustled like silk beneath his feet.

At the bottom of the big ravine he watched the river gently sleeping, a very small river, with banks far too big for it. He stopped and ate a handful of raspberries mechanically. A blood-red sun was setting in a sea of mist. Its last rays were flaming on the meadows, not green as they should have been at that time of year, but quite yellow, ready for the torch. The air was clammy with humidity, and the sweat running down his brow was salty in his eyes. Patira stood panting beside him, and the thirsty earth drank in his saliva.

They climbed back to the house at dark, the master with his head high, the dog following to heel. They sat out on the porch until it was quite dark.

Then Albert lit his lantern. He went from room to room, closing each door behind him, drawing the blinds at every window. He made a bundle of his clothes, like the one he had brought with him, no bigger, no smaller. And when it was black night he went to bed. When he woke up, it felt as if he had not been to sleep at all; yet his watch said four o'clock in the morning.

Outside the night was ending, but there was no coolness in the morning air. He looked up at the sky, but there were no stars; the earth seemed strangely silent. What was wrong with the birds that they had stopped singing? There were a few beans left from the day before; he ate them cold, with a bit of bread and a mouthful of water.

Outside a vague pale light was glimmering in the east from below the overhanging clouds. He must be quick.

Patira was in his kennel near the door. Albert heard him stirring in his sleep, hesitated, but did not call him.

Steadily he walked to the shed, and came out carrying his axe. He looked around a moment, then went down towards the field and found himself among the tobacco plants. No, that was not the place!

He turned towards the stream where there was a hollow with green bushes in the shade. He whistled softly: a bark answered him.

When Patira reached his side, panting from his run, he struck him down with the axe, without a word, without a caress. Then he began to dig a deep hole. He did not shed a tear, but his lips were tightly closed. He threw the axe away, as far as he could, with all his strength.

Then he went back to the house, picked up his pack, and started off in the grey light of dawn.

And now, a few houses farther on, a shadow slipped out from behind a group of fir-trees. Butch must have seen him from the attic window. She had put a dress on, but her shoes were untied and her hair was loose down her back.

'Hullo. Is that you, Marie?'

'Where're you going like that?' She pointed at his swinging pack.

'Oh, sure, sure,' he said, feeling that she had guessed. 'I'm going back to the city. This is no place for me.'

He had begun to walk on. Butch hesitated a moment and then walked a few steps beside him.

'You don't mind, going off like this?'

He shrugged his shoulders and did not reply.

'I would have liked you to tell me first.'

'Why?' He tried to make a joke of it. 'Would you have gone with me?'

She stopped still a moment in silence; then she touched his shoulder gently and he too was still.

'Go with you? Go away with you?'

There was silence between them. Little noises were beginning in the Vaillancourts' house. She said softly, and the words welled up from within her like clear water from a spring: 'Perhaps. Yes. I would have gone with you . . . if you had wanted me.'

Then he looked at her, looked right at her, all of her. With eyes clearer than they had ever been before he looked, as if he had never seen her before that wretched morning: her clean mouth with its strange smile, her slender waist, the strong straight legs above her untied shoes. He felt that in all this countryside she was the only thing that was not a foreigner, the only friendly thing, the only thing that was precious to him although he had never suspected it. The only part of his possessions that he wanted to take away with him.

'All right. Are you coming?'

He saw her hesitate a moment, turning round and looking back at the house which was not her home although she had lived in it so long. He knew that if she turned back, even to go and fetch something, he would have to go on alone.

But she simply bent down and tied up her shoelaces. Then she carefully twisted her long hair into a knot on the nape of her neck.

They set off.

They halted for the first time quite a way along the road. They had been walking almost an hour and had reached the summit of the long slope. They stopped for a while to take breath. Albert was standing, looking away to the east. She was sitting on the sand, at the side of the road.

Mechanically and with some difficulty she traced with her finger in the sand: ALBERT, BUTCH.

He looked down at what she was doing and she blushed. Then gently with his foot he rubbed out BUTCH and bending down wrote MARIE.

They got up again.

Through a hole in the mass of cloud a ray of sunlight came down on them. They looked towards the west far away. Above Grands-Pins there was a grey bank of clouds heavy with kindly rain, and in the slanting sunbeams they could see the long dark streaks of the downpour.

'See, Marie? They've got their rain!'

She added, almost in a whisper: 'They've got their rain . . . now that you're gone.'

'Yes,' said Albert steadily. 'And we've got the sunshine.'

Translated by Morna Scott Stoddart

ALAIN GRANDBOIS

May Blossom

The servant boy had an exceedingly loud gong. As soon as
he entered the tiny first-class saloon, where I was trying
unsuccessfully for the tenth time to light a damp cigarette,
he began his infernal banging. I was by myself. The saloon
was about twelve feet square. Possibly fifteen. Barefoot, naked
from the waist up, the boy stood in the doorway, beating on
his metal disc as if to smash it. I signalled that that would do.
He continued, louder than ever. I swore at him loudly, to no
avail, then I got up, took him by the shoulders, and spun
him around, complete with gong, and gave him a couple of
good swift kicks, but gently, gently—I'm not a brute after
all. He fled into the passage, but soon came back to say, 'Me
love gong! Me love gong!'

Then he left, laughing. And all the while keeping up the
most frightful racket.

Great fleshy, voluptuous orchids adorned the captain's table.
The captain was laughing. Everyone laughs in the Orient.
Except the old people and the children. The captain said to
me, 'It seems you don't especially care for the sound of the
gong?'

'On the contrary, I'm very fond of it,' I replied. 'It's just
that I think the gong-boy is trying to rival the trumpets of
Jericho.'

'You're out of sorts.'

'Perhaps. I have a slight fever.'

'Ah, I see . . . '

We were having a good stiff drink of whisky, with plenty of ice. That may not be the best treatment for malaria, but it's a splendid way to drive off discomfort. Momentarily.

The captain and I were old friends by now. We'd just spent several days together, right in the heart of Canton province, cut off like rats on the island of Shameen. All around the island, Canton seethed with riots, spitting out hatred and death. Every bridge was protected by barbed-wire entanglements, flanked by machine-guns manned by ragged, barefoot soldiers, constantly yelling and leaping about, who were very quick on the trigger. At night, from the hotel roof, we could see the birth of monstrous crimson flowers of flame, watch them shoot up and grow tall in the four corners of the city. On the evening of the fifth day, after some mysterious negotiations, we managed to get back to the ship. The *Ngao-men* was an old six-hundred-ton tub plying the route between Canton and Macao. It had three 'first-class' cabins, the small saloon, and the officers' mess. As for the rest of her, the between-decks appeared to blend into the hold.

The captain told me, 'We won't arrive in Macao before tomorrow evening. I've had to alter my course towards the south-west. These waters are infested with pirates. In troubled times they spring up like mushrooms after a warm rain.'

'It's all part of the job,' I said, just to say something.

'Yes . . . it is part of the job . . . but I've been sailing around these coasts for over twenty years. I know every nook and cranny of them. I . . . I'm tired of it. I feel as if I'm not a sailor any more, but a functionary. The kind of incident you witnessed takes place with depressing regularity, like clock-work, according to the season. Now the great thing would be for peace to take hold one fine day, and last—that would upset this systematic chaos.'

The boy refilled our glasses.

I said, 'Why don't you ask for another command?'

'Because . . . it's too late. I'm sixty years old. I'm married. My wife and I have a small cottage in Macao. It's surrounded by flowers. And I'm counting on your coming there to see us. In all probability that's where I'll end my days . . . I was born at Noordwijk, on the North Sea. I'll die at Macao, in the South Seas. That's life.'

Once again we heard the gong. The captain laughed and said, 'You see, my gong-boy takes his work seriously. That's how he makes himself feel important. While he's beating on that thing he thinks he's master of the world. There are two cabin passengers. He beats for two hundred. Soon we'll have no passengers at all. But, he beats just the same . . .'

At that moment May Blossom appeared. She was tiny, very slim, and her face was astonishingly beautiful. She wore a sheath of deep blue silk, embroidered with gold. Her arms were crossed, her hands hidden in the wide sleeves. Like a convent Superior about to address her novices. She bowed slightly to the captain. The captain introduced us. He had suddenly become very formal.

We sat down to dinner. The boys bustled around us. The captain said nothing, apart from ordering the meal. Occasionally, between courses, she glanced at the captain or me. She wore a look of remarkable gravity. She ate so daintily, so delicately, it was as if she were gathering lilies beside a perfumed fountain. When we had finished eating, she bowed and left us, following the *maitre d'*. The boy brought us brandy.

'She's sixteen years old,' the captain told me.

The captain and I were stretched out on the upper deck. The evening was drenched in sublime sweetness. A russet moon, ringed with northern lights, swayed lazily in the rigging. Every so often a large junk crossed our bows, her sail like the underside of a giant bat's wing, and we could see naked men gathered round a fire on the after-deck, still and glistening as if cast in bronze. The horizon was submerged in the southern mist. We drifted on a sea with neither beginning nor end. A sea of eternal space. Nothing existed. Neither Canton, nor Macao, nor Noordwijk, nor Paris, nor Québec. No thing, no person. It was like a slow progression through a ghostly limbo.

Suddenly we heard the sound of light footsteps and May Blossom was beside us. The captain invited her to sit down. Two, three hours went by. No one uttered a single word. The darkness began to fade. May Blossom stood up and spoke a few words in Chinese to the captain. Then he said to me, 'Miss Cheng asks if you would like to hear a short poem by Siu Tche-mo . . .'

May Blossom looked out over the water and began to recite. Her voice, a soft contralto, sounded strange, veiled:

> *Away, world, away!*
> *alone, I reach the mountain top;*
> *Away, world, away!*
> *I face the vault of heaven.*
>
> *Land of my dream, away!*
> *I drop the jade cup of illusion;*
> *Land of my dream, away!*
> *smiling, I greet the mountain and sea winds.*
>
> *All things, away!*
> *before me the mountains pierce the sky;*
> *All things, away!*
> *before me vast infinity unfolds.*

May Blossom vanished. She did not come to the captain's table the next day. She was indisposed. Towards the end of the day we arrived at Macao. By this time the city of every vice sent up a lurid glow from its many fires. I said goodbye to the captain, who repeated his invitation.

'I'm on forced leave,' he said. 'I'll have to wait until the Canton troubles cool down before I resume my command. I'm going to tend my rose garden.'

After lunch on the flowered terrace of the villa, the captain's wife, a beautiful woman of Chinese and Portuguese descent, served us fragrant tea. We were chatting about nothing in particular when the captain suddenly asked me, 'What do you think of my god-daughter?'

'Your god-daughter?'

'Why yes, Miss Cheng. May Blossom.'

'I had no idea . . .'

'I know, I know . . . it's a secret that I must ask you to guard closely, at least for the rest of your stay in Macao, because if old Cheng found out there'd be hell to pay.'

'Old Cheng?'

The captain lit his pipe.

'Old Cheng is May Blossom's father. He's the richest and most prominent man on the peninsula. The most lavish supporter of all worthy causes—regularly distributes rice, tea, and clothing to the needy along the coast, and even takes it upon himself to see that the dead are properly buried. He's also general advisor to the Governor of the colony. An extremely important person. That's the sort of success, according to conventional wisdom, that crowns a long life of good deeds and splendid virtues, wouldn't you say?'

'Indeed,' I replied politely.

But the captain went on excitedly, 'Indeed, indeed! But sometimes it happens, my dear young friend, that conventional wisdom has it all wrong. Because old Cheng is the damnedest fiend alive. He's the greatest brigand in the South Seas. Fifty years ago he was just a coolie in Canton. He turned pick-pocket, pimp, pirate. He became head of a gang. It wasn't long before he was masterminding a whole network of activities involving prostitution and drugs. During Dr Sun's revolution he managed to become a general. He bought and sold, rebought and resold, several armies. He conquered the North, where he picked up with some other warlords. In 1917 he supplied guns and ammunition to the Germans; in 1920, to the White Russians; in 1923, to the Bolsheviks; in 1925, both sides, the armies of the North and those of the South; today he goes three ways—Chiang Kai-Shek, the communists, and Japan. The ambassadors and consuls never know which way he'll jump. I don't know whether he knows himself, but he always lands on his feet. Here in Macao he controls the gambling houses, the bordellos, the race-tracks, the drug-trade, alcohol distribution, the loan-sharks, and, needless to say, all the local politics, which, believe me, are of a remarkably oriental complexity. He lives in Macao, under heavy protection, since he doesn't dare show his face in Canton or Hong Kong, where his life wouldn't be worth a cent. Occasionally a small bomb finds its way into the garden of his palace. But only the servants get blown up. So much for old Cheng. He is very highly re-garded. And scrupulous about observing the rites . . .'

'And the god-daughter?'

'The god-daughter . . . well, the old gangster, for reasons unknown to me, entrusted her education to the nuns of Con-vent X in Hong Kong. Cheng trusts me. As much as he can trust anyone, that is. To the extent that he has asked me to look after her when she's travelling . . . But two months ago May Blossom was baptized, without her family's knowledge, and I was the godfather . . . that's the story. But what do you think of her?'

'I . . . well, your god-daughter seems to be an awfully serious young person. She has a way of looking at you . . . she almost intimidates me. . . .'

The captain began to laugh. Then he said, 'I'm telling

you about her because she told me that she would like to see you again. She means to invite you . . . she's been asking me questions about you. She knows you're Catholic and that you write.'

'She knows a good deal,' I told the captain. 'Be that as it may, my visit here in Macao is far too short to spend it with young society girls. I would much rather meet old Cheng.'

'No doubt. But old Cheng has shown no interest in seeing you.'

I asked the captain, 'What on earth is all this about?'

'I'll be hanged if I know.'

'And what would you do, in my position?'

'You're free and adult. I never give advice. It's a waste of breath.'

'Then I'll tell the young lady that I'm far too busy, that I'm dreadfully sorry, and so forth . . .'

'You're a sensible man,' the captain said. But the captain's wife was smiling.

Someone knocked at my door. I called out 'Come in'. A boy handed me a letter. I opened it. Miss Blossom notified me that the next day, at eleven o'clock, a carriage would convey me to the palace. The boy never moved.

'Answer?' I asked him.

'Ya, ya, mastah sah, answah.'

I wrote to Miss May Blossom that I was grateful, that I was sorry, dreadfully sorry, and so forth, and put the sheet of paper into an envelope. Then I tore up the envelope and wrote to Miss May Blossom that I accepted her charming invitation with the utmost pleasure.

The following day at eleven I climbed into a carriage drawn by two small white horses. An elderly Chinese woman huddled in the back. She motioned to me to sit beside her.

It was May Blossom's governess. Her amah. She wore the scowl of someone who was extremely displeased. We

went over the Praîa Grande at a quick trot and found ourselves in a wide avenue shaded by the dazzling green foliage
of royal palms and carob trees. Lining the street were villas,
soft rose, pale ochre, faded blue, just visible behind the
profusion of greenery. Then the road began to wind, twisting
this way and that, like a snake. All at once the amah spoke
to me in a querulous tone:

'The master is terrible, really terrible . . . He must not
find out . . . It would be the end of me. Oh, I tried to
prevent Miss Blossom. I begged her, I wept . . . I'm only a
poor old woman. How in the world would I cope with the
master's rage? Now tell me honestly, what could I do?'

Whereupon she began sobbing in quick half-smothered
bursts. Then, 'Ah, I'm a poor old wicked, shameless
woman . . . I couldn't resist Miss Blossom. I've never been
able to resist her . . .'

She was silent. We were steadily climbing a hill. After
some time the wall that surrounded the palace came into view.
The amah, who had finished her sobbing, said: 'The master
has gone down the hill to see the Governor. One of the
servants is keeping watch over the ways out of the palace.
There are more along the road. They will give us warning
signals. You will go back the way we came. The master has
a fast car and will come home by the main road.'

She sounded like a general outlining strategy to his officers.
We drew alongside the wall and the carriage stopped in front
of a sturdy, dark wooden door. We got down. The amah
lifted a bronze knocker and the door opened. Like Sesame.
We were in a long covered walk-way. On either side were
marble-flagged courtyards, flower gardens, fountains ringed
by willows, pools embroidered with pink lotus, and pavilions
shaped like pagodas. The amah led me to a pavilion shaded
by an immense banyan tree. I entered a tall, square chamber,
its ceiling made of latticed beams along which brightly painted
dragons reclined at full length. Panels with delicate brush-

work characters hung from the walls. Black lacquer tables bordered in vermilion, some chairs, a divan, curios and ornaments of jade and ivory, a large bronze buddha, sleek and glossy.

May Blossom appeared. She was utterly beautiful. She bowed and indicated that I should sit down. A servant brought a tea tray. She presided over the tea in the same deliberate and fastidious manner that I had so admired at the captain's table. We drank our tea. The boy removed the tray.

She was sitting across from me.

She said, in her soft, low voice, 'The captain has undoubtedly informed you, since I gave him permission to do so, that I am Catholic . . .'

'Quite so,' I replied.

'In a week's time I must return to the Convent of X. I will spend three more months there. Then I am to return here, to my father's home.'

I must have shown some surprise because she quickly added: 'You will wonder why I'm telling you this. Well, here is why. I am supposed to return in three months, but . . . but I cannot return.'

I waited.

'I cannot come back here because they wish me to marry. My husband has been chosen for me. I do not know him. According to the rites, I will not see him until after the marriage. I know nothing of him, except that he comes from Yunan, and that his father is wealthy . . . I cannot come back because I cannot marry him. And I do not wish to. I am a Christian.'

Her lips trembled. Like a child's, on the verge of crying.

'I am a Christian. I would be obliged to live with his family. It would be forbidden me to worship my God freely. He would live the way my brothers do . . .'

Again I waited.

'I have three brothers. They are all married. They live here, in the palace. Their wives are my friends. They are refined and charming. My brothers spend their evenings at the theatre, or in the gambling casinos. They have taken concubines and brought them here to live, in the most beautiful of the pavilions . . . My friends weep in secret. What can I say to console them? I do not want that sort of life. I do not wish to weep secretly.'

Her angelic little face looked bruised. Her eyes were lowered. She got up and opened a small casket and then handed me an envelope. I bitterly regretted having come, having given in to my foolish curiosity. She said: 'The captain told me that you intend to visit Shanghai. Take this photograph. I would ask you to glance at it now and then. They say . . . that I am beautiful. I feel terribly ashamed of speaking to you in this way. But I must. And if, three months from now, you . . .'

The amah rushed in, very agitated. 'The signal, the signal has been given. The master has just left the Governor's palace.'

May Blossom went on, very quickly, 'If, in three month's time, you send this photograph to the Captain with your address written on the back, he will not understand what it means, but I will understand . . . and I will leave for Shanghai.'

She turned away slightly, and added in a very low voice, 'I would make you a most faithful and obedient wife . . .'

Then she looked directly at me. She was crying. She attempted a smile. I left. The amah led me again to Sesame and I returned to Macao. Later on, in Shanghai, I wrote to the captain. But I kept the picture of May Blossom.

Translated by Patricia Sillers

GABRIELLE ROY

Ely! Ely! Ely!

I still ask myself what could have prompted me that evening to go from Winnipeg to Ely, a village only some thirty miles away, by train. It was the Transcontinental, a huge train of rarely less than forty cars. It left Winnipeg shortly before midnight. It took forever to get under way.

And hardly had it picked up speed, it seemed to me, when it already slowed down again. Shortly afterwards appeared the train conductor who, looking rather disgruntled, took my heavy suitcases which he dragged to the platform—I was at the end of the train, in the very last car. He opened the door on a howling wind, on a landscape of apocalyptic darkness and into this abyss he intoned monotonously: Ely! Ely! Ely!

I knew the name since childhood because my father had established at Ely settlers from Québec, even some members of his family, and had always spoken about it. I had, however, never set foot there, not even felt attracted to it. A lot of circumstances had to occur to arouse the passionate curiosity that I experienced now for Canadian people and places: my living abroad, travelling to remote places in Essex and Provence, experiencing loneliness upon returning to Montréal and settling there; and perhaps above all feeling for some time homeless.

The conductor, having stepped down to the ground and

undoubtedly finding that I took too much time catching up with him, began to call out again, into the emptiness: Ely! Ely! Ely!

I got there. He gave me his hand. I found myself, close to him, in deep darkness, and without a sign of life except that of the train that right up to the last car was ready to take off again snorting with impatience transmitted by the engine that was so far up front that its suppressed power could only be guessed at.

'But where is Ely?' I asked.

The conductor pointed in the direction of some faint lights scattered in the distance. He jumped on the footboard, again took up his lantern which he began to swing, like a priest his censer, outside the train in the dark night. At once the train took off again, picking up speed quickly this time as if it had only waited to get rid of me. Apparently whistling with relief it announced: For a long time I won't have to stop again. Its rear light already disappeared in the silky infinity of the prairie night. Then I realized that it had put me off as close as possible to Ely, should its engine be level with the station. Thus with the head of the train at Ely, I myself must have been a good half-mile away from it out in the country.

I found myself in light sandals, far from any dwelling, in some mists of time, with two suitcases to drag . . . and I burst out laughing. Then, leaving in the high grass my heavy suitcases about which I certainly didn't have to worry, I set off on foot straight ahead.

Now the night, which I had thought was empty and lifeless, revealed itself full of gentle soothing sounds. These were a part of a nocturnal life which was abundant, although it was at first a bit difficult to make out. From some gentle vibrations, I could sense wheat fields which stretched far out on both sides of the railway. Sometimes when two waves of stalks happened to move against each other, a strange surging noise resulted. In these dry fields there is apparently, according to the wind's caprices, a kind of surf.

Sometimes, I also heard a muted grating. It wasn't quite yet the season of the fiddling insects. However, I could have sworn that one of them, a grasshopper or a cricket, long before the others was trying out its bow. And the railway tracks still hummed a bit with the rumbling of the train which had undoubtedly already reached the next village.

I went slowly. This strange night into which I had stepped as a stranger became familiar and friendly to me. Did I ever feel so much in Canada as on that night? With my hands free, my hair blowing in the wind, I remembered the hoboes of my childhood that one could see blackened by the soot of the train and who talked about the country like nobody else. A country's first link—wouldn't it be a physical link: a stream, a river, a path, a road, a railway? That could explain perhaps why our hearts remain attached to the railway while they are hardly enamoured with the plane, a superb bird without a home.

Now, the lights before me became more distinct and marked the outlines of the village: the main street was marked off by a few street lamps; a handful of houses whose windows were still lit up. Some black holes in between which were probably sleeping houses; finally a brilliantly lit entrance: no doubt the hotel.

I knew these little Western hotels, almost always the same everywhere, with their strange wooden ornamental fronts cut up by steps, their noisy tavern, their old drunks returning at the closing of the tavern to the hall or the big sitting-room filled with huge leather armchairs each with its spittoon beside it; with its familiar characters also practically the same from one end of the country to the other, retired farmers who were forever bored, bearded Poles, sometimes the teacher, sometimes a lawyer, but not necessarily. What these talkers had in common wasn't so much their age or their trade, but the unending need to probe the human condition.

With all doors open, there came to me now the flow of several conversations taking place simultaneously in the hotel hall and undoubtedly in several languages for they created in the distance the strangest racket.

Now suddenly there rose from this rumbling babel perfectibly audible, if I may be so bold as to say so, a 'damned traitor I tell you, if I ever see your damned face again . . .' The phrase reached me while I was still away from the village. Then the rough voice that had uttered it receded in the brouhaha as mysteriously as it had sprung up.

I thought I heard then: 'You, shut up, Charrette . . .' and couldn't get over finding myself in familiar country, so to speak.

With my hair tousled in the open air, my white linen suit stained with cinders, the strap of one sandal broken, I finally arrived at the village. I think my face also showed then signs of a kind of intoxication due to the strangeness of the night, the invigorating air and I don't know what exhilaration that this long walk had aroused in me while time had apparently stood still.

I appeared on the threshold of the hotel. The conversations ended abruptly. Sentences remained in suspense. Everybody was staring at me. And at first I myself was dumbfounded by the surprise I had created. Only afterwards did I understand. Nobody there had heard a car coming. As far as the train was concerned, if someone had remembered its brief stop, this had been so long ago, it didn't occur to anyone that I could have got off the train. In the eyes of these flabbergasted men, I had come from nowhere. And moreover, happy, because undoubtedly my face still showed my amusement at finding myself in such a predicament.

Among the dozen silent men, all scrutinizing me, I glimpsed a particularly striking figure with azure blue eyes and a dark beard, who wore a high black felt hat shaped like a stove pipe. I easily recognized a brother of the Hutterite sect. I told him at once in English that I had come to Ely precisely with the aim of studying the Hutterite colony in Iberville, close to this village; that I intended the very next day to ask the elder of the group for permission to visit them and that we would certainly meet again. From his bewildered look, which was like that of all the others, I realized that they thought I had made my story on the spot.

Then, choosing in this silent group a face that was perhaps a bit more friendly than that of the others, I asked quite by chance, in French, whether I could have a room for the night.

Luckily, I had hit on the right person. The man to whom I had addressed myself broke away from the group and went behind the counter where he began to rummage in a pile of torn magazines. He finally found the register whose cover was protected with wrapping paper. Then he looked for something with which to write. I had approached the counter and watched him. Suddenly, in a low voice as if it hoped it would pass unnoticed in spite of everything in such complete silence, I heard him asking me:

'Where do you come from?'

Was it the tone in which he had asked the question, the atmosphere of the anxious curiosity which surrounded me—all waited for my answer—the fact is that it seemed it was asked figuratively and I was tempted to answer that I had no idea.

My astonishing trip, the strange destination, the murmur of voices in discordant languages which had welcomed me on the threshold of this place, indeed everything, inclined me to get to the bottom of the pertinent question. Where, indeed, did I come from? From the neighbouring city where I was born and from where I could have gone a hundred times in search of Ely during my childhood and youth, although I had never thought of it then? From Québec, the place of my family origin where I felt I was summoned towards my deep roots? But if that was it, with which side should I identify myself especially? With the Roys, troubled people, strict, Jansenists according to what I had been told, but also idealists and dreamers? Or with the Landrys, vivacious, impulsive, gracious and smiling? Where should I turn to to learn from where I came? And wouldn't it be necessary to go even further back? Without realizing it I fixed my eyes beyond the open threshold on the black of the night. Vague, gentle noises from the close-by prairie came to die on this doorstep as if, sighing gently, it expressed its desire for company. I saw all these men hanging on my lips. I was tempted to ask them: 'Where do we come from? Do we know!'

Meanwhile, behind the counter, my man watched me closely. He repeated a bit more loudly:

'Where do you come from, Miss?'

I watched him in turn. He was a middle-aged man, with a pleasing look, rather heavy, of dark complexion, black hair and eyes. What prompted me to ask him:

'And you?'

He looked even more embarrassed than I.

'Originally?' I said.

He made a gesture which embraced an area difficult to determine 'from Wisconsin . . . Before, from Massachusetts . . .'

'And before, no doubt, from Québec?'

He seemed to remember then that it was up to him to ask and he began again:

'But, where do you come from now?'

Finally, I realized that he merely tried to find out the mystery of my arrival on foot, past midnight.

'You could have found the door locked, and everybody in bed,' he reproached me. 'It's only because of the heat that we're still open.'

'That's all I would have needed!' I said. 'Which reminds me: I left my two suitcases on the edge of a wheatfield, about half a mile from here.'

'You came by train? But it passed almost an hour ago.'
He reflected a moment, remembering. 'That's true. We
thought it had stopped . . . oh barely! . . . Sometimes just
long enough to drop off a parcel. So it was you!'

His curiosity being satisfied a little, he told me not to
worry about my suitcases.

'There, where you say you've left them, there's nothing
to fear. There isn't a soul about . . . I'll have them picked
up at dawn.'

Then he offered to show me to my room.

I climbed a narrow staircase behind him and followed him
into the hallway. He opened the door on a small room that
was clean and attractive but where all the summer's heat
seemed to have concentrated. He opened the window and
warned:

'You'll have to wait a while to let it cool down a bit.'

I went downstairs with him again. The conversation,
which had again been in full swing after we had left, died
down once more.

Since my man had taken up his place again behind the
counter and had begun to leaf through his old magazines, I
thought a long time of some subject for conversation.

'The hotel belongs to you?' I finally asked him.

'I bought it two years ago from a guy called Dybrowski.'

We took a long time to digest this sentence. Much later I
came back to my idea:

'You make a living with it?'

'With what?'

'With the hotel.'

He smiled amiably with a little smile that seemed to embrace all people of my kind.

'If it were only for the passers-by! . . . With the tavern,
yes, almost . . .'

Our eye was caught by a customer who cleaned his teeth,
his mouth wide open, with his fingers.

'Do you often stay up so late?'

'We don't like putting people out the door . . .'

With this, as if the reproach had been meant for him, the bearded Hutterite said: 'It is late . . .', then got up, came a few steps towards me and solemnly declared in English with a strong German accent:

'Upon your coming to visit the Hutterite colony of Iberville, do not forget to ask for me, Joe Wallman, the shepherd. I shall be honoured to be of some assistance to a young lady from Québec.'

Thus, at the end of his long observation of myself in which he had indulged, my story finally seemed convincing. But they were few who shared the sentiments of the Hutterite who had become so friendly. What was most damning against me, as I learned later, was that I spoke French with a slight accent which I had acquired in France and English apparently with intonations which remained with me from my stay in England. Only the German Hutterite wasn't particularly surprised about all this. He greeted me with his strange black hat and went away.

He had hardly left when their tongues loosened a little.

'Damned hypocritical people!' they said of him. 'They take vows of temperance, for anything you like, but they're always at the hotel trying to get a free beer.'

'Just because of a beer now and then, you shouldn't call Wallman a hypocrite,' the hotel-keeper objected. 'Wallman isn't a bad guy.'

The haggler looked annoyed. He jammed on the greasy cowboy hat, that had apparently been stuck on his head for many a month, and bid us a surly good-night. Once he had left, it was silent again, but even more so. Open suspicion could be read in everyone's face. It was wartime. People saw spies everywhere . . . Now I had said I had come by train, but what proof was there of that? Suitcases? A mile away and nobody had seen them! And how was it that I, a stranger, was forever asking questions instead of answering them, as would be proper?

For a while I tried to sustain their looks as they scrutinized me from beneath their old hats. Contrary to custom which allows the accused to wear his hat, out of respect for him, this disrespectable court of judges used head-dress which was permanently fixed. But I was tired, I was ready to drop with sleep. I was going to retire to my room, leaving these distrustful men to their conjectures. As I reached the stairs the hotel-keeper's voice called me back:

'You haven't signed the register.'

I retraced my steps. I took the prepared pen from the hotel-keeper's hand. I wrote my name and address after that of somebody called Wilkinson who had registered for one night a little more than a month ago. I was already quite settled in the mind of the 'listeners'. What got into me to surprise them even more by asking another ill-timed question? It was as if I couldn't help myself—their hostile curiosity provoking mine in retaliation.

'What did Wilkinson come here for?' I asked in spite of myself and probably in a severe tone.

The row of old hats suddenly got up. The hotel-keeper was startled.

'Wilkinson. Which Wilkinson?' And without delay, he asked anxiously:

'Are you from the government?'

'The Wilkinson here . . . on your register.'

'Oh! That one! He's a Fuller Brush salesman.'

'They are still around!'

'Of course.'

'The Pain Killer too?'

'That too . . . But yourself, whom do you represent?'

You'd have thought a scene from something like Gogol's *Government Inspector* was being staged.

'Nobody. I've come to gather material for an inquiry.'

'An inquiry? You're making an inquiry?'

'About Canada.'

'Canada!'

'Yes. What is Canada? And first of all is there a Canada?'

Perturbed, he examined me with obvious disapproval.

'Why, is there a Canada!'

'Everybody is asking himself about it.'

The little friendliness and politeness he had finally granted me gradually was suddenly taken away from me. In the corner of the room where they kept together, the old hats didn't stir any more. Suddenly I had enough, I drew the register with the brown cover toward me. Below the signature of the brush salesman, I put mine.

In turn, the hotel-keeper drew the book toward him, glanced at my signature, took a sudden interest in it.

'You are a Roy?'

His severity and animosity vanished visibly. Finally he smiled at me and I thought then there was something sympathetic in his face.

'I'm Dave,' he said.

'Dave?'

'Yes, Dave.'

I don't know what he expected of me. Having my doubts, I preferred to be on my guard. To keep a certain distance, or perhaps because of my embarrassment, I busied myself with the register. The last guest registered before Wilkinson was somebody called Marchand. I asked, without really fully realizing that I had begun asking questions:

'This Marchand, did he come from Québec?'

'What Marchand?'

I was surprised by the change that had again appeared in the hotel-keeper's features; every trace of friendliness had again disappeared. He had become cold, distant and seemed offended.

'What difference can it make to you if a merchant has been here!'

I shrugged my shoulders and rather stiffly bade them all

good-night. Before going upstairs, however, I had to be more friendly toward the hotel-keeper, for I had to ask him to have me woken up at seven o'clock and if possible, order a taxi for me for eight o'clock so that I would arrive early at the Hutterites.

'So your story is really true? You're really going to visit these people?'

I thought of studying one of their colonies, then different ethnic groups in Canada, without having a clear idea of where it would lead me. As a matter of fact, I was just beginning in journalism and quite awkward; but the rather cool welcome I had been given and the shyness with which I was then afflicted impelled me to want at all costs to give myself an air of importance. I therefore announced firmly:

'I am taking a survey throughout the country . . .' far from doubting that I would do it somehow, in spite of myself, one thing leading to another; that I would see myself in the end with enough material to write about Canada and its people for the rest of my life, and that even my whole life wouldn't be long enough.

'To know what?' he asked.

'The truth.'

The hats in the corner appeared to me to draw together as if to be at one against me. The hotel-keeper stiffened. I didn't know yet that announcing the search for truth puts everybody on the defensive. There was something like tangible fear around me.

Once again I said good-night and went up to my room.

At the agreed-upon time, the hotel-keeper stated curtly through the door:

'It's seven o'clock. Your taxi will be here at eight o'clock. It's five dollars for the trip to Iberville. Your suitcases are in the hallway.'

When I went down, he was behind his counter, looking drowsy, unshaven, still leafing through his old magazines. I wondered if it was possible that he could still find something new in them.

Obviously it was just to give himself an air of composure, for several times while I was drinking my coffee which he himself had served me, I noticed that hurt look of the evening before which puzzled me very much. At the same time he seemed on the point of addressing me with some reproach which he could hardly check. It was only when I was just about to go through the door that he assaulted me in the back: 'You're a queer one.'

'I?'

'A queer one,' he repeated. 'You come here. You question everybody. You make an inquiry, as you say. You invite confidences, but, who'd have expected it, you make sure that you won't reveal yourself!'

His strange expression exuding both a reproach and apparently a desire for a rapprochement finally upset me.

'I'm Dave,' he began again, hopefully.

Then from my deep store of vague, distant memories the name of David which I must have heard at home came back to me. Could he be the son of a nephew of my father?

I retraced my steps.

'Could you be? . . .'

'Of course!' He called out joyously and triumphantly. 'I'm your cousin Dave.' He didn't stop recalling:

'I said so too, I said to my wife, you'll see, she's going to make herself known. Are you coming for supper at the house tonight? With the family? . . .'

I went there. Dave with his wife Rosalee and his daughter Jacinthe lived in a charming little house with a pointed roof, quite low among tall trees and countless flowers. Hours ago the table had been set waiting for me. Rosalee had gone to a lot of trouble to prepare a meal worthy of this strange meeting.

We spent several hours very happily together. I wasn't

quite sure that they were my cousins. Certainly they cited from memory many of my father's sayings and expressions, but who in the village hadn't known him? Who at least didn't remember his colonizing work? Anyway, it didn't really matter. On the wall, there was just like at home, when I was a child, a portrait of Pope Benedict XV and one of Brother André of course. There was also the same picture of the Holy Family that I had always seen in our kitchen above mother's sewing-machine, and here it was also just above the sewing-machine. Obviously we were a family. Québec was everywhere present, wherever I looked, among people who, however, had never set foot there again since leaving their cradle, so to speak. But their gentle speech was Québec's. Their friendship that was so warm and caring belonged to it.

How strange! Long before the days of radio and television, the old Québec, Québec, alone and poor, sent out living waves. They spread out in all directions. They reached distant villages, lost hamlets, even solitary homes like the one where I was this evening, and they warmed them with humble flame that was felt everywhere.

My inquiry began well. Right from the beginning I rediscovered the mysterious flame of fellowship which had shone for me in the prairie and had made me in part what I was.

I said so to my 'cousins' who seemed touched. They then lavished on me a thousand pieces of good advice on how to approach the sensitive but reticent Mennonites: the Doukhobors who were at first unsociable but then so warm in their welcome; the Ukrainians who were sometimes abrupt but whose friendship was unequalled once they offered it. To sum it up, it seemed to me, they spoke to me of men in general.

A week later I made the Transcontinental stop again just for me. As long as people could remember that had never happened twice in such a short time. To stop the train you had to wave in front of the engine a kind of flag you took from a nail on the front of the station which at that hour seemed soundly asleep. Strictly speaking, it wasn't done. But I had read in the CN timetable that one had a right to do it. For greater efficiency I placed myself right in the middle of the tracks while I waved my flag. I waved my arms as soon as I saw the shiny eye of the engine. It stopped at the exact spot where I had just stepped back. In the total darkness, I surveyed the train in vain; nowhere did I see a possible entry in its smooth side: the first seven or eight cars were sleeping cars, all doors were tightly shut where the people slept, except perhaps for those who had woken up with a start and who must have asked themselves, 'Why on earth do we have to stop in this hole?'

Finally, much farther down, my cousin and I noticed the light of a lantern moving in a gesture which seemed to mean: 'Down here. Down here. And for heaven's sake, hurry up.'

It wasn't quite as far as where the train had let me off when I arrived but it was a good distance away. We ran, out of breath, with my suitcases, not daring to slow down because of the little puff of steam with which the gigantic train seemed to hurry us on.

At last I noticed a step that was quite small and by itself in this world of darkness, travelling, wandering and silence. Beside it stood the conductor. 'My' conductor. He said, less with blame it seemed to me, than with real satisfaction of finding me again in this vast Canada:

'So, it is you!'

He gave me time to say goodbye to my cousins.

We went up, the two of us, with the lantern, the suitcases, and the step, and instantly, as it took off, the train sent us hitting our nose against a wall.

I had a car almost all to myself. After he had put away my suitcases and checked my ticket, the conductor still didn't leave.

He wanted to know if I had liked Ely, and perhaps without admitting it, he too really wanted to know what I had gone there for. Especially, I think, he felt like talking to another human being. These long night trips through the monotonous prairie that was almost without lights and seemed to have returned to its original state must have bored him profoundly. At times I had sensed that no one on earth gets as bored as he who belongs to the race of travellers, but up to then I hadn't thought of including train conductors among them.

Today I regret not having listened to him. But he seemed about to tell me his whole life: his childhood in Liverpool, his years in Montréal, then in Winnipeg, well, his existence which apparently couldn't be separated from that of the CN.

My own thoughts called me. I listened absent-mindedly. He ended up noticing it. He went away regretfully.

Then I let my head rest against the back of the seat. I relished my recent memories. I had even greater expectations for tomorrow. The long train whistles that now tear at my heart then delighted me. Oh, how happy I was! Going ahead, as receptive to the unknown of our country as to the whole future that was still possible for the world.

Translated by M.G. Hesse

CLAIRE MARTIN

The Gift

As I was leaving the movie theatre that night I saw Francis Thierry arm-in-arm with a slinky redhead—wearing green, naturally. Women with red hair are born knowing they look spell-binding in green; they know it makes their white skin look silvery and that the red hair flaming above it makes them look like something conjured by an alchemist. If they happen to have green eyes as well, you expect them to cast your horoscope or conduct you to their nocturnal revels. Circe was probably a green-eyed redhead. Poor Thierry, do you suppose he knew anything about Circe?

Up until then I had only seen him with sentimental, soulful little blondes whom he could easily sweep off their feet. Thinking a poet was in love with them, they felt they had to look plaintive, to sigh languidly, and roll their eyes heavenward at every turn. Thierry wrote them syrupy little verses that made them fall all over him. That was all right. To each his own weapons. But later on he published the poems. That was not all right.

The whole thing started when he was only about fifteen. In the throes of puberty and lacking money for ice-cream, he discovered that the best way to make conquests of the neighbourhood girls was to present them with extracts from *You and Me* that he had copied out and reworked to suit each one. The little girls, used to the coarseness of the other boys, drooled all over him, as we used to say. Gradually he got the idea of giving birth to some of these little hearts-and-flowers poems himself, though he never got beyond 'my dearest, my darling, my adorable one'. And the things sold. Well, why not? For one thing, he was extremely fickle. And every girl wanted to own the book with her poem in it. Besides that, there were often as many as eight or ten girls, each thinking a particular poem was written for her alone. Thierry never lost his head though, not even over the most adorable of his little sweeties. Poetry, as everybody knows, doesn't necessarily exclude practicality. And then too, there were those who patiently waited their turn, working themselves up vicariously by observing the mood of the others. Taking one year with another, all this produced a nice little nucleus of readers.

He wrote a weekly half-hour program for the radio station where I worked. You could have drowned in the gallons of lavender-water that gushed from it. So what? The ratings were good. The sponsor was happy.

The author used to come in person to oversee the show. Wild horses couldn't have kept him away. He interrupted rehearsals to kindle the proper feeling in us, to find out whether we thought we were really getting it. Only after he'd begged each one of us to strain for it, and been assured that, yes, we had it, were we allowed to continue. Then, just before the stand-by, he went around patting the actors on the shoulder, hugging the actresses, kissing hands, cheeks, hair, gently repeating, 'with feeling, my dears, with feeling.' While the show was being broadcast he would shut his eyes and contract his nostrils slightly during the most tingling passages.

The half-hour was barely over when all the phones began ringing at once. The switchboard operators were inundated, overwhelmed, worn out. But Francis lapped it up. Comfortably ensconced in an easy chair, like a great purring cat, he spoke to dozens of admirers, treating most of them like intimate friends. He never failed to use the husky, soothing voice that he'd taken such pains to acquire. For nearly an hour he would repeat over and over, 'I wrote this sketch with you in mind, my sweet.'

After that came the autograph-signing. We called it 'the recruiting' because it was during this operation that Francis made most of his conquests. It sure did the trick.

Then along came this redhead. God knows where he dug her up. Certainly not at the recruiting; that wasn't her style. Her name, appropriately, was Sonia, and she seemed to view the world as if from the top of an iceberg. She also appeared to intimidate our Thierry tremendously, which seemed to astonish him more than anyone else. Not long after that evening at the movies he brought her to the radio station to hear the program. To show her what a marvel he was, no doubt. Poor guy!

We would have preferred it if he'd taken her to the listening studio. But Thierry wanted to show himself off in all his glamour and to appear fully in control. He also wanted to keep her by his side.

She perched herself next to the sound engineer, and through the big window separating the control room from the studio, all we could see was that glacial smile of hers. It was clear that Thierry's prose cut no ice in that quarter.

The actors, who needed plenty of encouragement to enable them to spew out all this saccharine, became flustered every time they looked up to see that white chin pointed at them, apparently consigning them to a horrible fate. Embarrassed by their lines, as if to admit that they actually were pathetic, they tried to play it down a little. But on the heels of seven or eight run-throughs in the ecstatic mode, it was a disaster.

When it was over Sonia, with the air of a goddess heading back to Mount Olympus, got up and left the control room. Thierry followed. A few minutes later, when we were leaving the studio, he introduced her to the manager, with whom she stayed to chat until the phone calls were over.

From the next week on, it was obvious that Thierry was smitten. You could see it plainly at the times when his admirers used to call. He had tried to change his style and it just didn't come off.

After that week, Sonia chose to stay in the listening studio, keeping the manager company. And it was the same thing every week. Thierry kept trying to pull himself together, without success. After every broadcast he'd come looking for her, his manner both grovelling and meek, as if anticipating defeat. But little white chin was completely unresponsive. And the ratings plummeted.

In August Thierry was summoned to the manager's office and informed that his contract wouldn't be renewed—but they needed someone with a bit of a way with words to write publicity material. After offering his services, in vain, to all the other radio stations in the city, he had no choice but to accept.

That same week he received a short letter, which he showed me with tears in his eyes. In four lines Sonia declared that they were not meant for each other.

Whereupon we were treated to the most unexpected, unimaginable spectacle: Thierry, who'd been dazzling little blondes for as long as we could remember, was downcast, drawn, haggard; his eyes hollow, his lips grey. This little lady-killer was paying for all the hearts he had wrecked, and paying dearly.

But the worst was yet to come. He thought he'd been thrown over because he was nobody any more, as he put it, poor soul. He told anyone who cared to listen that all she'd ever seen in him was the successful author. When the new season started though, he dropped the subject. His half-hour had been taken over by Sonia.

He tackled his dull job, tight-lipped and, needless to say, ignored by everyone. Within a few days he acquired a bilious look that he never lost. He was to have put out a book of poems around Christmas time but he published nothing at all and seemed not to care. Alone in his cubby-hole he wrote ceaselessly; no publicity writer has ever written with such frenzy. From morning till night he typed away and many times I would see his mouth working and his features contorted with fury. Not pretty. I whispered about it to the others behind his back for a while but then I got used to it.

The months passed. Sonia ruled the roost at the radio station. Her sketches, admittedly excellent, were a great success and everyone was quick to puff them up. She'd made a name for herself and was on excellent terms with the manager. We all played up to her. As for Francis, he seemed to be living on another planet. He wouldn't even look up when the green skirt went by.

Came the month of May. One day at noon, I'll never forget it, I was discussing some work with him when his phone rang. Before answering it he glanced at the clock and turned a bit pale. And then, as he listened, I saw the most extraordinary expression come over his face. It was like the anguished gasp that contorts the face of a sprinter reaching the finish-line. But it was short-lived. He hung up with an air of exhaustion, pretended not to notice my questioning look, excused himself and went out in a rush, leaving me starved for information.

I'd stopped thinking about it when a gang of people, gesticulating and squealing, emerged from the newsroom. Francis Thierry had just won a big literary prize for his novel. We were dumbfounded, and, I have to say, our faces were red. They still were when he showed up at his desk again the next day. You should have seen us, one by one, sneaking around to congratulate him. Sonia and the manager were the only ones to do it unselfconsciously. Francis shook everyone's hand with the same bitter smile and then instantly stuck his nose back in his typing.

A few days later the book was in the stores. We already

knew from the newspaper reviews, magazine articles, and interviews that it was anything but a love-story, but we could never have imagined . . . Well! Let me tell you, it was a far cry from 'my darling', 'my dearest'. Had Thierry called his heroine 'my darling' we'd have been sure that the words had come to mean something entirely different to him. There was no place in this book for words like that. It was an astonishing work. You'd have said it was driven to completion by the crack of a whip. A firm, harsh prose conveyed a load of hatred and cruelty that weighed down every page—as if the author would never tire of unburdening himself.

At first Sonia tried to weather the storm. Beyond a shadow of a doubt this novel was about her, but she let on that she had no idea. So did we. What she finally couldn't stand was the shower of honours that rained on Thierry. For a while not a day went by without his receiving some new accolade. The US wanted an English translation; South America wanted one in Spanish. Hollywood planned to make a film. A publisher in Paris phoned to ask for a contract to do his second book. Meanwhile the rest of us, all agog, swarmed around Thierry. Sonia packed up and left for an extended holiday in Mexico.

A second book never did appear. Hatred, I must say, is very effective. Far more deadly than love. It's platonic, self-sustaining. It doesn't need to be reciprocated, doesn't require the stimulus of bodies. It slips right through your fingers. Things changed for Thierry; having no lack of girls to choose from he married a little blonde, pink and sweet, had babies galore, all blond and pink. With the Hollywood money he bought a magnificent property. And he forgave her—the one to whom he owed his little moment in the sun.

Then he went back to using his real name: Gaston Dupont.

Translated by Patricia Sillers

YVES THÉRIAULT

The Whale

On every boat and quay from Gaspé to Paspébiac the news spread like wildfire: Ambroise Bourdages claimed that—singlehandedly—he had landed a whale!

The fishermen were all getting a great kick out of it. Now if Ambroise had claimed that he had caught a two-hundred pound cod that had later managed to get free of the hook, everyone would have made a solemn show of believing it. That would have been an admissible exaggeration, quite in keeping with local instincts, habits, and customs . . . But a whale?

Stretching his arms wide Ambroise insisted: 'I'm telling you, a whale! Colossal! As big as a boat—bigger even! Ahhh, my friends, my friends . . . I spot it sunning itself. Quick as I can I grab a rope, I get a hook on it, I bait it with a herring, I attach a floater, and then I let it out behind the boat . . . the whale spies the bait and starts making for it. I let out the line . . . a hundred, two hundred feet. The whale swallows the bait—and it's hooked!'

'This hook of yours, how big is it?' asked Vilmont Babin.

'A big cod hook. Maybe an inch and a half . . .'

'And it hooked the whale?'

'Yes.'

A tremendous burst of laughter shook the whole quay.

About a dozen fishermen were listening as Ambroise related

his adventure. A few girls were there too, as there always are when the boats come in. Among them was Gabrielle, who smiled too much at Adélard these days—at least in the opinion of Ambroise, who had eyes only for her.

Unlike the others, who found his story too good—and too funny—to be true, she listened gravely and did not laugh.

There was a look in Gabrielle's eyes that Ambroise could not quite make out. It was a serious expression that suited her natural reserve and good manners—manners very different from those of the rude, obnoxious Adélard.

He was there too, laughing with the others at Ambroise, making fun of him.

'Did you stow your whale in the hold?' he asked Ambroise. 'Or weren't you strong enough to haul such a big trophy into your boat?'

This produced a great roar of laughter. Everyone wanted to slap Adélard on the back. Here was a match for Ambroise! Someone with the answer to a tall tale!

'Call me a liar,' he said with dignity, 'it doesn't bother me. Just remember this: if I were on my deathbed and my mother asked me to repeat every word I've just told you, I'd do it. I didn't lie to you. My men were asleep below. We were heading out towards the Shippegan banks and I was at the tiller. I landed a whale . . . and anyone who doesn't believe me can forget it. I know what I did. I hooked a whale with a cod-hook.'

He spat on the timbers of the quay, turned on his heel, and left.

Naturally it wasn't long before they were talking about Ambroise Bourdages's alleged miraculous catch in every village on the Coast. As it made the rounds from one quay to another the story was altered and embellished out of all recognition. Ambroise was floored by the version that got back to him.

It was Clovis, the prissy, affected son of the banker in

Port-Savoie, where Ambroise lived, who brought back the first of this bizarre gossip.

'Do you know what they're saying at Paspébiac?' he asked Ambroise. 'My poor friend, you'd never believe it! It's really terrible!'

'What are they saying?'

'I said it's terrible, but to tell the truth it's mostly funny.'

'Let's say it *is* funny. What is it?'

'Good heavens you're tiresome! So impatient . . . Well, to hear them talk it seems you caught a whale with your bare hands, held on to it for dear life all by yourself, fought like the devil to haul it by the tail into your boat, and in the end it got away.'

Ambroise groaned.

'Ah, no, no! They're all making fun of me!'

Just at that moment Gabrielle came out of the Company store. Her hair floated on the breeze and her smile was as bright as a sunflower.

'How beautiful she is,' thought Ambroise, 'so tall and graceful. If only she could like me!'

But as she passed close by Ambroise she gave a sarcastic little laugh.

'I have to get proof of my story!' cried Ambroise, when Gabrielle was out of earshot. 'Clovis, no one would ever take you for a liar! A banker's son isn't allowed to tell lies!'

'Of course I mustn't tell lies. Lying isn't nice. Besides, I wouldn't want to disgrace my father.'

'All right then! Tomorrow you and I are going out to sea. You'll be my witness. We're going to catch another whale, and this time it won't get away!'

Next day they headed out on the water. Despite the sunshine the seas were heavy and sullen. The boat rolled and pitched for seven long miles. But then, just at the end of the run, they saw a jet of spray rising from a whale that was frolicking in the waves—not six yards from the boat.

To summarize the day's adventures we'll say that Ambroise, using all his fisherman's skill, managed to catch the whale with his cod-hook. This was not easily done. The sea monster gave a magnificent display of its strength and agility. On three different occasions, while diving furiously in an effort to get free of the hook, the whale almost capsized the boat. Finally exhausted, it rose calmly to the surface. Ambroise fastened the rope and took the tiller. Slowly he towed his trophy towards the moorings of Port-Savoie.

He was bursting with joy. It had been accomplished despite all the doubt and sarcasm. Even Gabrielle would have to agree that he, Ambroise Bourdages, had not lied about capturing a whale. In fact it was so far from being a lie that a week later he went out and caught another.

This was the way to silence the scandalmongers.

At the same time it ought to establish him as the greatest fisherman and the most respected man on the Coast.

It is not every day that a man catches a whale with such simple tackle. And even if there is an element of luck in it, there is also an element of know-how and gumption that cannot be overlooked.

But just as they were about a mile from Port-Savoie the whale suddenly came to life. With one powerful sneeze it spat out the hook—as if to show that it had only been toying with them and could quite easily have escaped earlier, if it had wanted to.

Then it dived and disappeared under the water.

This loss, however, did not bother Ambroise too much.

He had a witness with him. An honest man, a banker's son, a person to corroborate his story who would be believed without question.

As he jumped up onto the quay he let out a great cry.

'Ahoy!'

About fifty people, all aware of the expedition, were waiting when Ambroise and Clovis returned.

Even Gabrielle was there.

Ambroise quickly told what had happened. He described everything in detail. And as the ripples of laughter began to spread: 'Listen Ambroise,' said Vilmont Babin, 'you can get away with it once, but the same lie twice—it won't work!'

With a great sweep of his arm Ambroise pointed to Clovis.

'Clovis was there. He's my witness. An honest witness. He saw it all. He'll tell you that the whale got away just about a mile from here.'

But Clovis was sporting a smile that looked more like a grin. Then, in his piping voice he declared: 'Ambroise is a liar. I never saw him catch a whale!'

The shouts and threats that followed this declaration were so clamorous, and poor Ambroise was so crushed by Clovis's double-dealing, that all he could think of was to run away as fast as possible.

Two hours later he risked going outside again. Clovis was standing by the Post Office. Ambroise hurried over to him. The young man waited for him imperturbably.

'Snake in the grass!' Ambroise yelled at him. 'Liar! Worse —you're a perjurer! I'll have you arrested!'

'Just a minute, my friend,' said Clovis stiffly. 'There's something you don't know. I have my eye on Gabrielle too. Do you really think I'm going to let you impress her with your whale-fishing story? I've decided to fight—with my own weapons! The fortunes of war, old fellow, I'm sorry.'

But Ambroise, disconsolate, had already left. He felt trapped, beaten. Farewell dreams! He'd lost Gabrielle forever to wilier men. Clovis, for one. And Adélard. While he, Ambroise, was fighting shadows.

Once again he raced for home.

But as he was entering the house the sun suddenly reappeared and joy began to revive his hopes. Gabrielle was there, in the kitchen, with Ambroise's mother.

'Ah!' said Ambroise . . . 'Gabrielle?'

She smiled at him.

'Ambroise, I apologize. Forgive me . . . I misunderstood your lie about the whale!'

'But,' said Ambroise, 'it wasn't a . . .'

Gabrielle waved aside his explanation.

'When you tried to tell your story for the second time today, I admit I was disgusted. I knew you were trying to impress me. But after I got home I began to think about it. Do you know what I decided, Ambroise?'

'No . . . no.'

'It's a lucky girl that has a fellow who'll go against everyone just for her, simply to impress her, to win her . . .'

Ambroise was about to protest strongly again, but suddenly he thought better of it. A sly gleam appeared in his eye. So this was the way the land lay? Well, then.

'Gabrielle,' he said softly, 'it was the least I could do. A lie like that about a cod would never have been enough—not grand enough! But a whale, an impossible catch . . . It was a matter of gallantry, of giving it enough weight—you know?'

'Of course. That's why I'm here . . .'

So Ambroise took her by the hand and led her out into the village and walked with her so that everyone would plainly see that in spite of everything he'd made the best catch of his life . . . and to hell with the whale!

Translated by Patricia Sillers

ANNE HÉBERT

The Torrent

As a child, I was dispossessed of the world. By the decree of a will higher than my own, I had to renounce all possession in this life. I related to the world by fragments, only at those points which were immediately and strictly necessary, and which were removed from me as soon as their usefulness had ended. I was permitted the scribblers which I had to open, but not the table on which they lay; the corner of the stable which I was to clean, but not the hen perching on the window sill; and never, never the countryside which beckoned through the window. I could see the large hand of my mother when it was raised towards me, but I could not perceive my mother as a whole, from head to foot. I could only feel her terrible size, which chilled me.

I had no childhood. I cannot recall any time that was my own before the singular adventure of my deafness. My mother worked incessantly, and I participated in this work with her, like a tool in her hands. She rose with the sun, and the succeeding hours of her day dovetailed with an exactitude which left no possibility of digression.

Other than the lessons which she gave me until I entered secondary school, she never talked to me. She was uncommunicative by nature. For her to depart from this rule, I had to commit a sin. That is to say, she only spoke to me in reprimand, before punishing me.

As concerns my studies, there again everything was planned, calculated, with never a day's holiday and never a vacation. When she had finished a lesson, her countenance became that of a total mute, her lips tightly sealed, as if closed by a bolt from inside.

As for me, I would lower my eyes, relieved that I had no longer to follow the working of her powerful jaws and her thin lips as she pronounced each syllable of the words 'chastisement', 'God's justice', 'damnation', 'discipline', 'Hell', 'original sin', and, above all, that distinctive phrase which recurred like a leit-motif:

'One must master oneself utterly. We have no idea of the evil forces within us. Do you hear me, François? I will master you myself.'

At this, I would begin to shiver, and tears would fill my eyes, for I knew what would come next:

'François, look me in the eyes.'

And then the long drawn-out punishment would begin. My mother would stare at me mercilessly, and I was unable to raise my eyes to meet hers. Then she would add, as she stood up:

'Very well, François. The lesson is finished. But I shall remember your ill will, when the time and place have come . . .'

Indeed, my mother took minute note of the slightest misdemeanours, in order to bring me to account some other day, when I had almost forgotten them. Just when I thought that I had evaded her, she would pounce upon me, implacably, forgetting nothing, itemizing for each day and for each hour those things which I believed to be the most hidden.

I could never understand why she did not punish me on the spot, all the more because I sensed obscurely that self-restraint was so difficult for her. Afterwards, I understood that she had acted in this way out of self-discipline, in order to 'master herself', and also, certainly, to impress me all the more, and to establish her hold upon me as deeply as possible.

There was another reason, which I only discovered much later.

I have said that my mother worked without stopping, whether in the house, in the stable, or in the fields. To correct me, she would await a pause.

The other day, I found a little notebook that had belonged to her in the shed, on a beam behind an old lantern. In it the schedule of her days was carefully inscribed. On a certain Monday, she was to put the sheets out on the grass to bleach, and I remembered that it had suddenly started to rain. I then saw that on the same Monday this strange woman had struck out 'Bleach the sheets', and written in the margin, 'Beat François.'

We were always alone. Although I was almost twelve years of age, I had not yet looked upon another human face, except for my own shimmering reflection when I leaned over the stream to drink. As for my mother, only the lower part of her face was familiar to me. I did not dare raise my eyes up to the angry pupils and the broad forehead, which I was later to see so atrociously ravaged.

Her chin imperious; her mouth tormented, in spite of the attitude of calm which she strove to maintain by means of silence; her bodice black and armoured, with no tender place in which the head of a child might nestle; such was the maternal universe in which, so young, I learned hardness and rejection.

We lived too far from the village even to go to mass. But that did not prevent my passing almost the whole of a Sunday on my knees, at times, in punishment for some misdeed. This was, I believe, the maternal fashion of sanctifying the Lord's day at my expense.

I had never seen my mother pray, but I had suspected that she did sometimes, when closeted in her room. At that time I was so dependent on my mother that the least stirring within her had repercussions inside me. Oh, I did not really understand anything of the drama of this woman, but I sensed, as one senses a storm, the most subtle changes in her moods. And, on the evenings when I believed my mother to be praying, I did not dare move on my straw pallet. The silence was as heavy as death. I awaited some unknown tempest which would sweep us both away, we who were so bound together in a common and sombre destiny.

One desire grew within me daily, and weighed upon me like nostalgia—to see another human face, close up and in detail. I tried to scrutinize my mother stealthily, but almost always she turned abruptly towards me, and I would lose heart.

I resolved to go and find the face of a man, not daring to hope for that of a child, and promising myself to flee if it were that of a woman. To this end, I decided to post myself by the side of the main road. In time, someone would surely pass by.

Our house stood, remote from any line of communication, in the centre of a stretch of woods and fields and water in all its moods, from the calm of the stream to the rush of the torrent.

I went through the maple grove and across the great, stony fields which my mother persisted in ploughing, her teeth clenched, her hands gripping the handles, the shocks at times causing her to lose her hold. Our old horse, Eloi, had died of this work.

I had not thought the road was so far away and I was afraid of getting lost. What would my mother say when she returned to milk the cows and noticed my absence? I shrank beneath her blows in advance, but I continued on my way. My need was too pressing, too despairing.

After crossing the burned-over clearing where my mother and I picked blueberries every summer, I found myself by the road. Out of breath, I stopped short, as though a hand had touched my forehead. And I wanted to cry, for the road was bare and forlorn in the sunlight. Unvarying, soulless, dead. Where were the processions I had imagined I would discover? Over this ground had passed feet other than my mother's or my own. Where were those footsteps now? In what direction had they gone? They had not left a mark. Surely the road must have died.

Not daring to walk on it, I followed the ditch. Suddenly, I stumbled over a form stretched out in the deep grass and fell headlong in the mud. I got up, dismayed at my dirty clothes. And I saw a horrible man beside me. He must have been sleeping, for he was now slowly sitting up. Glued to the spot, I was unable to move, expecting to be killed, at the least. I did not even have the strength to hide my face with my arm.

The man was filthy. Dried and fresh mud by turns covered his clothing and his face. His long hair mingled with his beard, his moustache and his eyebrows, which were so heavy they hung over his eyes. My God! what a face, full of bristling hair and spatters of mud! I saw the gummy mouth with its yellow teeth. I wanted to run away, but he seized me by the arm. Taking hold of me as he tried to get up, he made me fall head over heels.

He laughed, and his laugh was as beastly as he was, matching him perfectly. Once more I tried to escape, but he made me sit down on the edge of the ditch beside him. His foul odour mingled with the smell of the swamp. Under my breath, I muttered an act of contrition and thought of God's judgement, which I believed would follow upon the terror and disgust which this man inspired in me. He kept his coarse and dirty hand on my shoulder.

'How old are you, sonny?'

Without waiting for my reply, he added:

'Do you know any stories? No, eh? Well, I know some. . .'

He put his arm around my shoulders. I tried to squirm

away, but he tightened his grip, laughing. His laughter spewed close to my cheek. And at that moment I saw my mother in front of us. She had in her hand the large stick which she used to bring in the cows. For the first time, I saw her in her entirety—tall, strong, a clear image and more powerful than I had ever believed her to be.

'Let that child go!'

The man got to his feet with difficulty, surprised, and as much fascinated by my mother as I was. My mother addressed me in the tone one uses for a dog, shouting:

'Go home, François!'

Slowly, my legs giving way beneath me, I started down the path towards the clearing. The man was talking to my mother. He seemed to know her. In his drawling voice, he was saying:

'Well, if it isn't beautiful Claudine! . . . And to find you here! . . . So you left the village because of the youngster, eh? . . . A fine little boy . . . yes, very fine . . . But to find you here! . . . Everybody thought you were dead . . .'

'Get out of here!' thundered my mother.

'Big Claudine! Not over-shy in those days . . . Don't be mad . . .'

'I forbid you to be familiar with me, you pig!'

Then I heard the dry crack of a blow, followed by the dull thud of something falling. I turned around. My mother was standing there at the edge of the woods, immense, the cudgel shaking in her hand; the man was stretched out at her feet. She must have used the heavy end of the stick to hit him on the head.

Big Claudine (I called her this mentally from then on) assured herself that the man was still alive, gathered up her skirts, jumped over the ditch, and set off again on the path towards our house. I preceded her, running. The echoes of my flight resounded in my ears, together with the sound of my mother's robust stride behind me.

She caught up with me by the house, and entered the kitchen dragging me by the arm. She had thrown the stick away. I was frightened and aching all over; nevertheless, I felt an inexplicable curiosity and attraction. I understood obscurely that what was to follow would be as awesome as what had just happened. My senses, dulled by a life of monotony and confinement, were awakening. I was living through an impressive and terrifying adventure.

My mother said, in a cutting voice:

'A human being is a beautiful thing, eh, François? You should be happy now that you've seen one close up, face to face. Attractive, isn't it?'

Shattered to realize that my mother had divined my inmost secret, I raised my eyes to her, having lost all self-control. The conversation went on with my wild eyes held by hers. I was paralyzed, magnetized, by big Claudine. 'The world is not beautiful François. You must not touch it; renounce it, right now, freely. Don't lag behind. Do as you are told, without looking around you. You are my son and you are the continuation of me. You will fight against your evil instincts until you achieve perfection . . .'

Fire shot from her eyes. Standing in the middle of the room, her whole being erect, she expressed the violence she could no longer contain. I was transfixed with fear and admiration. Then, her voice softening a little, as though talking to herself, she kept repeating, 'Self-possession . . . self-mastery . . . above all, never give in to oneself . . .'

My mother stopped. Her long hands were already calm, and from them calm spread through her. Her expression was withdrawn, only her eyes retained a spark, like the remnants of a feast in a deserted house.

'François, I will go back to the village with my head high. Everyone will bow to me. And it will be my victory! My victory! I'll never let a dirty drunk slobber over me or touch my son. François, you are my son. You will overcome your

evil instincts and attain perfection. You will become a priest!
You will be respected! Respect! What a victory over all of
them!'

A priest! The idea crushed me, above all this day when I
had been so hurt in my search for a kind face. My mother
had often explained to me, 'The mass is the sacrifice. The
priest is both the sacrificer and the victim, like Christ. He
has to immolate himself upon the altar mercilessly, with the
Host.' I was so young, and I had never been happy. I broke
into sobs. My mother almost threw herself upon me; then,
she turned on her heel, saying in her curt voice:

'Cry-baby! Weakling! I have received a reply from the
principal; you will go to the *collège* on September 4th, next
Thursday. Go and get an armful of kindling, so I can light
the stove for supper. Go on. Move!'

My school-books had belonged to my mother when she was
young. That evening, under the pretext of preparing my
things for school, I examined these books one by one, looking
avidly at the name inscribed on the fly-leaf of each volume.
'Claudine Perrault' . . . Claudine; beautiful Claudine, big
Claudine.

The letters of her first name danced before my eyes, twisting
into fantastic shapes like flames. It had never before struck
me that my mother's name was Claudine. Now it seemed
strange to me, painful. I could no longer tell whether I was
reading this name or whether a voice close to my ear was
pronouncing it, a railing and demoniac voice, the breath
touching my cheek.

My mother came in. She neither brightened the atmosphere nor reassured me in my depression. On the contrary,
her presence gave weight to the supernatural quality of the
scene. The only spot of light in the dark kitchen was projected
from the lamp onto the book that I was holding open. My
mother's hand moved quickly within this luminous circle.
She seized the book; at one moment the 'Claudine', written

in a lofty and wilful hand, seemed to draw all of the light to itself; then it disappeared and in its place, in the same haughty handwriting, was 'François', 'François', in fresh ink, and 'Perrault' in the old. Thus, in this narrow light, in the space of a few minutes, the long hands played, and sealed my destiny. All my books were thus dealt with. My mother's words hammered in my head: 'You are my son. You are a continuation of me.'

When this eventful day had passed, I forced myself to erase it from my mind, upon the orders of my mother. Moulded for so long by her iron rule, I succeeded well enough in rejecting any conscious memory of those scenes, and in accomplishing mechanically the work imposed on me. Deep within me, however, I experienced at times an unwonted, an inexpressible richness whose slumbering presence astonished and troubled me.

The practical effect, if one could call it that, of my first encounter with the world was to put me on my guard, and to lock up within me any spontaneous gesture of human sympathy I might naturally have had. My mother had scored a victory.

This was the state of mind with which I entered the *collège*. Shy and uncommunicative, I observed my companions. I rejected their advances, whether timid or bantering. Soon a vacuum formed around the new student. I told myself that it was better this way, that I must not become attached to anyone or anything in this world. Then, I imposed penance on myself for the unhappiness I felt in my isolation.

My mother wrote: 'I am not there to teach you. It is up to you to devise your own mortifications. Above all, fight against your principal fault—softness. Never allow yourself to become sentimental over the mirage of any particular friendship. All of them, both teachers and students, are in your life at this time only because they are necessary to your development and instruction. Take advantage of what they *must* give you, but *keep your distance*. At all costs, do not give of yourself freely, or you will be lost. Moreover, I am kept informed of everything that happens at the *collège*. You will give me an exact account during the holidays; and you will account also to God, on Judgement Day. Do not waste your time. As for recreation, I have an understanding with the principal. You will help the farmer with the stable and the fields.'

I understood farmwork, and I preferred occupying myself in this way to taking recreation with the other boys. I did not know how to play or how to laugh, and I did not feel that I belonged. The teachers I considered, rightly or wrongly, to be the allies of my mother, and I was particularly on my guard with them.

All through the long years of school that followed, I studied. That is to say, my memory registered dates, names, rules, precepts and formulae. Faithful to my mother's teaching, I wished to retain only the external symbols of my studies, and I excluded from myself that real knowledge which is an experience and a possession. Thus, on the subject of God, I attached myself with all the power of my will to the innumerable prayers recited each day, building a rampart within myself against any possible shadow of His naked face.

My marks were excellent, and I habitually took first place, as my mother demanded.

I considered the structure of a classical tragedy, or of a poem, to be a mechanism of principles and recipes bound together only by the author's will. However, once or twice, I was touched with Grace, and perceived that the tragedy or poem depended solely on its own inner necessity, a condition of any work of art.

Such revelations touched me painfully. In an instant, I could measure the emptiness of my existence. I had a presentiment of despair. Then, I would stiffen my resolve, and absorb whole pages of chemical formulae.

When the marks were read out, and especially when the prizes were given, I experienced the same feeling of profound disenchantment, which I could not overcome in spite of my efforts.

The year that I studied rhetoric, I was at the top of my class and took a large number of prizes. My arms loaded with books, and my ears buzzing with the polite applause of those same classmates for whom I had not ceased being a stranger, I went from my seat to the platform, and experienced an anguish so poignant and a despondency so great that I could barely move.

When the ceremonies were over, I stretched out on my bed. The dormitory was bustling with the coming and going of students who were getting ready to go home for the holidays.

Suddenly, I glimpsed what my life could have been, and a brutal, almost physical regret seized me, an oppressive tightening in my chest. I saw my companions leaving, singly and in groups; I could hear them laughing and singing. I had never known joy. I was unable to know it. My isolation was now more than an interdiction; what had begun as a refusal on my part had become an incapacity, a sterility. My heart was bitter, ravaged. I was seventeen years old!

There was now only one boy left in the dormitory. He seemed to be having difficulty closing his trunk. I was about to offer my help, but as I was getting up from my bed, he asked:

'Help me close my trunk, will you?'

Surprised and put out at being anticipated, I played for time.

'What did you say?'

My words echoed in the deserted room, putting my teeth on edge. My voice was curt and rasping; it was always disagreeable and irritating for me to hear it.

I lay down again, my lips tight, clenched fists grasping

my pillow. My companion repeated his request. I pretended not to understand, hoping he would say it again. I counted the seconds, for the feeling reached me that he would not ask again. And I did not move, but lay there experiencing the richness of doing something irreparable.

'Thanks for nothing, and have a good holiday, you damned twerp!'

Then this classmate, whom I had secretly liked more than the others, disappeared, bowed down beneath the weight of his trunk.

My mother never came to meet me at the station, nor did she watch for me at the window. She awaited me in her own way, that is, in her everyday clothes, occupied with some task. Upon my arrival, she would interrupt her work long enough to ask me the few questions she felt necessary. Then, assigning me some chore to be done before the next meal, she would return to her work.

That day, in spite of the great heat, I found her on her knees weeding a bed of beets. When she saw me, she squatted on her heels and pushed her straw hat back on her head with a brusque gesture. Wiping her hands on her apron, she asked:

'Well, how many prizes?'

'Six books, mother; and I won the scholarship.'

'Show me.'

I held out the books. They were similar to all prize books—red, with gilt edges. How absurd, how ridiculous they seemed to me! I distrusted them. I was ashamed of them. Red, gold, false. The colours of a false glory, the emblems of my false knowledge. The insignia of my servitude.

My mother got up and went into the house. She took out her bunch of keys—a great knot of metal wherein all the keys of the world seemed to be massed together.

'Give me the money!'

I put my hand in my pocket and took out the purse. She almost snatched it from me.

'Well, give it to me! Do you think I have all day to waste? Go and get changed, and help me finish the beets before supper . . .'

Unflinching, I looked at my mother, and there entered my mind an irremediable certitude: I realized that I detested her.

She locked the money in the little writing-desk.

'Tomorrow, I will write the principal for your registration forms. Lucky that you won the prize . . .'

'I am not going back to school next year.' I enunciated this statement so clearly that it seemed to be the voice of another person. The voice of a man.

My mother flushed. I saw the colour flood her sunburned throat, her face, her forehead. For the first time, I saw her waver. Her hesitation gave me great pleasure. I repeated:

'I am not going back to school. I will never go to the seminary! You had better not count on me to gild your reputation . . .'

She sprang at me like a tigress. I was observing the scene lucidly, noting the supple strength of this tall woman, even as I recoiled towards the door. Her face was contorted, almost hideous. It occurred to me that I too would be thus disfigured, some day, by hatred and death. She was brandishing the mass of keys in the air. I heard them jingle, and glimpsed their metallic sheen as they struck me like a bolt of lightning. My mother struck me several times over the head with them. I lost consciousness.

When I opened my eyes, I found myself alone, stretched out on the floor. There was a violent pain in my head. I had gone deaf.

From that day on, a crack opened up in my oppressed life. The heavy silence of deafness possessed me, and a tendency to daydream appeared as a kind of accompaniment. No voice, no sound from the world outside would ever reach me again, of this I was certain. Neither the cry of the cricket nor the roar of the falls. But I could hear within me the existence of the torrent, of our house, and of the whole farm. I had never possessed the world, but there was a change now: part of the world possessed me. The stretch of water, mountains and secret hollows came to me with a sovereign touch.

I believed myself to be free of my mother, and I discovered a new kinship with the earth.

My eyes would dwell upon our house. The other buildings, which were in the same style, faced it; long and low, they were identified with the austere soil. The cultivated fields scarcely marred the woodlands, which unfolded to the broken rhythms of the wild surrounding mountains. And I felt, above all, the presence of water—in the freshness of the air, the various species of plants, and the song of the frogs. Streams, and the calm river; pools, clear or darkened; and, near the house, boiling through the rocky gorge, the torrent.

The torrent suddenly took on an importance that it should always have had in my existence. Or, rather, I became aware of its hold on me. I struggled against its domination. I could sense the spray mounting from the falls, floating invisibly over my clothing, my books, over the walls and the furniture, imparting to my daily life an indefinable sense of water, which seized my heart. Of all earthly vibrations, my poor, deaf head had preserved only the intermittent tumult of the waterfall beating upon my temples. And my blood flowed to the precipitous rhythm of the howling waters. At times, when I was almost calm, I did not suffer from it so much, for it became a distant murmur. But on those terrible days when I would re-examine my revolt, I felt the torrent so strong within my skull, crashing against my brain, that my mother striking me with her knot of keys had not hurt me more.

This woman never spoke another word to me after that famous scene when, for the first time, I had opposed my will to hers. The summer's labours followed their course. I knew that she was avoiding me. I, too, arranged to be alone, and abandoning the mower, the hay, the vegetables and the fruits, I would give myself over to the spirit of the country-side. I would remain for hours contemplating an insect, or the movement of the shadows over the leaves. I also spent entire days evoking those times, even the most distant, when my mother had mistreated me. Each detail was still present to my mind. None of her words, not one of her blows, had passed out of my memory.

It was about this time that Perceval came to our farm. Al-though she had broken in many horses, this one, which was almost wild, would not be humbled by big Claudine. He resisted her with a shrewdness, a boldness, a perseverance that enchanted me. His black coat covered with foam, his nostrils steaming constantly, he was that being of fire and passion that I myself wished to become. I envied him. I would have liked to consult him. To live in the immediate vicinity of this undaunted fury seemed to me an honour, a source of strength.

I would get out of bed in the evening, after my mother had retired, and go out to the stable, where I would perch in the hay-loft above Perceval. I was delighted, astonished, to see that he never slackened the force of his passion. Was it his pride that would not allow him to sleep while I was observing him? Or did my motionless and hidden presence irritate him? He never ceased his sonorous breathing, nor the volleys of his hooves against his stall. From my shelter, I could see his beautiful, black coat, shimmering with blue reflections. Electric currents ran up and down his spine. I could never have imagined such a feast. I savoured the real and physical presence of passion.

I would leave the stable almost maddened by the roaring and pounding inside my head and ears, like the surf in a storm, holding my head in my hands, for the shocks were so tumultuous that I feared I would die. I would resolve not to remain in the stable so long the next time. But the spectacle of Perceval's anger attracted me so much that I could bring myself to leave him only when the roar of the torrent within me prevented any other focal interest.

Then I would be drawn to the edge of the falls; I was not free to stay away. I moved towards the movement of the water; I brought to it its own song, as though I had become its unique depository. In exchange, the water showed me its compulsive writhing, its spuming foam—necessary complements to the blows beating within my head. And there was not just one great cadence, involving the total flow of the water, but a spectacle of exasperated forces, of many currents and internal movements in ferocious conflict.

The water had hollowed out the stone. The rock on which I stood jutted out over the water like a terrace. I visualized the stream beneath, dark, opaque, fringed with foam. False peace, profound darkness. The reserves of fear.

Springs filtered in at various places. The rock was muddy. It would have been easy to slip. Several hundred feet of fall! What fodder for the gulf, which would dismember and decapitate its prey . . . mangle it . . .

When I returned to my pallet on the floor of my room, I was not really separated from the torrent. Falling asleep, I could hear its roar, which had become an integral part of my self, the image of my impetuous fever. The elements of a dream. Or of something to be undertaken? I sensed that there would soon emerge from my torment the monstrous visage of either the one or the other.

The day of school opening was approaching. My mother had steeled herself, and was only waiting for the right moment to do an about-face, her vigour stored up and enhanced by her long and apparent resignation, which was really only a victory over her vitality. Not one of my moments of idleness

in the fields, of loitering at the falls or in the woods, was
unknown to her.

I knew she was in full possession of her powers. Strangely
enough, the continual setbacks she encountered in the breaking of Perceval left her unperturbed. She rose above everything, sure of her final triumph. It made me feel small. I knew
that it would soon be impossible to avoid a confrontation
with the gigantic Claudine Perrault.

I turned to Perceval.

That evening, the horse was beyond constraint. On entering the stable, I almost turned back, for he was so violent
that I feared he would smash his stall. Once in the shelter of
the hay-loft, I watched his astonishing rage. The foam on
his coat was streaked with blood. He had been cruelly
hobbled, moreover; yet that did not prevent him from
struggling.

I think that my first feeling was one of pity to see such a
superb creature wounded and tortured. I did not realize that
what I found most intolerable was that a hatred so ripened
and concentrated should be so bound and confined. The
horse's rage made my own hatred seem inferior and cowardly.

This captive demon, at the height of his powers, dazzled
me. In both justice and homage, I owed him this much—to
permit him to be himself in the world. For what evil end did
I wish to free him? Was it to unleash the evil in me?

Within my skull, the torrent suddenly roared with such
force that I was filled with terror. I wanted to scream. I
could no longer draw back. I remember being deafened by
the howling mass that struck my head.

And then, there was a blank that since that time, I have
worried over trying to fill in. And when I sense the possible
approach of the dreadful light in my memory, I struggle to
be free of it, and I attach myself desperately to the darkness,
however troubling, however menacing it may be. The in-

human circle, the circle of my thoughts unending, the material of my eternal life.

The torrent shook me from head to foot, subjugated me, engulfed me in an eddy that almost tore me to pieces.

The impression of an abyss, an abyss of space and time, where I fell down a void, succeeded the tempest. Yet I broke through the limits of this dead space. I opened my eyes to the luminous morning. I was facing the morning, and the sight of the sky blinded me. I was unable to move. What struggle had exhausted me in this way? A struggle with water? It was impossible. Moreover, my clothes were dry. In what abyss had I been drowned? I turned my head with difficulty. I was lying on the rock, at the edge of the torrent. I saw the foam gathering into the yellow spray. Was it possible that I had returned to the torrent? What atrocious battle had consumed me? Had I fought the Angel face to face? I did not want to know. I pushed back consciousness of it with gestures that rent the air.

The horse had been set free. He had made his terrible gallop through the world. An evil passage for anyone who had been in his way. Then I saw my mother, lying flat and still. I looked at her. I measured her size as she lay outstretched.

She was immense, covered with blood and stamped with hoof-prints.

I have now no point of reference. No clock marks my hours. No calendar marks my years. I am dissolved in time. Discipline, rules, rigid barriers—all have collapsed. The name of God is dry and sterile. For me, no God will ever inhabit this name. I have known only empty symbols. I have borne my chains too long, and they have had time to put down roots. They have undone me from within. I shall never be a free man. Too late did I desire my freedom.

I walk upon the wreckage. A dead man among the ruins. Anguish alone distinguishes me from the dead symbols.

Nothing is alive except the countryside around me. Not that I regard it with a loving and aesthetic appreciation. No, my bond with it is more involved and more profound: I am identified with the landscape. Delivered over to nature. I can feel myself becoming a tree, or a clod of earth. The only thing that separates me from the tree or the clod is anguish. I am open to anguish as the earth is to the rain.

The rain, the wind, the clover, the leaves have become the elements of my life, the real limbs of my body. I belong more to them than to myself. But terror runs along the surface of my skin. I pretend not to believe it; but at times it enables me to distinguish my arm from the hay beneath my scythe. If my arm trembles, it is fear that causes it, suddenly. Grass does not live with fear, but only with the wind. I abandon myself to the wind in vain; fear alone sways me and stirs me.

I am not yet ripe for the ultimate flight, for the final commitment to the cosmic forces. I do not yet have the permanent right to say to the tree, 'My brother,' and to the falls, 'Here I am.'

What is the present? On my hands I feel the warmth and lingering freshness of the March sun. I believe in the present. I raise my eyes, and see the open door of the stable. I know of the blood there, and of the woman stretched out on the ground with the marks of rage and death upon her. These are as present to my eye as the March sun. As real as when I first saw them fifteen or twenty years ago. This dense image rots the sunlight on my hands. The limpid touch of light is forever spoiled for me.

When I return home, fear alone distinguishes my muddy steps from the mud of the path leading to the house.

In an old pine, the oldest and the highest one, a crow is perched. He must be singing of his return from the south, but I can see only his contortions. I have lost sound and singing. And speech no longer exists. It has become a mute grimace.

The torrent is silent, with the heavy silence that precedes the spring flood. My head is silence. I analyze the fragments. I reshape my unhappiness. I complete it. I clarify it. I take it up where I had left it. My investigation is both lucid and methodical. Little by little, it corroborates what my imagination, or my instinct, had led me to suppose.

I admire my detachment; I marvel at it. Then, suddenly, I know that I am deceiving myself. I believe myself to be without self-pity, yet I am aware that I am evasive, that my currents fork to avoid reality. I am lying. What good is my self-questioning? Of what use is my self-deception? The truth lies heavy upon me. It weighs me down from within. It corrupts even the simplest of my gestures. I am in possession of this truth, and from it I know that not one of my gestures is pure.

I cannot remember ever having felt such calm . . . It disquiets me. With what increased fury will the next assault of inner tumult come upon me? Will this pause indeed bring a sweetness to my life? I do not believe in sweetness.

The desire for a woman has come back to me in the desert. No, it is not a promise of sweetness. It is as unpitying as everything else within me, a desire to possess and destroy the body and soul of a woman, and to watch the woman play her role in my own destruction. To seek her is to give her this right.

I have gone to find her. I am retracing the steps of my childhood, towards the highway: the journey of my youth's innocence, when I sought a friendly face, and was denied it.

After so many years, I rise once more to the surface of my solitude. I emerge from the dark depths of the pool. I await the lure. I know today that it is a trap. But I, too, shall overcome it and taste the fresh food of flesh.

At the edge of the road, pedlars have set out their wares. On my property. Two of them, standing there like grey trees, formless, draped and hooded. Their hands are immobile in the air above the fire, as if in ultimate benediction, coloured by the little fire made of twigs.

My muscles stiffen and my breathing grows heavy. At last, I shall measure my strength by expelling these intruders. They have cut some small trees—I can see this at a glance. They are camping on my property. As impassive as Druidic stones, they watch my approach, but do not move. Ah, my anger, gather your proven powers!

I challenge them, but they give no response whatsoever. What if I have lost the art of speech, after so many years of silence? I shout; I roar. I do not know what words escape from my throat. Do they express my thoughts? I do not know. In any case, they reach these dolmen. There is movement beneath their cloaks. The hands leave the fire. One of the two shadows approaches me. It is a man, middle-aged, greying, sly-looking. He is rather ridiculous in his bizarre and falsely solemn clothing. It pleases me.

Before my clenched fists he dissolves in a profusion of apologetic bowing. He talks incessantly, but his babbling is lost upon me. I fell him with a single blow. He rebounds from my outstretched arm like a ball. I laugh. My laughter must have a sound, but I do not hear it.

He gets up, his cloak covered with mud and melted snow. He redoubles his greetings and apologies. It seems that he is offering me his merchandise in restitution. He gathers an armful of necklaces, rosaries, almanacs, knives and other knick-knacks from his handcart, and puts them in my arms with gestures of false regret, a regret that is more for his bleeding cheek than for any injury he has done me. The meaning of the entire scene could be expressed very simply: 'Take anything you like, but please don't beat me up! I will leave your property as fast as I can . . . just let me get my things together . . .'

I put all the assorted trinkets on the ground, keeping only

a necklace of glass beads, which please me by their naïve vulgarity. I look at the man. He signals me to keep it. Happy to get off so cheaply, he smiles; or rather he purses his lips. I offer him money, but he refuses it, shaking his head with a gloomy look.

Still advancing, I now draw near to the second figure which is crouched by the fire, the hood down over the eyes. Taking this form by the shoulders, I stand it up in front of me. It is a woman. Raising her face to mine, she laughs. Disconcerted, I draw back a little. The man also attempts to smile. They seem to be mocking me. By way of reply, I approach the woman so close that I can feel her breath on my neck. I tear off her cloak. I want to strip her of all her finery, just as I would strip the bark from a birch tree. She does not try to escape . . . she continues breathing in my neck. She is laughing into my neck. She flouts me with her dazzling teeth. I can feel her heart beating, its rhythm undisturbed by the laugh I cannot hear. She is holding her arms in an arch above her head, her hands behind her neck, as though hiding something.

Did I really speak, or did I only think these things? I wanted to know what she was hiding. Still close to me, she removes the loose shawl she was tying around her thick hair. Her hair falls free about her shoulders—long, black hair; a mass of hair, blue-black. I draw back. Now it is she who comes towards me. Her eyes are bluish-green; her brows are dark and curved, emphasizing the perfect setting of the eyes.

I turn and cry out to the fellow, who is following the scene with a bored air:

'Is this your daughter?'

He shrugs.

Gesticulating, and attempting speech, I explain to him that the girl is the only thing that tempts me in his whole bazaar, and that if he does not let me have her I will smash his face. Still pressed against me, she laughs more softly, and I can feel the warmth of her breath on my chest. She lowers her head a little. Her scent is in my nostrils.

The man is dismayed. I throw handfuls of money to him. (I can't understand all this money in my pockets.) He retrieves it here and there from the ground, hopping excitedly. His eyes roll in ecstasy. Ingratiatingly, he bows low.

Then I put an end to the demonstrations of this tramp, signalling him to put out the fire and get out with his belongings. He hurries around, cleaning up, and when everything is piled into the handcart he stands there, hesitating. The woman goes over to her accomplice and speaks with him. Listening, he shakes his head. Now she is coming back to me. By her attitude, I know that I have won my prize.

The role of solitude has been reversed. Solitude is now the burden of the pedlar. I and my partner are a couple. The man goes his way alone; I do not.

The woman has put back over her head the sort of burnoose she is wearing. She goes over to the wagon and pulls out a little bundle of clothing. Her expression is withdrawn. I notice how blooming and full her mouth is when at rest. This sensation is super-imposed upon that of her laughter.

And suddenly I find myself giving her a name. I, the wild man, feel the name of a woman mounting to my lips, like a gift which I would offer. I, who have never received anything, will taste the miracle of the first gift. I call her Amica. Probably she has some other name, but I shall never hear it, and this one I have just uttered for the first time. I heard it composing itself within me, and welling out for her to take it. She has accepted it, because she is mine now, and I have acquired the right to give her a name.

I waited then a long time after the man had disappeared down the road, trundling his handcart. Then I lead Amica on a circuitous route through the mountains, in order to confuse her memory forever about the path leading to my property.

I imagined that she would ply me with questions, such as: 'Where are you taking me?' 'Is it very far?' 'Are you going to keep me very long?' 'Do I really please you so much?' 'Did you get the necklace for me?'

But no, not a word. Her mouth stays closed in a sulky pout.

She walks at my side, enshrouded even more within her cowl. Her eyes are watchful. At times, her passive expression is broken as she darts towards me a glance so piercing that it makes me tremble. Too late! I am already bound to her. Nor am I awakening from an illusion; on the contrary, from the moment I saw this woman, what attracted me more than anything else was just this hint of craftiness and evil in her eye.

I continue through the bush, never retracing my steps. I will go on to the end, to the fulfilment of this evil which now belongs to me alone, and of which I knew nothing even this morning. When we are within sight of the house, and of the torrent, I shall feast my eyes upon her face. When she realizes that we are miles and miles from the nearest neighbour, I shall acquaint her with the torrent. I will initiate her to the vision of my solitude. She will shiver when she sees that of the two, I am the more to be feared . . . I will pull her to me, and feel her shivering against me, my hands on her throat, her eyes pleading.

I observe her; I scrutinize her expression. Twice, I pulled back her hood, and she neither protested nor did she emerge from her apparent apathy. We enter the house, and I close the door behind us. Her expression remains unchanged; not a muscle moves on her face. Yet the feeling of this house is sinister. Dark and unkempt, it bears the imprint and odour of the dead, and of the dreadful one who is still alive. Amica, impassive, penetrates my drama, appears in my home with neither fear nor repulsion.

Amica is the devil. I have invited the devil to my house.

She laughs, putting her arms around my neck. Her arms are beautiful and firm, yet they seem to me to be unclean, destined to play I know not what role in my downfall. I resist their enchantment. (What are these cold snakes that have entwined me?) I pull them off brusquely, but they persist, and their resistance pleases me. I twist them. Although this also pleases me, it does not reassure me. The use of physical force indicates all too well the defection of my spiritual force. Brutality—the last recourse of those who have lost their inner power.

I go outside, and am refreshed by a breath of damp air against my brow. But already I have only one desire—to return to the snare of Amica's embrace. The evening air means nothing now. I know another freshness, a new turmoil.

She is standing at one end of the room, cutting bread, when I open the door. I throw my armful of wood on the floor, and, without moving over the doorsill, I cry out to her:

'Good day, my wife!'

Facing one another, we eat our meal. The flame of the lamp is brighter, because she has cleaned the glass. Her shawl is on a chair, her mantle hangs upon a nail. What peaceful household is this which I see around me? Nothing seems to penetrate my mind any more. I see an unknown woman eating opposite a stranger, the one as secretive as the other. No, I have never lived here; nor this man, either.

I welcome the woman into my bed, and the man who accompanies her.

How long is it since I took possession of my mother's big bed? I had not had the strength to take over her whole room;

but, one evening, I brought the great bed up into my attic as a replacement for the straw pallet of my childhood. Was I afraid the horror of my nights would diminish? I irritated the wound. I am it, and it is me. But what is the use of discussing the reasons for my gestures, my compulsions? I am not free.

I introduced Amica into the bewilderment of my nights. Oh, you do not know, you of the long blue hair, you of the phosphorescent pupils, you whose arms are cool and fresh, what this bed means—this bed that receives you and your deaf companion! You do not know what old insomnias lie about, what fevers and unnameable terrors. And when sleep comes it is scarcely better. A descent into the deepest gulf of the subconscious, where I can neither play nor defend myself, even as feebly as when I am awake.

I observe this strange couple on their wedding night. I am the guest at their wedding. Amica shows an aptitude and an ease in her caresses which fill me with a dreamy astonishment. She is sleeping now. My familiar demons begin to move among the dark carvings of the bed. Oh, I will no longer be the only one so tormented! . . . But no, they spare her calm slumber. They deploy themselves around her, at a distance. She is a calm island in this bed of the damned.

Dawn is breaking. I sense the distant murmur of the torrent, on its way, within me. I must be dreaming! Why are those little shoes at the foot of the bed? And on the chair, those delicate materials? What is this sleeping head doing on my breast?

I take it in my hands, like a ball. It wearies me and embarrasses me; it disconcerts me. What am I going to do with it? Throw it away? I feel a dryness throughout my being. No desire, no voluptuous inclination. Dryness. Utter drought. Thus has an arbitrary fate always robbed me of the springs of emotion and of joy within me. Oh, my mother, I had not known the extent of your destruction within me!

I get up and lean out of the window to avoid the vision of

this strange wedding-night. I move discreetly, as if I did not want the sleeping couple to perceive my frustrated presence in their nuptial chamber.

Days pass, and a kind of continuity is established. Amica occupies herself with the meals and the housework; I, with the stable. It is not yet the time for field and garden. I do not want to leave her alone in the house for one instant. I follow her unceasingly. My nerves are taut. Anything might happen.

Why did I not take her back after the first night? Already she was a burden to me. But I feared the highway. I feared the itinerant pedlar, who might have gathered a gang of idlers to come and find me; to question me, perhaps, with the intention of coming here. The idea was unbearable. I believed myself sheltered by my retreat. I had cut the bridges to the inhabited universe. And I had also cut off the trail of Amica. She had wanted to become a witness to my life. Now she will not leave it so easily.

A witness—the words grip me, obsess me. Amica is a witness . . . A witness of what? A witness of my home, of my existence, of myself. The idea gives me a chill, as though there were a large mirror in which my gestures and my expressions were held in ineffaceable images. At no price can I release my witness to the world.

Sometimes at night when I wake up, I see her sitting at the foot of the bed, combing her hair. I am invariably surprised at the extreme attentiveness of her eyes as she stares at me. She observes me tensely, ready to flee at the slightest warning. I can feel her watching, even when my eyelids are closed. Her gaze presses on my sleep with a strange weight. It awakens me through its concentration. It is almost like hypnotism. What is she trying to do? Must she possess me entirely? I will kill her, before that.

Once, unable to stand her exasperating insistence any longer, I made as if to strike Amica. In one movement, she leapt to the floor. The litheness of her action was such a rev-

elation that I did not think of running after her. The deep
uneasiness I felt when her eyes, too wide-open, were fixed
upon me, was completed by the impression of this supple leap.

It reminded me of a certain cat.

My mother would never keep a cat. Probably because she
knew that a cat is never servile. She could accept only those
animals which could be tamed and made to obey, trembling,
at her feet. (Ah, Perceval, who were you, then?) I have never
seen a cat here, except during the last days of my mother's
life. At that time, there was a cat prowling around. He would
only show himself, strangely enough, when I was alone. I
remember being troubled and irritated by the sensation that
the animal was lying in wait for me, with his dilated pupils.
He seemed to be following a latent intention forming within
me, one which escaped me, and whose inevitable outcome
only he could penetrate.

When I saw the cat for the last time, I was eyeing the
broken body of my mother. The beast, conscious, out of
reach, kept staring at me, a look fixed from time immemorial.
Someone had surprised me, then? Someone had been contemplating me without interruption, untiringly? Someone
had known me, at that moment when I no longer had any
knowledge of myself?

Amica has the same eyes as that cat. Two great orbs,
immobile in appearance, but palpitating like flames. She ex-
amines me when I am asleep. She stares at me when I no
longer see. She can discover in my dreams those gestures
indicating my absence, gestures which have fled into the
most obscure regions of my being, which sleep takes up again
at leisure, and which leave this bitter, stale taste, just enough to
nourish the torments of the day.

I never saw that cat again. I often had a very strange feeling
about it. It seemed to me that this malignant beast had entered

within me. It existed within me, and knew everything, bearing me down with the entire burden of its certitude.

And so, today, I find this woman, with eyes so astonishingly similar, riveted upon me. Thus I imagine my witness appearing in the light of day. My hidden witness, emerging from my conscience, facing me in all clarity. The witness tortures me! It wants me to confess. Why has this sorceress come here? I do not want her watching me! I do not want her to question me! I know very well that I shall never be able to get rid of her! . . . There was a creature who knew me at the moment of Perceval's flight. This witness now interrogates me from without, directly, without my collaboration, a separate being, like a judge. It pursues me into my most secret refuge, which was its true home. It violates me more profoundly than my conscience . . . I know nothing! I know nothing! If this creature knows something, it has nothing to do with me. No! No! Do not smile, Amica. It has nothing to do with me. As for me, I know nothing.

The shawls and skirts in which she drapes herself seem to be held only by the moving clasp of her hands, that tighten or loosen according to the whim of her movements, now lively, now relaxed. A cascade of folds slips from her hands and reappears further down in serried waves. The interplay of folds and hands; in one hand, a knot of folds clasped at the breast, the glistening silk stretched taut at the shoulders. The broken design, recreated elsewhere. The silk slips, leaving the shoulder naked, revealing the arms. Fingers so brown on the red skirt. The skirt swiftly drawn together in handfuls, now, as she mounts the stairs. The limbs perfect, the ankles fine. A knee shows. Then everything disappears. The skirt sweeps the floor, the hands are free, and the bodice unconfined.

This morning, I found Amica at the table, with the few spoons, forks and knives in my possession set before her. She seemed to be considering them. When she saw me, she indicated the shabby lot with forceful gestures, and spoke with animation. I could not understand at all what she was trying to tell me. Then, for the first time, she wrote something for me on a piece of paper. 'Are they silver?'

I burst out laughing, and wrote on the paper underneath her question, 'Of course not, stupid.'

Amica bit her lips, with a furious and spiteful glance.

Odd, indeed. Why was she so anxious to know if my cutlery were made of silver?

Amica has a strange way of keeping house. She will scour—one could say, ferret—in the same corner for hours, or in the same cupboard, while there are other tasks that she never undertakes at all. She never blackleads the stove, for example, nor does she scour the pots. Watching her, I would think she was looking for something. What has she come here for? What if our meeting had not been by chance? What if, on the contrary, she had awaited me with the express purpose of inquiring here as to the living and the dead? Why did I bring this woman here? Now, I can see no way of getting rid of her. Shall I measure her capacity for suffering against my own? No. I shall have to humour her. I fear too much that she will take my secret away with her, while I am asleep.

To keep watch. To keep watch over oneself. In the end, that is what is so unrelenting. I watch myself. I live only within myself. The only voice which comes to me is from within. No lips translate those words, no intermediary gives them form. But they strike my being, as sharp as arrows. I have plunged into the depths of myself without let-up. Following upon a childhood tortured by the absolute denial of self-knowledge, I was suddenly faced with the deepest of human gulfs. I foundered in the abyss.

While still alive, I partake of the last judgement: the confrontation with my real self. It is too much for a human to bear. I am burning. Oh! I am not always lucid! The sickness in my head distorts the voices. But it is enough to know that they speak, that they accuse me. And that I accuse myself.

At times, thoughts come to me which could be an alleviation, a kind of Grace; if I could believe in alleviation, and if Grace had not been refused me. Each person bears within himself an unknown crime, a draining wound, which he expiates.

When I was little, I used to go to sleep deadened by fear and work. Sometimes it happened, for an instant, that I could feel a presence which was a kind of consolation, superior to anything that I had ever suffered. I dared not abandon myself to this bliss, which my mother called the temptation of softness. I would stiffen, conscious perhaps of killing an angel in my refusal. To justify myself, I would tell myself that it must have been a bad angel, for the good ones are the policemen of God, and they punish little children who are too tender-hearted.

The experience of God had been forbidden me. And yet they had wanted to make a priest of me! Very early, I was turned away from the possibility of tasting God.

If Grace exists, I have lost it. I have refused it. But it goes deeper than that; someone before me, whose continuation I am, refused it for me. Oh mother, I hate you! And I have not even yet explored the fields of your devastation within me! A phrase haunts my nights. 'You are my son, a continuation of myself.' I am linked to the damned. I am a part of her damnation, as she of mine . . . No! No! I am responsible for nothing! I am not a free being! I repeat to you that I am not free! That I have never been free! Oh, what strikes me with such fury? The torrent surges through my head. And I am not alone! This woman whom I plucked from the roadside is before me, observing me, spying upon me. She must not see me in this state. I am drawn close to the falls. I must behold my inward image. I lean over the boiling gulf. I lean over myself.

How many hours have passed? What instinct drives me to go back up the rocky gorge? The instinct of the burrow, that draws home the wounded animal? If I return, it is because the torrent is not yet my absolute domain. The household of my childhood still holds me; and perhaps Amica, as well . . .

I am not yet prepared for the definitive integration with the fury of the falls, nor for the even more profound abyss within me. I still seek to escape from myself. The outcome, the final flight into my despair, remains in suspense. For how many hours, or days? To consent to my destiny does not depend on my own will. The next crisis will carry me away.

The springs among the rocks are swollen with the recent rains. I am walking in the water. I am so weak that I find I have to stop at every step.

I drink at the pump and splash my head with water. Amica is not there. I go to bed with my clothes on, my head aching. I do not yet feel uneasy that she has not come in. (I think so slowly.) Usually, I do not let her out of my sight. Moreover, she never goes far from the house. What can she be doing? It is already evening; and I have told her of the wolves on the mountain.

Amica has returned. I am too weary to question her. More sultry than usual, she seems to promise a richness of unknown caresses. She has reached her full powers. I want to send this sated woman away. Why am I so fastidious? What sort of a companion does my humiliation require?

She lays her hands upon my forehead. I cannot help but enjoy her hands, gentle against my burning. Suddenly, I have a revelation which panics me. I did not know that I had opened my mouth, but thought that I had only mentally desired to have some water. But Amica nodded assent, and helped me to drink, raising my head like that of a child. My eyes rolled in stupefaction. She is laughing.

I know now with certainty that I possess no control over my voice. I do not know whether I am speaking aloud or whether I only continue my silent thoughts. Amica can read my mind. My thoughts are open to her. I had not imagined this end of my horror! I am delivered to this slut! I bite my lips, so that not a word will escape them. Amica laughs.

I do not have the strength to rise. I exhaust myself with futile efforts. My head is bursting. I want to get rid of Amica. Since her arrival, she must have surprised me often in this way. Just what does she know? She is giving me more water to drink. Her skin has an unwonted odour. A different odour, which outrages me. For I think that I recognize this particular aroma. The odour of a human, not very young; of tobacco, old paper and ink . . . I have smelled it before. It reminds me of the chief of police who interrogated me after my mother's death . . . I scream, but am aware of it only by the contraction of my chest, and by the way Amica starts back, and stands there, rigid and pale. Her shawl has tumbled to the ground, revealing her bare shoulders and arms. I would like to rend her proffered body with my teeth and nails.

I have now no inner shelter. The sacrilege has been committed. The most secret corner of my being has been invaded. I am naked, in the open, facing this informer. She will find out even more than necessary for a police report. She will penetrate my torment.

I am burning with fever. If I speak aloud in my delirium, I do not hear myself. And she replaces my lost hearing. She usurps my role as my own principal listener. I communicate with her instead of with myself. My soul is violated. I had been told that God alone has this right and this power. A slut will pass the final sentence! At this moment, I would like to believe in God, in His terrible righteousness and perfect grandeur. Let Him read me and absorb me in my own truth. Not this woman! This miserable nobody! Oh, the Devil, then, is very powerful. And I am his accomplice.

I smell the freshness of springtime through the window, mingled with the odour of the falls. I have the sense of smell of a dog. Since my deafness, this sense has developed and increased to a strange degree. As would a hunted animal, I feared the scent of the police on Amica. But could I be mistaken? . . . There is no hint of ink and paper . . . Ah! I believe it is the rancid odour of the pedlar! . . .

Amica tucks me in like a baby in its cradle. I struggle, and she laughs. What I would give to hear the sound of her laughter! All that I know of it is this grimace which becomes more and more ferocious . . .

She has gone downstairs. She must be ransacking everything. The way is clear. She has a free hand. She is trying to find material proof of the crime. I myself have searched for twenty years. Will she do better? There are certain parts of the house that I have forbidden her. And in the stable, a certain stall, a certain place in the musty hay, now twenty years old. A certain dulled part of my memory which is sealed up . . . To Amica, nothing is forbidden here; she will enter everywhere, even into the precincts of a scarcely hidden terror.

The coroner's verdict stands before my eyes: accidental death. Then why has this girl come to snoop around? There is nothing to find out. The itinerant pedlar will know nothing. He will not have anything at all to take to the police; nor Amica either.

The fever is freezing me; it consumes me. What is Amica doing? What can she discover? Is it possible that she will find something? I do not have the physical strength to get up, but when she returns, I will strangle her. Or better still, I shall await the return of my strength, and then I shall throw this spy into the water. For one instant, she will hang from my arms over the precipice. She will struggle. I will not hear her cries, but I shall feel the convulsions of her terror. Then Amica will be decapitated and dismembered. The remains will be dashed down among the rocks. No! No! I do not want her dissevered head lying upon my breast. I want none of her! Nothing! And her long blue-black hair around my neck—it suffocates me.

I must have slept. It is morning. Amica has not come back. She has fled. I am certain she has fled. Does this mean, then, that she has found what she was looking for? By what clues? In what drawer? In which trunk? Oh! the rough floor of the stable, where the black blood is being absorbed!

The mountain must be encircled. The police and their dogs will be lying in wait for me. Amica has betrayed me. She is paying me back, the baggage that I bought in cash from the pedlar! I have been sold in my turn. By her, and by myself. Was I aware of the price? The price of my poor tormented body? . . . What surfeit of agony? I cannot expect any reprieve. Soon, I shall be only a burning torch.

How was I able to get up? I drag myself downstairs. Everything is in disorder, the cupboards all open and rifled. The door to my mother's room has been broken open. I stop before the presence that even the meanest objects, scattered pell-mell, reveal so potently. Everything that my mother has touched bears her imprint, and opposes itself to me.

The lock on the writing-desk has been broken. The one and only time that I dared to open this desk was on the day I acquired Amica. It was there that I had taken the money she cost me. In my impatience to be on my way, I had paid no attention to a certain sealed envelope, which I had torn open after having felt it. Nevertheless, one precise detail remains in my mind. After having filled my pockets, I am sure that I replaced the envelope, still half full, in the big ledger my mother had kept, from which I had taken it in the first place.

The ledger is lying open. I leaf through it. No trace of the envelope. I do not know how to explain the curiosity which draws me to go through these pages. I do this with the greatest care, minutely, even, torn by a kind of avidity. I find that my mother's efforts at book-keeping, which were at times unorthodox, were aimed at the extinction of a debt. On the last page, I read the final phrase inscribed in her large handwriting: 'The wages of sin are now paid.'

I stoop to pick up the torn and empty envelope. I can piece together the same words as are in the ledger: 'The wages of sin' and, in smaller letters, 'To be burned tonight'. Then follows the exact date of my mother's death.

This is what Amica has done. She has escaped with the devil's money. She will go into the world, and tell of what she found here, and that I am the offspring of sin, the son of big Claudine. The whole world will know that I was chosen by evil from the first breath of my existence.

What do I have left to renounce? Unless it be myself, and my own drama? I have never thought of the renunciation of one's self as a precondition for the purity of being. Moreover, I am unable to be pure. I shall never achieve purity. I deliver myself to my own end. I absorb myself into myself; and I am nothing. I cannot imagine my ending as outside of myself. Therein, perhaps, is my error. Who shall teach me the way? I am alone, alone within myself.

I am walking. I can take a step forwards, or a step back. Who says that I am not free? I am weak, but I am walking. I can see the torrent, but I can scarcely hear it. Oh, I would never have believed such lucidity could exist! Awakened, I play with the elements of my fever, which is now abating. The water is black; it is all whirlpools; it spits yellow foam. I can see Amica's head above the waves. That head—I don't know what to do with it. Perhaps she lives within me. Everything lives within me. I refuse absolutely to come out of myself. Her hair floats in the wind like a shadowy veil. It mingles with the water, in long coils, a turbulent blue-black, bordered with white. Her hair flows towards me in the eddies. It smells of the fresh water of the falls, and of Amica's own perfume. Her head is torn off. No! I don't want it! It spins like a ball. Oh, does anyone want to buy it? As for me, I have paid too much for it.

I weary of watching the water and the fantastic images within it. I am hanging over the brink as far as I can. I am within the spray. My lips taste its flatness.

The house, the long and dour house, born of the soil, is dissolving within me also. I can see it crumbling away in the backwash. My mother's room is turned upside down. All the objects belonging to her life are floating out over the water. Such poor things! Oh! I see the silver mirror someone gave her. From within it, her face is contemplating me: 'François, look me in the eyes.'

I am leaning out as far as possible. I want to see down into the gulf, as far down as I can. I want to lose myself in my own adventure. My sole and fearful wealth.

Translated by Gwendolyn Moore

ROGER LEMELIN

The Stations of the Cross

It all began one June evening in the main hall of the Provincial Museum.

'Monsieur le curé Ledoux! What a surprise! I did not know that modern painting interested you!'

'Perhaps, perhaps,' the old priest stammered, smiling mysteriously.

The speaker, an eminent ecclesiastic and a discriminating connoisseur of art, looked in perplexity after curé Ledoux, who, like a waggish spy, was threading his way through the groups of guests. This particular evening happened to be the first night of an exhibition of the works of a young painter, Paul Lafrance. He had just arrived back from Paris, where, for three years, he had busied himself in imitating Picasso. Paul Lafrance was almost six feet tall and did not weigh more than one hundred and thirty pounds. His long, mouse-coloured hair, his pale blue eyes, the Parisian's sceptical smile on his lips, his check suit and the short, fat women surrounding him, all contributed to making him appear more scrawny and more dejected. The weird designs and the violent colours of the canvases gave the walls an air of ludicrous astonishment. Some so-called connoisseurs, Provincial Government officials, were scrutinizing, criticizing, and appraising each work with pretentious gestures and glances. They had no money. The other guests, holding Martinis, were chatting about fishing and politics and glancing absent-mindedly at the paintings. These dilettantes, these business men flocking to an opening night through a taste for fashionable gatherings, behaved like gapers invading a circus famous for its five-footed giraffes. They are very extraordinary giraffes but the gapers don't buy them. Paul Lafrance had not yet sold one canvas.

'Monsieur Ledoux, you here?'

The old priest nodded, smiling artfully, his eyes almost closing. His cassock, greenish from being worn too long, was a trifle short and revealed his dusty boots, topped by thick, black, woollen socks. Now and then he rubbed a nervous hand through his tousled grey hair, and with the other crumpled a large chequered handkerchief into a ball in the opening of his roomy pocket.

Apparently unaware of the astonished murmurs that followed in his wake, he reached the first canvases and began to examine them one by one with an outstanding gravity, as if he had to condemn them to heaven or hell. Whatever was he doing at this exhibition? Those who knew him had reason to be astonished.

Monsieur Ledoux was rector-founder of Saint-X parish in the poorest district of Québec. For some time there had been a great deal of talk about him all over the city. After fifteen years of untiring apostleship he was seeing his parishioners of early days (swearers, drunkards, thieves) become exemplary citizens. But it was through his new church that old curé Ledoux had become famous. This temple was costing three hundred thousand dollars. Very good. His parishioners must be working men of heroic calibre to have consented to such a sum. Again very good. But all that would not be enough to have Monsieur Ledoux talked about at every social gathering. Monsieur Ledoux's famous church was not like the others! That was why! Gothic in style, it was the only one in the city without pillars! The high altar was visible from every seat. That isn't all. Monsieur Ledoux had had air-conditioning installed. It was probably the first innovation of its kind in all the churches in America! It had been said for a long time that curé Ledoux, son of peasants, was an uncouth and uncultured man. But what about this air-conditioning, this absence of pillars?

Monsieur Ledoux glided from one canvas to another with a concentrated air that one would not have expected of him. Someone offered him a Martini which he refused with a gesture of annoyance. After some twenty minutes' examination he buried his large nose in his chequered handkerchief and glanced furtively around him.

'Make up your mind, Thomas, make up your mind!'

Monsieur Ledoux was talking to himself. He often did that. Everybody called him 'Monsieur le curé', so Monsieur Ledoux often said to himself: 'Thomas! Eh! Thomas!' The priest walked towards the painter, Paul Lafrance, whose back was turned, and pulled discreetly at his sleeve.

'Monsieur l'abbé?'

'Curé Thomas Ledoux. Your work interests me. It's modern. Give me your address.'

The pale blue eyes gazed at the old priest as Paul Lafrance mechanically recited his address. Monsieur Ledoux, having moistened his pencil with saliva, wrote down the number in a little notebook. He closed it, smiling like an accomplice.

'Perhaps you will hear from me.'

He shuffled off towards the cloakroom. The painter and the guests, piqued with curiosity, gazed after him.

Monsieur Ledoux boarded a streetcar. With his chin sunk in the fleshy cushion that prosperity had placed round his neck since the erection of his famous church, he appeared to doze in heavenly bliss. His head swayed from left to right with the jerks of the streetcar and in rhythm with the rolling wheels on the rails. All at once the old priest sat bolt upright and opened his eyes watchfully. By an intuition peculiar to clergy, he had sensed the nearby presence of a church.

It was the Basilica of Québec. Monsieur Ledoux stared at it intently with an affectionate expression that gave way to one of triumph. The celebrated Basilica, the Cardinal's chapel, was filled with unfortunate pillars and had no air-conditioning system. Not like Monsieur Ledoux's church! His chin disappeared once more into its cushion and Monsieur Ledoux, having made sure of Paul Lafrance's address, began to doze again.

Monsieur Ledoux got off the streetcar in his parish and walked toward the presbytery. It was ten o'clock at night. Like a proud landowner he sniffed the air of his domain and glanced fondly at the humble homes of his flock. All at once he found himself in front of the unusual temple that crowned his saintly ambitions and filled him with pride. He stopped and, swaying with his hands behind his back, eyes half-closed as though in ecstasy, he gazed at it. His lips curled into a blissful smile: 'Thomas, Thomas it's really true, it is your church, your church, you old Thomas, you!'

His rapture was suddenly interrupted. Two devout women, faithful parish workers, were standing beside him and admiring the temple with him.

'What a fine church, eh, Monsieur le curé! The electric organ has been bought. All we need is the Stations of the Cross.'

Monsieur Ledoux turned round abruptly to them and said with puerile haste:

'We'll have them in a month. They'll be unique, these Stations of the Cross. The first of their kind in America, even in the whole world, perhaps, Thomas says so.'

Open-mouthed, the two housewives, delighted by this news and slightly shocked by the unexpected 'Thomas' of Monsieur Ledoux, watched him go away. Monsieur le curé, less repentant for having said too much than annoyed by this familiar use of Thomas that he had not been able to restrain before these good women, went into the presbytery furiously sniffing up a pinch of snuff. He went up to his office and on his way was addressed by the youngest of his curates, abbé Constant, the door of whose room was open. Comfortably seated in a leather armchair, he was busy reading James Joyce's novel, *Ulysses*. Abbé Constant, who had been ordained two years before, put himself in the category of the young clergy with advanced ideas who clamour for a youthful Church, suited to the needs of the time. He often smiled at certain of Monsieur Ledoux's old-fashioned preferences but he was very fond of him all the same.

'Are you beginning to sleep away from home, Monsieur le curé?'

'I've just come back from the Museum, from the first night of an exhibition of modern painting,' Monsieur Ledoux replied, blushing.

Wide-eyed with astonishment, abbé Constant gazed at his superior without saying a word.

Monsieur Ledoux, annoyed at having blushed, added defiantly: 'Yes, I have decided that our Stations of the Cross will be modern art. The first in America. And I think I'm going to choose this artist, Paul Lafrance.'

'But . . . Monsieur le curé,' ventured abbé Constant, who was beginning to collect his wits, 'don't you think our parishioners are scarcely prepared for . . . for Stations of the Cross like that?'

Then Monsieur le curé stiffened haughtily and said with triumphant solemnity:

'And it's you, young man, who reproached me for being old-fashioned! I have eliminated pillars, have had air-conditioning installed, and now it's the turn of modern art. Well, good-night. Don't go to bed too late. You say five o'clock mass tomorrow morning.'

Abbé Constant was too astonished to go on with *Ulysses*. He went to bed.

The young curate's objection hastened the execution of

the project because the curé could not tolerate anyone to doubt the worth of his ideas. Monsieur Ledoux rarely consulted his churchwardens where the financial affairs of his parish were concerned. He made his decision and, as a matter of form, called them together in order to tell them about it. As Monsieur Ledoux was cunning enough to make them believe that he had acted under their influence, these gentlemen (a fruit merchant, a grocer, and a streetcar conductor) nodded their heads gravely in approval. In the matter of the Stations of the Cross, Monsieur Ledoux presented them with the accomplished fact.

The artist Paul Lafrance set the price of his work at twenty-five hundred dollars for fourteen pictures representing the different stages in the Passion of Christ, according to the rules of modern art. Moreover, the surrealist painter promised to visit all the churches in the city, in order to make sure that his Stations of the Cross would be completely different from the others. Monsieur le curé promised to pay for the cost of the canvas, the paint, the frames, and to board the artist while he was doing his work. The brightest room in the presbytery was turned into a studio by the painter and the curé. The latter was anxious to keep up a daily inspection of his Stations and to become acquainted with the mysterious caprices of Modern Art.

The sight of the long-haired artist and the fabulous price of twenty-five hundred dollars made the churchwardens open their eyes wide, but Monsieur Ledoux remarked with a knowing smile:

'Churchwardens like you are blessed by God, who allows you to buy something more rare and beautiful for a church already unique.' These gentlemen puffed out their chests, looking at one another. What a curé!

It was an extraordinary experience for Paul Lafrance. Newly arrived from Paris where, many a time in front of his artist friends, he had made fun of the French Canadian's lack of taste for painting and where, before anti-clerical dilettantes, he had slandered the Canadian clergy, he now found himself with an order for fourteen surrealist paintings from the priest of a parish of working men, when as yet he had not sold a single canvas during his exhibition. This was a great piece of news in all the artistic circles of Québec and many of the painter's friends insisted on visiting his studio and meeting Monsieur le curé Ledoux. For a whole week the rumour circulated about Saint-X Parish that Monsieur le curé had had a celebrated artist brought by aeroplane from Paris. But Monsieur Ledoux remained impervious to questions. 'Wait until Sunday at high mass.'

The Sunday arrived. The church was packed to the doors. The absence of pillars and the air-conditioning were never so appreciated as on that day. All the flock were craning their necks in order to get a better look at the artist, Paul Lafrance, seated among the altar boys on a kind of throne usually reserved for visiting bishops. Lafrance, who had acquired pagan ways in Paris and given up his religion, was thinking that Art leads everywhere, even to Rome. He compared himself to Michelangelo and with some satisfaction imagined himself becoming a prince of the Church. All these glances raised towards him, the proximity of the altar and the religious propriety which surrounded him, prompted him to recall his prayers. He smiled imperceptibly at the thought that he was paid twenty-five hundred dollars to rediscover his faith. Monsieur le curé climbed into the pulpit.

'My very dear brethren:

'Heaven sends us a messenger of beauty from Europe. It is quite in keeping that Providence should direct his steps to our temple which, without doubt, is one of the dwellings on earth preferred by the Almighty. This church has been built in the most modern style and it would be illogical if the Stations of the Cross which will decorate it should be in the style of past centuries. If the art of building has been perfected to such a degree as to result in a work of art like ours, the art of painting has also evolved, and we must make it a duty to require as much of painting as of building. Thus, in honouring progress, we honour the Lord who is kind enough to bestow it upon man. My very dear brethren, you have before you, in the chancel, the celebrated painter, Paul Lafrance, who, tomorrow, will begin your Stations of the Cross, a work of which your grandchildren's children will be proud and which will make our church even more famous.'

During the days that followed, the presbytery became, in the parishioners' eyes, a mysterious laboratory where a magician armed with brushes devoted himself to all kinds of artistic alchemy. Many curious ones tried to obtain the favour of casting a glance at Lafrance's work, but Monsieur le curé kept this privilege for himself. Out of consideration, Monsieur Ledoux did not visit the studio for the first two days. Paul Lafrance took his meals at the same table as the curé and his curates and long discussions on cubism, impressionism, and surrealism took place between the abbé Constant and the artist, who seemed to get along with each other very well. In the course of these conversations, which he did not understand in the least, Monsieur Ledoux often blew his nose, pretending he had a cold in order to excuse himself for having nothing to say.

However, at the fourth meal, tired of blowing his nose, the curé became impatient and determined to find some books which would deal with these mysteries. But he dared not ask the painter in front of abbé Constant. He rose from the table briskly, during the dessert, and very politely, asked:

'Is your work progressing, Monsieur Lafrance?'

'Yes. The first picture is finished. Some last touches and it will be perfect.'

Monsieur Ledoux, warped by fifteen years of financial administration, gave himself up to a rapid calculation. One picture in two days, fourteen in twenty-eight days, ninety dollars per day. He was a little disappointed. It had seemed to him that, because of the importance he attached to this work, it should take some months to complete.

'Do you wish to see it?' asked the painter.

The two men went off to the studio and Monsieur Ledoux, on catching sight of the picture, cried out in stupefaction.

'Don't you like it?' the painter ejaculated, distressed.

Monsieur Ledoux shook his head and frowned.

'I think the feet and the arms of the Christ are unusually long. It gives an odd effect. Don't you think so?'

The painter, already inflamed by the fervour of the artist defending his work, opened his mouth to make a declaration of his principles, but a second's reflection and a brief glance at Monsieur Ledoux persuaded him to change his tactics.

'It's because it's new that it takes you by surprise. You'll become accustomed to it and then you'll like this style. Painting has changed a great deal. It's no longer photography. Moreover, you insisted that my Stations of the Cross should be an innovation.'

'I don't deny it.'

Monsieur le curé, chin in hand, was reflecting. To tell the truth, a disturbing conflict was going on inside him. Just what demon had urged him to choose this painter? Moreover, from the first glimpse on the opening night at the Museum he ought to have foreseen the dangers with which modern art threatened his Stations of the Cross! The word 'modern' and the success of his church had blinded him. Obviously, he had not acted with his customary prudence in paying a thousand dollars in advance to the painter. It was now too late to retreat. He could not dismiss the painter after the enthusiastic recommendation he had given him. Monsieur Ledoux abruptly put an end to his reflections.

'Monsieur Lafrance, I'm not disputing the beauty of your work and I think that in the long run I shall understand it.

But I do not forget that I have eighteen thousand parishioners who are not so well prepared as I to appreciate your work. And they are the ones who pay for it. So please shorten those arms and feet a little. Anyhow, you know what I mean.'

The painter seemed highly shocked but the curé had already left. With clenched fists, Monsieur Ledoux went to his room muttering: 'Thomas, you're nothing but a proud old peacock. You've got yourself into a fine mess. Because you have a new church without pillars and with air-conditioning you think you're the hub of the universe. You old fool, go and pray a little while and ask God to get you out of this tight corner. Above all, thank Him for the blow to your pride.'

He met abbé Constant in the hall.

'Well, now, Monsieur le curé, what do you think of Monsieur Lafrance's work?'

'Stupendous! Stupendous!'

Monsieur Ledoux did not add anything further but went up into his room and knelt down. His prayer lasted an hour and, apparently, the Lord advised him to persevere in his project in order to punish him.

Regular torture then began for Monsieur Ledoux. He made an effort to show a great enthusiasm for the Stations of the Cross but his common sense told him: 'Thomas, you know very well that these paintings are dreadful. You're courting disaster.' In order to be convinced of the beauties of modern art he consulted a clergyman renowned for his artistic knowledge. Monsieur Ledoux even obtained some large books on the subject. All to no purpose. The frequent visits he paid to the artist's studio only succeeded in adding to his despair. Artists like Paul Lafrance are as uncompromising as the Ten Commandments. The painter went on with the work in his own way and the further it progressed the longer, it seemed to Monsieur Ledoux, the feet and arms of the Christ became. Those violently coloured paintings with monstrously grotesque figures appeared to Monsieur Ledoux like a Mardi Gras masquerade. The good curé lost his appetite and the fleshy cushion around his neck decreased considerably. He never mentioned the Stations of the Cross in the pulpit and his parishioners, who were waiting impatiently for the unveiling, were astonished. What was happening to him?

Then something most unfortunate occurred. The verger, who was a very inquisitive man, succeeded in getting into the studio while the curé was away, and glanced at the pictures. Immediately word went round the parish that the People of the Passion were all crippled and walking in paths of blood. Alarmed, the housewives called on the curé and confessed their anxiety. He smiled, closing his eyes.

'Ladies, I suspect you of inventing rumours in order to force me to satisfy your curiosity. They're all untrue. In the meantime, if it will give you any pleasure, I can tell you that the Holy Women in our Stations of the Cross are the portraits of the most devout ladies in the parish.'

Delighted and flattered, the ladies left the presbytery quite content. Monsieur le curé, overwhelmed, did not know what to do. While feeling so downcast, he came face to face with abbé Constant. Forgetting his pride, he confessed hesitantly to him:

'Monsieur l'abbé, I think you were right. I have made a mistake. Our parishioners are not ready to appreciate our Stations of the Cross. What am I going to do?'

Abbé Constant, who for some days had known his curé's state of mind, behaved himself as befits a good priest. He did not laugh at him but cheered him up and offered to help him. The two priests set to work and prepared a ten-page circular in which the symbolic beauty of modern art was praised with forceful adjectives. The circular was printed and distributed to the parishioners by the altar boys. In the face of this incomprehensible action, the parishioners began to be seriously alarmed.

The work was finished one Saturday afternoon and the

painter's satisfaction equalled the curé's distress. The artist received the balance of his payment, thanked the curé, and left like a great lord. To put an end to the great martyrdom he was enduring the good curé announced that the exhibition of the work would be on Sunday morning, a quarter of an hour before high mass. Certain remarks of dissatisfied parishioners about the circular on modern art had reached the curé's ears and he fearfully visualized the moment of the ceremony. He passed a dreadful night and every time he woke up he implored Heaven to calm his anguish and to see to it that his parishioners would bow down in admiration before the Stations of the Cross.

At half-past nine, the verger, whose rising indignation was mingled with fits of laughter, hung the pictures in the empty church. Monsieur le curé, hidden behind the altar, perspired profusely while waiting for the doors to be opened.

A crowd of parishioners interested in the fate of their church stamped and jostled outside the entrances. Finally the doors opened and there was a rush into the temple. There was not a single sound from the thousand gaping mouths, so great was the stupefaction. Then there burst out fourteen rounds of horrified cries which were relayed from picture to picture in a kind of chain of explosions. The women protested the most violently.

'They're frightful. Look at the Christ! The arms are longer than the legs, the feet longer than the thighs, and the hair does not curl. Horrible! Just look at the face! The chin is pointed, the eyes are all wrong.'

Among the group of good ladies who thought themselves represented by the Holy Women of the Passion were some white with anger and others who were crying, for the Holy Women of the Stations of the Cross looked like enormous frogs. The churchwardens seemed to be in a bad humour and were whispering: 'Twenty-five hundred dollars for these daubs! A child could do them!'

Other men threw up their hands, expostulating: 'The cross

is much too small and it's snowing flowers into the bargain! Just look, will you! The hands are pierced with nails and don't even bleed!'

A rebellious atmosphere reigned in the church. The parishioners were all coming to the same conclusion: Had Monsieur le curé gone crazy? Every eye searched for him.

Behind the altar, Monsieur le curé Ledoux, face white as his surplice, mopped his brow. To cap everything, the air-conditioning system had gone out of order the day before. It was July and the heat was tropical.

Ten o'clock mass began and no one paid any attention to the service. The church was full of whispers and ripples of muted laughter. How shameful! Such a shocking thing in such a beautiful church! Monsieur le curé went up into the pulpit more dead than alive. He would have preferred to be at Rome, prostrate at the Pope's feet and thinking only of the beauties of Christianity. 'Face the music, Thomas!' His voice was weak and his hands trembled.

'My very dear brethren:

'I am only an old man whose dearest wish, as you know, is to give you a church finer than all others. For a long time I have dreamed of acquiring a magnificent Stations of the Cross for you. At last, it is in front of you, but instead of the admiration that I expected, you show dissatisfaction. I do not hide the fact that I am broken-hearted by your attitude. But I pray heaven that your eyes will become accustomed to this work and recognize its beauties in the end. My very dear brethren . . .'

Monsieur Ledoux felt himself grow faint and made no effort to resist swooning. The churchwardens, while carrying him to the vestry, remarked: 'Not surprising that you fainted! Throwing twenty-five hundred dollars to the devil like that!'

Monsieur Ledoux's fainting had sown consternation in the hearts of his flock, but not to the point of changing their opinion on his famous Stations of the Cross. These events filled the parishioners' conversation for several days and Monsieur le curé deemed it wiser to keep to his bed. As long as there was anxiety about his condition no one complained about the Stations of the Cross. But although Monsieur le curé kept out of sight he was, nevertheless, most active. From various sources of information he learned that his faithful flock were attending church less and less frequently and that those who came to the religious services spent their time laughing at the ridiculous paintings. On the other hand, the temple was invaded by a curious crowd from neighbouring parishes attracted by the peculiar Stations of the Cross.

Monsieur Ledoux's greatly celebrated church had become a kind of museum where one forgot to kneel and took the liberty of talking and laughing boisterously. Monsieur Ledoux endured many bitter moments. After having enjoyed too briefly the importance of his church, he was already suffering from its decline. Then it was that Providence deemed him to have been punished enough and inspired him with an ingenious idea. Why hadn't he thought sooner of the Mother Superior of the Convent?

She had some talent for painting and Monsieur le curé had often gone, on Sunday afternoons, to see her paint saints, ships, rivers, and roses in delicate colours with a dainty brush. He had her roused at ten o'clock at night and the good Mother Superior, all of a tremble, ran to the presbytery. When she left Monsieur Ledoux, she said these words: 'I can paint these fourteen pictures in two weeks, I promise you. But I repeat that I am not equal to the task. Pray God I may succeed.'

The Mother Superior's work was kept a great secret. Monsieur le curé went to the convent three times a day and all those who met him wondered why he wore such a cheerful expression when the church continued to be profaned by inquisitive folk who came from all over. Ten days after the

Mother Superior's visit, Monsieur Ledoux telephoned to a very important person who nearly fainted after hearing the curé's words. But that is another story. Two days after his telephone call, on Saturday night, about eleven o'clock, a Government truck stopped at the side door of the church and two workmen, under Monsieur Ledoux's direction, carefully carried fourteen packages from the church to the truck.

The next morning, at ten o'clock mass, the church witnessed the finest sight imaginable. The frightful Stations of the Cross had disappeared and were replaced by fourteen beautiful paintings in delicate colours, with handsome men, beautiful women, and a Christ that resembled Clark Gable.

The flock were filled with rapture that was soon transformed into deep piety. Many good ladies shed tears of joy and all the deeply affected parishioners raised grateful glances towards the altar. The church was exorcised and restored again to the bosom of the Lord. Monsieur Ledoux went up into the pulpit in triumph.

'My very dear brethren:

'Your joy moves me to the highest degree. The magnificent Stations of the Cross that you see before you are due to the brush of the Convent Mother Superior who deserves all our gratitude. As for the other Stations of the Cross, I thought those pictures were meant, after all, for experts. So I gave them to the Provincial Museum. My very dear brethren, let us rejoice in the Lord. Our church has resumed its march toward celebrity; it is the first in the city without pillars; the only one in America to possess an air-conditioning system, and the first in the world to make a gift of the Stations of the Cross to the Museum.'

Translated by Mary Finch

GÉRARD BESSETTE

The Mustard Plaster

The old man slammed the door behind him. His wrinkled face was livid, and his lips quivered with rage. Grasping his cane firmly in one bony hand, he started down the stairs. *They'll never see me again. It's all over.* At each step he had to feel in front of him with the cane, like a mole dazzled by daylight. No longer would they insult him, or make fun of his advice, or ignore his eighty years of experience. *I shall never give in.* From now on their promises and sweet talk would fall on deaf ears. After all, they were the ones who had begged him to come and live with them. ('You'll see. You'll be just fine. We have a beautiful big room waiting for you.') *The hypocrites! It was because of my pension of course. If only Léon hadn't brought that great big Englishwoman back from Europe after the war . . .* The old man had never quite been able to accept the fact that Shirley, that stranger who didn't even speak French, was his daughter-in-law.

On his return to Canada, Léon had naturally found himself unemployed. He'd never been much good at making his own way. And because he had been a lieutenant during the war, he had imagined that a lucrative job would be his for the asking. While waiting for this to happen, he 'put out feelers', looking for 'something suitable, something worthy of his talents . . .' His veteran's allowance ran out before he found anything. And at that point he and Shirley had redoubled their insistence that Mr Denaud should come and live with them. And the old man had agreed. They had been living together for about five years now. Léon had eventually had to take back his old job as a cashier in a bank. And at the end of every month, in addition to the generous rent he already paid them, Mr Denaud was obliged to give them a little extra to keep the household solvent. Shirley had no sense of the value of money, or of how to keep to a budget. The moment she got her hands on a few dollars, she wasted them on extravagances. *What a fool I've been!* He should have left them earlier, when he was stronger and could see more clearly. *Never mind. Better late than never.*

Testing the surface by tapping his cane before him like the antenna of an insect, the old man advanced along the sidewalk with small, careful steps. A fall would be catastrophic, for he knew he would never be able to get up again without help. Since he was well known in the neighbourhood, he would be taken back to the house; or, worse still, someone would go and get Léon. This had happened four or five times during the last few months. Recently, Mr Denaud had suffered inexplicable momentary blackouts which he had not admitted to a soul, but which made things spin around him in a dizzying nightmare. *I really should make up my mind to go and see a doctor.* The thought occurred to him, but he had plenty of other things to occupy his mind. Didn't he have to find another place to live, to have his things moved, his furniture? He grinned at the thought. Once his furniture was removed, Léon's place would be pretty empty. Mr Denaud imagined Shirley's stricken expression on seeing her almost empty rooms. What, in fact, would be left? A stove, a table, three or four chairs, a bed, and that's about all. The sofa in the living-room? *Yes, obviously I shall have to leave them the sofa.* Young Richard slept on it, and Mr Denaud could not take it away from them—especially now that the little boy was ill. It was, in fact, because of that . . . The old man swallowed painfully. He didn't want to think about that for the moment. The difficulties of walking, and the unevenness of the sidewalk took all his attention.

Mr Denaud reached Sherbrooke Street, which, at this point, seemed as wide as a river. The thought of crossing it terrified him. Beads of sweat stood out on his wrinkled forehead. Cars rushed by at ridiculous speeds and with deafening roars from their exhausts. He would have to cross this vast space with no other guidelines than the two faded white strips that marked the pedestrian crossing. The old man could not trust the traffic lights. He saw them out of focus as diffuse globes of light that blended with the adjacent red and green neon sign of a drugstore. Mr Denaud always avoided this dangerous intersection on his daily walks. He would go four blocks further along, where a safety island allowed him to cross the street in two stages. But what would happen now if he had a dizzy spell in the middle of the traffic? His throat was dry, his eyes were smarting. Today he could not indulge in his customary detour. He would have to save his energy. *Of course, I could always ask a passer-by to help me.* But he rejected that possibility. It would have been an admission of failure, of his dependence on Léon and Shirley that he was unable to shake off. This reflection gave him courage. He waited until the stream of traffic in the cross-street started across Sherbrooke, then set out across the road himself, walking as fast as he could and tapping with his cane.

By the time he reached the far side he was bathed in sweat. There was a throbbing in his ears and he had to lean against the drugstore window to catch his breath again. Only then did he wonder where he was going. Until that moment he had thought only of escaping, of getting away as quickly as possible. Conflicting possibilities made his head spin. Nevertheless, a decision would have to be reached. *But not here. I can't decide anything here.* He would have to find a place to sit down, to relax and reflect. He set off again towards Ontario Street, using his cane to counteract the steep incline of the sidewalk. *Where shall I go?* The Ladies of St Edward Club, where, from time to time, he met a few cronies? *No, if I go there they'll make fun of me.* They would question him, old man Chartier especially, and he would end up making 'a clean breast of it', and telling them all the details of the argument with Léon and Shirley. Chartier also lived with his son. *Poor old Chartier!* Every month he had to hand over his entire old-age pension to his son, without a murmur, so afraid was he of being sent to an old people's home. *I'd be in the same fix if I hadn't managed to put away some savings.* No, the club was out of the question. Besides, he would not see his pals again now. He was going to start again from scratch, a totally new life. But where was he to go in the meantime? A restaurant, perhaps? No good: he wasn't hungry. Anxiety lay like a weight on his stomach. Besides, tea or coffee gave him palpitations, and carbonated drinks gave him heartburn. Of course, he could always order something and then not drink it, but such waste was unacceptable to a man of his strict and parsimonious habits. He had so often reproached Léon and Shirley for their extravagances that he could hardly fall into the same trap himself!

While deliberating he reached Ontario Street. Once more he was covered in sweat. He felt worn out and weak. He took a few more faltering steps when his nostrils were assailed by the smell of malt and yeast which a large ventilator was blowing across the sidewalk. A glass of beer might do him some good. There was a humming in his ears, and he was only vaguely aware of his surroundings as he wandered into the tavern, stumbled into another patron—who continued on his way, muttering insults—and collapsed into a chair by a small white table. At last he could rest and collect his thoughts. No doubt a tavern was not the ideal place. And, indeed, Mr Denaud had not been inside one for years. His father, many years before, had been in the habit of knocking back rather more than was wise, and of coming home somewhat the worse for wear of a Friday evening, when he would shout down the recriminations of Mr Denaud's mother. But that had all been so long ago it no longer had any meaning. He, Mr Denaud, was now an octogenarian, a widower without a family, so to speak, since Léon no longer counted, and since his daughter, Adèle, had married an American and lived in Miami.

The old man swallowed some beer. There were those who said it was good for the health. According to old Chartier, it stimulated the circulation. And surely dizzy spells were caused by defective circulation? Mr Denaud remembered having read this information in some medical article. He wiped his moustache with the back of his hand, feeling better. *My Dad died at ninety-five. He never had dizzy spells. And he drank his daily half-dozen bottles of beer.* But he put these thoughts out of his mind. It was not his health that was at issue. A much more urgent problem had to be dealt with: the question of finding somewhere to live, and arranging to have his things moved.

He sighed and gazed around the room through watery eyes. At a neighbouring table two men were drinking and discussing the race-track news. One of them had won three hundred and fifty dollars the day before, and was jubilant. The other had not had any luck and the two horses he bet on had finished among the last. He spoke with a lazy drawl like Léon's. Mr Denaud took another swallow. And then the circumstances that had led up to his leaving the house struck him with unusual force and clarity for a man whose memory of recent events was inclined to be hazy.

The drama, for that is what it had been, had started with his grandson Richard's illness. No wonder the child had fallen ill. Time and again the old man had warned Shirley not to let him sleep in a room with an open window. She, of course, simply did what she felt like doing. She insisted it was good for his health. And, of course, it hadn't been long before the little one caught a cold and began to cough. And still the window remained open. The old man had had violent arguments with his daughter-in-law. He had even warned her that the boy's lungs were inflamed. He might as well have saved his breath. By the time she finally got around to calling the doctor, Richard had a temperature of a hundred and four.

Mr Denaud took a gulp of beer, and dabbed at his moustache with his handkerchief. Beside him, the two men were still discussing horses and the pari-mutuels. New customers were drifting into the tavern and there was a buzz of conversation. From the very first sign that he was ill, what that little kid had needed was a mustard plaster. Mr Denaud had recommended it to Shirley, and to Léon. And they had made fun of him, saying that it was an old-fashioned, a pre-historic remedy! Nowadays it was all penicillin, oleomycin, antihistamines and things like that—all of them worthless inventions for taking away poor people's money. Mushroom mould for curing an inflammation of the lungs! What was the world coming to? And the doctors and the druggists kept getting richer. Well, then, one simply had to protest. But when the old man tried to intervene, the young doctor had practically ordered him to mind his own business. And, as usual, Mr Denaud had had to pay for the prescription because Léon had been broke.

With a sigh he raised his glass once more. A waiter asked him if he wanted another and without thinking he nodded his assent. *These young doctors nowadays are a bunch of incompetent hotheads.* And the proof was that the penicillin hadn't done any good. After a temporary improvement, Richard's fever had risen to 103.7. And all the time there had been a proven, effective remedy for inflammation of the lungs. The sight of his grandson's red, congested face, as the child twisted and turned in bed, made Mr Denaud decide to take charge.

Without saying a word to anyone he went off to the corner

grocery to buy a box of mustard. He knew all about plasters.
Many's the time he'd prepared them in the past. And it was
the simplest thing in the world. All you did was make a
paste with mustard and water, spread the paste between two
pieces of cotton and apply it to the patient's chest. Proud of
his shrewdness, Mr Denaud had quickly slipped into the bath-
room with his box of mustard and a thin linen towel. As he
prepared the plaster, he wondered whether it might not be a
good idea to add a little flour to the mustard to lessen its
sting. He vaguely remembered his mother doing something
like that when one of the kids was sick. But he didn't have
any flour. Should he try and get some from the kitchen? But
if he did that, Shirley would be sure to notice, and the whole
project would miscarry. *After all, it doesn't really matter.* And
he decided only to apply the plaster for about ten minutes.

Still sitting at his table in the tavern, his cane propped
against the edge of the table, Mr Denaud shook his head.
Once more he raised his glass to his lips to drown his anger.
As long as he had been allowed to do things his own way his
project had advanced without any problems. On entering
Richard's room he had peered at the alarm clock to see what
the time was, and then had applied the mustard plaster. But
from that point on things had gone wrong. He had barely
put back the covers when Shirley entered the room with a
pill and a glass of water in her hand. It was time for the
child's medicine. *I should have just let her get on with it and not
said a thing*, said Mr Denaud to himself. But it had been too
much for him and he had protested vehemently against these
newfangled quacks' remedies. Hadn't the child's temperature
gone up again, after all? So why persist with these stupidities?
His daughter-in-law had simply shrugged her shoulders and
briskly suggested that he mind his own business. Mr Denaud
had been about to reply when, after taking a couple of sniffs,
the Englishwoman had remarked that there was 'a funny
smell' in the room. So saying, she had looked straight at

her father-in-law, who had blushed and made a great point of admitting that perhaps in the end she was right about the pills. After all, what did he know about modern drugs? The old man was annoyed to recall how he had humbled himself. *For all the good it did me . . .*

He looked around the tavern. It was half full. Groups of labourers had dropped in for a drink on their way home. Two men sat down at his table, roaring with laughter. One was almost bald and had a huge strawberry-coloured nose; the other was a sort of dwarf who wore a baseball cap with a plastic visor and chewed a long cigar. Before Mr Denaud could protest, they had stood him a glass. He drank with them, muttering thanks which they ignored. *If Léon could see me, he wouldn't believe his eyes.* For a moment, the old man wished his son were there so he could tell him that he had no need of him and was perfectly capable of looking after himself. But he rejected this thought which, in itself, was a sign of dependence. *I must put all that sort of thing behind me.* Léon had been as much to blame as Shirley—perhaps even more, in a sense, for after all he was his own son.

The plaster had been on Richard's chest for exactly nine minutes when Léon returned unexpectedly from the office, two hours earlier than usual, just after Shirley had left the room. The old man had been peering at the alarm clock just as the door opened. He started and quickly suppressed an expression of annoyance. Léon rushed into the room still wearing his overcoat. Richard seemed to be dozing. His eyes were closed and the breath whistled gently through his half-open mouth. The little blond head with the flushed face just lay there against the pillow without the slightest movement. Obviously the plaster was beginning to take effect. If only Léon hadn't lingered so long in the room. The old man had become more and more nervous as he watched the minutes go by on the clock. Léon had also noticed the bitter smell in the room. The old man pretended that the smell came from some menthol nose drops, an explanation Léon accepted with a shrug. And finally he had left the room. Mr Denaud rushed to the bedside at the very moment when Richard woke up suddenly and cried out in pain. Quickly the old man had removed the plaster and, on hearing Shirley's and Léon's footsteps in the corridor outside, had thrown it in desperation into the waste-paper basket. But by now the air was so saturated with the bitter odour of the mustard that there was no point in trying to hide it. Léon had immediately found the plaster in the waste basket, while Shirley had bent over the child's chest and yelled with rage: 'He'll kill him! That's what he's going to do! He wants to kill him!'

Apparently the little boy's skin had been covered with yellowish blisters. But Mr Denaud had seen none of this. He had not been allowed to get close to the child. Besides, would he have been able to see them with his poor myopic eyes? Shirley had become more violent. She had insisted on remaining mistress in her own house. She was not prepared to allow her child to be killed by an old lunatic. And if that didn't happen to suit Mr Denaud, he had only to leave the house. And Léon had said nothing: he hadn't even protested! His own son.

'You got a light?'

The old man jumped, then turned his head towards the man who had spoken to him. He started going through his pockets, then remembered that he hadn't smoked since he'd started getting those deaf spells.

'No, I'm sorry.'

But by this time, the man had turned away to ask someone else. And Mr Denaud resumed his reflections. 'She practically threw me out,' he muttered. If, at least, he had left of his own free will he would have felt less bitter.

He finished his glass and continued to sit there, collapsed in his chair with his head slumped down on his chest. His breathing became more difficult, his vision more blurred.

I'm going to have a dizzy spell. He began to panic. What would become of him, so far from home, in this tavern where nobody knew him? No doubt it was the lack of air; the atmosphere was filled with smoke. *I must get a breath of fresh air outside.*

Grabbing his cane, he got up with difficulty, steadying himself with one pale hand on the enamel surface of the table. After a moment he felt better and risked a few steps. *I'm not all that weak, not that incapable, I* . . . At that moment his foot struck the leg of a chair. He tried to lean on his cane but it slipped in a puddle of beer. He felt himself falling forward, then a hard object hit his skull near the temple.

When he came to, the waiter was dabbing his forehead with a cold napkin. A warm viscous liquid was trickling down the side of his face.

'Feeling better, Dad?'

The old man nodded weakly, then closed his eyes again.

'Somebody'll have to take him home. Anyone here know him?'

'No, no,' murmured Mr Denaud, 'not home.'

At the same time he felt a hand going through his pockets and removing his wallet. Were they going to rob him? He made a gesture as if to reclaim his property. But all they wanted was his address.

'It's not far from here,' said a voice. 'I'll call a taxi.'

'No,' said the old man, 'I don't want to.'

'You're sure not in any shape to walk, Dad,' said the waiter. 'Go on, take a taxi. That's the best thing to do.'

He felt two powerful arms lift him up by the armpits. He made a feeble attempt to free himself but the room, the tables, the walls were spinning. A sudden overwhelming fatigue made him go weak at the knees. *Just to lie down in a bed, anywhere, but just to lie down.* If no one had been supporting him, he would have lost consciousness again and collapsed. He couldn't get the air into his lungs. He breathed with a raucous whistling sound. Someone put his hat back on his head, and he was practically carried to the taxi. Two men sat on either side of him in the back seat of the car. He was barely conscious during the journey. Going up the stairs, still supported by the two men, he belched and his mouth filled with bitter foamy liquid. Then he heard Léon's voice:

'Now what's happened to him? He had to go out by himself, naturally, even though I warned him. There, careful now, we'll put him to bed.'

'He was in the tavern,' said one of the men. 'All of a sudden, there he was stretched out on the floor. Must have hit his head on one of the tables. Look, you can see: it's still bleeding a little.'

'What did you say?' It was Shirley's drawling voice. 'The tavern? He was in the tavern? That's the limit! If he's going to start drinking, that's all we need! Thank you, thank you very much. We try to keep an eye on him, you know, but today our son was sick, and he slipped away when no one was looking.'

'Yeah,' said one of the men, 'looking after old folks isn't easy. My Dad's like that, too.'

The old man made a violent effort to sit up in bed. He was not going to allow such flagrant distortions of the truth without registering a protest. Neither Shirley nor Léon had ever forbidden him to go out. But he only managed to raise his head slightly.

'Would you like some coffee? There's some hot in the kitchen,' said Shirley.

The two men declined. Mr Denaud heard the door closing. It seemed to him he was left alone for ages. *No one looks after me. They wanted to get rid of me. It's me who supports them, and they wanted to get rid of me.* Suddenly he thought of Richard. How could he have forgotten him for such a long time?

'Léon, Léon!' he shouted in a hoarse voice.

Léon came rushing in. 'What is it? You're not still in pain?'

The old man felt his heart thumping away in his chest, and he needed a few moments to catch his breath again.

'Richard . . . how is . . . how is he?'

'He's better,' said Léon. 'The doctor came and gave him an injection. That calmed him.'

Mr Denaud's features relaxed.

'It was the mustard plaster,' he announced with some difficulty. 'It was the plaster.'

'We won't talk about that, please,' said Léon. 'That's over with.'

'It's the plaster, I tell you.'

Léon said nothing. The old man's lips formed a smile. His breathing was easier now. *I knew he'd end up on my side. He's just ashamed to admit it, but he knows he was wrong.* Mr Denaud was filled with intense joy at the thought that because of him Richard was better. It had hurt him so much to see the little chap suffering, lying in bed with his flushed face swollen with the fever. *It's when they suffer that one realizes just how much one loves them.* The old man closed his eyes, and shook his head. *How could I have even considered the possibility of leaving the little one? How could I have lived without him?* It was unthinkable. After all, it was better to put up with Shirley's sneers. *Shirley . . .* The old man was so proud of having 'saved' his grandson that he was prepared to think more kindly of his daughter-in-law. Though she was too proud to admit it, she must be ashamed of her behaviour. And, besides, wasn't she Richard's mother? So was it not she who unwittingly had provided the old man with a reason for living, a consolation for his declining years?

'Léon.'

'Yes, Dad?'

'You may tell Shirley that I forgive her.'

'That you forgive her? What do you mean?'

'You will tell Shirley that I forgive her,' repeated the old man.

He saw Léon shake his head.

'Okay. I'll tell her. You have a rest now.'

With a deep sigh of contentment Mr Denaud closed his eyes. *Life will go on as before. I won't have to move. I'll see the little one every day.* A pleasing warmth spread through him at the thought. With a smile on his lips he saw himself once again applying the mustard plaster that was to cure Richard. *I am still useful. Even Léon didn't dare deny it.* His heart beat more calmly. Slowly and voluptuously he filled his lungs with life-giving air. Then he slipped into peaceful sleep.

Translated by Anthony Robinow

JACQUES FERRON

Mélie and the Bull

Mélie Caron had only thirteen children. She expected to have more, one a year until she died; but after the thirteenth, Jean-Baptiste Caron, her husband, said to her, 'Stop, Mélie!'

So the poor woman stopped, not yet fifty years old. She remained unsatisfied, deprived of her due, all warm and trembling like an animal checked in full career. However her trouble was not without remedy: did she not still have her thirteen children? Thirteen children is not much; but it is a family. Alas! the consolation was shortlived. One by one her children left her. She had fed them too well: full of ardour were the boys, ripe and tender the girls; once fully grown there was no holding them back. In the end Mélie lost them all. She remained alone with her old man.

He, like a prisoner whose sentence is served, now found his freedom. He was no longer to be found at home, but spent most of his time with the other freedmen of the village, old eccentrics of the same breed as himself, parleying and laying down the law, drinking whenever the opportunity arose, and then pissing, drop by drop, the burning fire of his repentance. Mélie would take advantage of this to offer herself: 'Let me help you, old man.'

The suggestion was enough to make the waters flow again. Forty years of married life had taught the old man much; he knew that at the slightest sign of weakness his wife would get him into her clutches and not let go till she had molly-coddled him into senility. He remained on his guard.

'Thank you, Mélie. I'm all right now.'

Now it came to pass that the old lady, deprived of children and husband, her corpulence notwithstanding, began to feel confined, loath to be restricted to her own company. Humours began to rise to her brain. At first this made her head swim, then she felt unsteady. It was the end of August. Alone in her kitchen, with her fly-swatter in her hand, she listened; not a fly in the house. This silence astounded her. In the absence of flies she was prepared for much worse: for the appearance of snakes, of preposterous frogs, of demons armed with scapularies, against which her fly-swatter would have been useless; prepared for an attack of raving madness. She was on the point of screaming when she heard a moo which saved her. Fleeing her monsters, she rushed out.

Outside, giving shade to the door, there rose a cherry tree, with flashes of sunlight and the redness of cherries moving among its leaves: beyond that there stretched a garden, then, as far as the river, a field. Mélie crossed the garden. The calf in the field saw her; with his tail in the air he came up towards her with faltering little leaps. The fence which separated the field from the garden brought them both to a stop. The old lady leant down; the calf raised a round, wet muzzle; they looked at each other. And suddenly Mélie Caron was moved by a feeling which was worthy of her heart. This muzzle, this trust had overwhelmed her; tears came to her eyes; had she been able to cry tears of milk, she would have wept buckets to satisfy the appetite of the poor animal.

That evening when Jean-Baptiste Caron came home, she announced to him: 'In future I shall look after the calf.'

The soup was steaming on the table.

'Fine,' said the old man, sitting down. Discussions have never been known to keep soup hot. Better polish it off now and talk later. When he had eaten his fill: 'Why look after the calf, Mélie?' he asked.

She replied: 'Because I want to.'

'Have I by any chance not taken good care of him?'

'Good or bad, you'll not take care of him any more.'

'Fine,' said the old man, who in actual fact was not particularly concerned about the calf.

He was nevertheless surprised a few days later to see his old lady in the field, sitting under a huge, black umbrella, which protected her from the sun and whose light shade, far from hiding her from view, made her most conspicuous.

'What are you doing there, Mélie?'

'Knitting.'

And so she was.

'Perhaps you'd be more comfortable knitting in the house.'

'No, old man, I'm more comfortable here.'

And she added: 'Besides, I can't leave him now.'

He asked anxiously: 'Leave who?'

'Come now, old man, the calf, of course!'

The animal was lying at Mélie's feet. The picture was not lacking in charm. But to Jean-Baptiste it gave not the slightest pleasure.

'Shall I tell you something, Mélie? Shall I?'

She made no objection.

'Well,' he said, 'you look like an escaped lunatic, and that's a fact.'

'Old fool, yourself,' she replied.

You cannot reason with a woman when she is in full possession of her faculties, much less when she loses them. Reason attacks front on; such bluntness is a drawback; with the weaker sex you have to use some stratagem, or simply take them from behind.

'If Mélie were twenty years younger,' the old man said to himself, 'a few little pats on the behind would bring her to her senses.'

In fact he could have done with shedding a few years himself; he had long since lost the art of those little pats. So how was he to bring about a recovery? What could he do to stop the old lady's madness becoming the talk of the village?

'It'll be quite simple,' thought Jean-Baptiste Caron. 'Since she's mad over a calf, I'll sell the calf.'

In this way he hoped to cure her. The remedy was simple indeed. He went off at once and made the necessary arrangements with the butcher. The next morning at daybreak along came his man, paunch bulging beneath a white apron. He had donned for the occasion a bowler hat. He took away the calf. Soon afterwards old Mélie, still heavy with sleep, came out of the house suspecting nothing. The cherry tree, branches held high, for it had not yet lowered its panoply, revealed a strangely slender trunk. The sun was coming up. Dazzled, the old lady stopped a moment to blink her eyes, and then set off along the garden path, calling: 'Littl'un! Littl'un!'

She reached the fence; there was still no sign of the calf. Again she called him, but with no better luck. Then she made a thorough search: she searched high and she searched low, but, from the garden to the river, the field was empty.

'Ah, mercy me!' she cried.

And back she rushed, the sight of the water having convinced her that the animal had drowned. Is it Christian to put rivers at the bottom of fields? This arrangement of Nature's filled her with indignation. In her haste she bumped into the cherry tree, who, preoccupied himself, had not seen her coming, absorbed as he was in his foliage, distributing his fruit to the birds. The birds flew away, cherries fell to the ground, and the wicked servant was caught in the act at his very roots. Much to his surprise the old lady continued on her way. So he signalled to the birds to come back.

Mélie Caron went back into the house.

'Old man, old man, the most terrible thing has happened.'

This most terrible thing roused no interest.

'Can you hear me, old man?'

He could not hear her, and for a very simple reason: he was not there. The old lady ran to his room: she searched high and she searched low, but the bed of Jean-Baptiste Caron was empty.

'Ah, mercy me!'

But at the sight of the chamber-pot she was not alarmed. No old fellow who has trouble pissing is ever swept away by the flood. Besides the pot was empty. However, this incapacity of her husband's for drowning did not altogether lessen the mystery of his disappearance. Mélie Caron remained as in a dream. At first her dream revealed nothing; on the contrary it masked her view; the veil was coloured for she was dreaming with her eyes open. Suddenly the veil was drawn aside: she saw a knife, and behind the knife, holding it, his paunch bulging beneath a white apron, wearing for the occasion a bowler hat—the butcher.

'I'm dreaming,' she said to herself.

With which statement the butcher agreed, closing the curtain. Then old Mother Mélie rushed into the wings, and off to the butcher's she trotted. On her way she passed the church.

'Mother Mélie,' said the priest, 'you're tripping along like a young girl.'

'Yes, yes, Father, if you say so—like a young girl. But have you seen my old man?'

'I saw your old man and your calf, one joyful, the other pathetic.'

'Oh, the poor dear! Oh, the ruffian! Pray for him, Father.'

And the old lady continued on her way. She arrived at the butcher's. The butcher, who had not had time to remove his hat, was surprised to see her again so soon.

'Good day, butcher. Where is my calf?'

'Good day, ma'am. I don't know your calf.'

'Oh, don't you now!'

She paused in the doorway just long enough to blink her eyes. The morning was behind her, radiant, making the room in front of her dark. However she was soon able to distinguish the carcasses hanging there.

'There are many calves here,' said the butcher, showing her the carcasses. 'Only they all look alike since we undressed them.'

'I see one that seems to have kept its coat on.'

'Where's that, Mistress Mélie?'

'Here.'

And pointing her finger, she touched a very shamefaced Jean-Baptiste.

'That's your old man, Mistress Mélie.'

'Cut me off a leg all the same.'

'He's very skinny.'

'Cut it off, I tell you!'

The butcher refused. The old lady took away his knife.

'Then I'll help myself to that leg.'

Whereupon Jean-Baptiste Caron intervened. 'Don't act so foolish, Mélie. Your calf's here.'

He handed her a rope; the poor dear animal was on the end of it, his eyes startled, his muzzle round and wet.

'Littl'un!'

'We weren't going to hurt him,' said Jean-Baptiste Caron: 'only cut him.'

'A calf develops better that way,' volunteered the butcher.

'Quiet, you liars! My calf shall remain entire, as the Lord made him.'

Having made sure that he still had all his vital parts, including his little phallus, the old lady set off with him. The priest, who had not yet finished his breviary, was still in front of the church.

'Well, Mother Mélie, I see you've found your calf.'

'Yes, Father, but I got there just in time: they were about to cut him, the poor dear animal. I stopped their cruelty.

You see, Father, he still has all his vital parts, including his little pointed phallus.'

'So I see, Mother Mélie, so I see.'

The old lady continued on her way, pulling her calf behind her. Soon afterwards the old man, Jean-Baptiste, appeared on the scene, looking very dejected indeed.

'It appears,' said the priest, 'that you're jealous of a calf. Your old lady showed me what you were planning to deprive him of.'

'She showed you! Forgive her—she's not herself any more.'

'Forgive her for what? I don't take offence at that. Surely you wouldn't expect her to put drawers on her calf?'

The bell for mass began to ring. The priest was obliged to leave the old man. One month later the latter called at the presbytery. He was looking even more dejected; he walked bent double. When he sat down the priest noticed his face: he thought he seemed worried.

'Worried, no. Let's just say I'm weak.'

'Well now! You're getting older.'

'That may be, but it's not just age; for the last month I've eaten nothing but mash and grass.'

'No!'

'Yes, mash and grass.'

'The same as a calf?'

'You said it, Father; the same as a calf. I like meat, beans and lean pork. This food doesn't suit me at all and Mélie won't listen to me. She says we're all one nation.'

'What language do you speak at home?'

'We still speak like people, but only because we don't know how to moo.'

The priest began to laugh. 'It's just the same with French Canadians; they still speak like people, but only because they don't know how to speak English.'

Jean-Baptiste Caron nodded his head. 'It's quite possible that calf is English,' said he; 'he's taking my place.'

'Your place! You mean you live in the stable?'

'No, Father, we don't live in the stable. But the calf is living in the house.'

'You don't say,' said the priest, 'he must be an English calf.'

'He must be: he's not at all religious.'

The priest rose to his feet. 'We must drive him out.'

This was also the opinion of Jean-Baptiste Caron.

'But how?'

Jean-Baptiste Caron also wondered how. The priest put a finger to his forehead, and this was very effective.

'Return to your house,' he said to the old man. 'But first pull yourself together and look cheerful. Once home, eat your mash as though you enjoyed it and be loving to the poor dear little animal.'

'I won't be able to.'

'You will. After a week or two Mélie will think you share her feelings. At the same time, bring other animals into your house.'

'You must be joking, Father!'

'Cats, dogs, mice, rabbits, even hens. I don't say you should bring cows or pigs. Just domestic animals Mélie will grow attached to and so become less attached to the calf. Then it will be possible to use a stratagem.'

Jean-Baptiste Caron: 'A stratagem?'

The priest: 'You will tell Mélie that you are worried about the calf's future.'

'I'll tell her the truth: in six months he'll be a bull. It seems to me that's something to worry about.'

'Exactly, this is what we must prevent. After all he's an English calf: mating isn't for him.'

'All the same, we're not going to send him to school!'

'No, not to school: to a seminary.'

The priest added: 'A professional in the family is no disgrace.'

'You're right, Father; a professional in the family is no disgrace.'

At times advice is worth heeding, especially when it comes from one's priest. Jean-Baptiste Caron decided to make use of that offered him. Under the circumstances there was little else for him to do. He therefore declared himself to be in favour of calves, which won him the confidence of the old lady. Then he brought up the subject of education.

'Well now, it's no joke; a professional in the family is a worthwhile and honourable thing.'

Mélie Caron knew it was no joke. But completely wrapped up in her calf, she was not particularly concerned about honour or the family; she wondered which of the two, the bull or the professional, would suit her best. Her heart inclined to the one, her reason to the other, and the animal looked at her puzzled. She too was puzzled.

'What are we going to do with you, poor little fellow?' she asked him.

'Moo, moo,' replied the calf.

This reply did not help her in the slightest. Then she reflected, not unreasonably, that once educated the animal would express himself more clearly. So she opted for the professional, telling herself that if by chance he did not like this condition he could always go back to being a bull. Without further delay she went to the priest and told him of her decision.

'A good idea, Mother Mélie! And since you want him to be educated, send him to the Québec Seminary: that is where I studied.'

The old lady looked at the priest. 'You don't say!'

The priest was forced to climb down a little. 'We mustn't exaggerate,' he said. 'But all the same I do think, with his intelligence, this little fellow could become a lawyer or even a doctor.'

The old lady seemed disappointed.

'A doctor, that's no joke!'

The old lady knew it was no joke. She simply said 'Pooh!'

'A lawyer then?'

She preferred the lawyer.

'Then the matter's settled, Mother Mélie; next week they'll come for your little one: a lawyer he shall be.'

As had been arranged, one week later to the very day the Father Superior of the Québec Seminary sent his representative, a great giant of a man, part beadle, part deputy, who arrived with much to-do in a carriage drawn by three horses. The carriage drew up in the courtyard of the presbytery. Immediately the postulant was brought forth.

'*Ali baba perfectus babam,*' cried the representative.

Which is to say that at first-sight, without further inspection, he had judged the calf fit to become a lawyer. On hearing these words the animal moved his ears. The priest noticed this.

'Well, well, he understands Latin!'

Mélie Caron did not understand it. She said 'Amen', however, with a heavy heart.

This amen had an effect she had not foreseen: the representative rose to his feet and standing up in the carriage, pointed his finger at her:

'Thou, Mélie, *repetatus.*'

'Amen,' repeated the old lady.

Then the giant of a man leapt from the carriage, seized hold of the calf, and carried him off into the church barn.

'He's not as good as the Father Superior of the Québec Seminary,' said the priest, 'only being his representative, but you'll see, Mother Mélie, he still knows all about giving an education.'

Indeed, no sooner had he entered the barn with the calf, than he reappeared, alone, holding in his hands a long object, which he gave to the old lady.

'Thou, Mélie, *repetatus.*'

'Amen,' said she.

And the terrible pedagogue went back into the barn.

'But it's my Littl'un's tail!' cried Mélie Caron.

'Yes,' replied the priest, 'it is your Littl'un's tail. Keep it. He no longer has any use for it.'

At that same moment the door of the barn opened, and who should appear but the calf, stiff, in a long black frock-coat, walking like a little man.

'Littl'un!'

He stopped and slowly turned his head toward the old lady. This head did not fit, it was shaky and too high, its features motionless. And he stared at her with vacant eyes.

'Littl'un!' the old lady called again.

He did not even twitch his ears. The old lady did not know what to think. What had they done to her little one in the church barn that he should come out looking so distant? They had cut off his tail, to be sure; they had put clothes on him, true; he was walking on his hind legs like a prime minister, so much the better! In short they had educated him, but did that mean they had to make him blind and deaf? This being the case, education did make the farewell easier.

The seminarian calf, drawing a white handkerchief from his frock-coat, waved it, but distantly, oh so distantly: the fingers holding the handkerchief were already human. Mélie Caron made no attempt to hold him back. He climbed into the carriage beside the representative of the Father Superior of the Québec Seminary, and there sat upright on his little behind, he who had never used it before. The carriage moved off and soon disappeared from sight.

'Well?' asked the priest.

Well, what? The old lady did not know, so she made no reply.

'Well, yes,' the priest began again, 'he is gifted, that little fellow! He's not even at the Seminary yet, and all there is left of the calf is its head. Education is for him. A lawyer he shall be, and what a lawyer!'

'What lawyer?' asked the old lady.

'Why, Lawyer Bull! A famous lawyer. Come, come, be proud: he'll be a credit to you.'

Mother Mélie was holding the calf's tail in her hands, and it hung there pitifully. Proud? with her head down and her tail, so to speak, between her legs, she did not feel in the least like being proud. 'I'm very happy,' she said; and very sadly she went off. To see her leave like that worried the priest. The next day after mass, without stopping to have lunch, he went to call on her, and found her in her garden, feeding the hens.

'I was afraid I might find you in bed, Mother Mélie.'

'I very nearly did stay in bed, Father. When I woke up I had no desire to do anything, only to die. Surely at my age I'm entitled to a rest. Then I heard the clucking of the hens, the barking of the dog, the animals making their morning noise, and I thought of my poor rabbits twitching their noses without a sound. Who else would have looked after all these animals but me? So I got up.'

The priest took off his hat while he recovered his breath. His plan had worked, the calf was out of the way, the old lady cured; what more could he ask, under the circumstances? He was satisfied; he remembered that he was hungry. Mélie Caron gave him a meal and he ate till he could eat no more. When he rose from the table she was still not satisfied: 'Just one more little mouthful, Father?'

'So you're not cross with me, Mother Mélie?'

She was cross that he had eaten so little. Apart from that she had nothing against him, considering him to be a good Christian.

'But what about your calf, Mother Mélie?'

She saw no reason why she should be cross about that. Hadn't she parted with her calf so that he could become a lawyer? It had been for his own good; of what importance was the sacrifice she, poor woman, had made?

'Besides,' said Mélie Caron. 'I am used to these separations.'

She was thinking of her thirteen children, well fed all of them, full of ardour the boys, ripe and tender the girls, who had left her one by one. And where had they gone? One to Maniwaki, another to the States, a third out West. As for the rest, she did not know. Besides, Maniwaki, Maniwaki . . . she had never been outside of Sainte-Clothilde de Bellechasse: what could Maniwaki mean to her? Or the States? or Abitibi? or the Far West? 'I lost my children, Father; I can part with a calf. Besides I still have my hens, some rabbits, a dog, a cat and some mice, enough to keep me going for some time yet. My supply still hasn't run out.'

'You'll die one day, all the same.'

'The worms will console me.'

'Come, come, Mother Mélie? And what about the good Lord?'

'After, once the worms have eaten their fill.'

The priest thought of his position; there was nothing in the Scriptures to prevent Mélie Caron having her bones cleaned off by worms before going up to join the Almighty. 'Very well,' he said, taking his hat and preparing to leave. Whereupon Mélie Caron, still not satisfied, asked him if he thought that at the Seminary the little fellow would keep his head.

'His calf's head? Of course not.'

'Then how shall I recognize him?'

The priest thought of his position and either because he had forgotten his theology or because the question had not been dealt with he could think of nothing very Catholic to say in reply. He hesitated, feeling somewhat ill at ease in his cassock.

'Mother Mélie,' he said at last, 'there exists something which, as a young bull, your little fellow would have worn in all innocence, but which as a lawyer he will have to conceal; it is by that incorruptible root—for education cannot touch it—that you will recognize him.'

And doubtless judging he had gone too far, without explaining himself at greater length, he went off, leaving the old lady with her curiosity, naturally, unsatisfied. So when Jean-Baptiste Caron came home she eagerly asked him for an explanation. Jean-Baptiste Caron, who was not inhibited by theology, answered without hesitation: 'It's the phallus, pointed in the case of a calf which has become a young bull.'

'And in the case of Littl'un?'

'Likewise, since education cannot touch it. He'll keep his root even though he's a lawyer, and in this way will be easy to recognize.'

And so, reassured, Mélie went back to her daily routine, and the months passed, the winter months, then spring, and the cherry tree bloomed; then came the summer months, June, July, and the ripe hay was harvested. In August the newspapers announced the famous fair to be held at Québec in the early fall, and which Jean-Baptiste Caron had been wanting to see for a long time.

'Old girl,' said he, 'we really should see the Provincial Exhibition before we die.'

The old lady burst out laughing. 'Have you gone crazy, old man?'

In order that she might judge for herself he handed her a page of the newspaper. On it she found this professional announcement: 'Maître Bull, lawyer.'

'Anyway,' she said, 'it's not such a bad idea.'

So to Québec they went, their hearts heavy, their eyes wide. The city, the fair, amusement and pleasure soon lifted the weight from their hearts. Fatigue came more slowly; however, after two or three days, they could hardly keep their eyes open, and were beginning to miss the peace and quiet of Sainte-Clothilde.

'But,' said the old lady, 'before we go back, there's someone I have to see.'

Jean-Baptiste Caron was not in the least surprised.

'Someone you have to see?' he asked.

'Yes, old man! Just because we've never had any fallings out, that's no reason why we shouldn't see a lawyer before we die.'

Old Mélie was right: they should see a lawyer. It was unfortunate, however, that the lawyer had to be Maître Bull. Jean-Baptiste Caron could see no good coming of the encounter. It is one thing to recognize a young bull under a gown, but quite another to get the lawyer to agree to the test. At any rate, Mélie should go alone.

'I'm thirsty,' said Jean-Baptiste Caron. 'I'll wait for you at the Hôtel de la Traverse.'

So Mélie went alone. To Maître Bull's office she came. 'Come in,' cried he in a beautiful deep voice. She went in and found, in a dusty little office, a young man dressed in black, handsome as an archangel, sad as an orphan, who, after the normal formalities, asked for her name, first name and place of residence: Mélie Caron of Sainte-Clothilde. And the purpose of her visit: whom did she wish to bring action against?

'No one,' the old lady answered.

Surprised, he looked at her; and said, with relief: 'Thank you.'

It was the old lady's turn to express surprise. He explained to her that the lawyer's profession served as an alibi.

'Who are you then?'

'A poet,' he replied.

'Oh,' said she.

'I keep it a secret; if men knew they would look upon me as some kind of animal.'

Mélie Caron lowered her eyes at this modesty.

'Your name again?' the lawyer asked her.

'Mélie Caron.'

'I do not know why,' he said, 'but that name brings to my mind the image of a field and the sound of a river.'

At these words, no longer doubting that this was her Littl'un, the poor dear animal, old Mélie pulled from her bag the pitiful object which she had kept, and let it hang beside her. Meanwhile the archangel, the orphan, the young man in black, went on in his beautiful deep voice, saying that it was not the sound of a river, but that of the wind in the grass, the wind whose waters bleach it white in the sun.

'Earth's back is dark and stains the hand, but when the wind passes she forgets her sorrow and, moved, turns over, showing her white belly, where the grass is soft as down, where each blade is a nipple gorged with milk.'

'Poor dear,' thought the old lady, 'he badly needs to graze!'

'Do you sometimes hear a voice,' she asked him, 'a voice calling you: Littl'un! Littl'un!'

'Yes, I hear it.'

'It is mine,' said Mélie Caron.

'I did not know,' said the lawyer. 'Besides I cannot answer. I am imprisoned in a cage of bone. The bird in his cage of bone is death building his nest.* There was a time when I hoped to free myself by writing, but the poems I wrote then did not render my cry.'

'Poor dear,' thought the old lady, 'he badly needs to moo.'

'Are you married, Littl'un?'

The young man gave a horrified start; his archangel's wings trembled; he was deeply offended at being thought capable of something so low.

*TRANSLATOR'S NOTE:

> L'oiseau dans sa cage d'os
> C'est la mort qui fait son nid

These lines are taken from 'Cage d'oiseau' ('Bird Cage') by the Québec poet Hector de Saint-Denys-Garneau (1912–43).

'Quite so, quite so,' said the old lady, 'I didn't mean to offend you. I only wanted to find out if you were free.'

'I am free,' he said, 'subject only to the will of the ineffable.'

She handed him the hairy member.

'Then take back your tail, Littl'un, and follow me.'

She led him to the Hôtel de la Traverse where Jean-Baptiste Caron was waiting for them.

'Old man, it's Littl'un!'

Of this she seemed so sure that the old man lowered his eyes, embarrassed. Together they returned to Sainte-Clothilde. 'Well, well!' called the priest, 'it's back to the land, I see!' And back to the land it was! Though they had surpassed the prophesied return. Indeed, once he had grazed, it was not long before Maître Bull had recovered his coat. Meanwhile his gown was falling to shreds. Soon there was nothing left of the fine education he had received at the Québec Seminary. One day, at last, he was able to utter his poet's cry, a bellow such as to drive all the cows in the county mad. Faithful to his root, he had found his destiny. From that day on, before the wondering eyes of old Mélie, he led an existence befitting his nature, and left behind him in Bellechasse, where they called him The Scholar, the memory of a famous bull.

Translated by Betty Bednarski

NAIM KATTAN

The Neighbour

I used to see him several times a week, a brown briefcase under his arm. We lived in a building on Durocher Street and his apartment was next to mine. I never heard him, no visitors or music. He was small, thin, alert and bright-eyed, with a high-pitched Asian voice. Was he Vietnamese? Chinese? Burmese? I didn't dare ask, nor did I feel the need to know. It often used to happen that we would be going up or down the stairway together. He would greet me briefly with a nod and a barely perceptible smile. We crossed paths by either speeding up or slowing down. We always avoided speaking to each other. Were we afraid to break the silence and, in so doing, destroy an intimacy we were obviously determined to protect?

One rainy morning I called a taxi. I was getting in when I saw my neighbour taking his umbrella out of its case. He was about to brave the downpour. Without thinking, I invited him to share my cab. He accepted impassively, without showing any annoyance or relief.

He was going to St James Street, not far from my office.

'Mr Young,' he said, holding out a hand and indicating with the other that he meant himself.

I introduced myself and added, 'Mr Young, that's a very English name.'

'No,' he said without a smile, 'it's a Chinese name. I'm Chinese.'

'So you work at the bank,' I said.

'Yes, for the past ten years.'

He didn't ask me any questions. We were embarrassed. How could we go back to being silent, sitting next to each other like that, our knees touching at every sharp turn and sudden stop?

'Quite a downpour!' I said.

'Oh, yes,' he agreed.

What did he do at the bank? He would find that a prying question and it would encourage him to question me. I looked out the window of the cab door; a stream of water was enclosing us on all sides and rushing down on us like a cataract.

When we parted he took my hand discreetly and thanked me without any warmth.

After that, our paths crossed now and then at the entrance to the building, in the halls or on the stairs. In the morning Mr Young always wore a white shirt and a plain brown or green tie, and under his arm, the brown briefcase. Sometimes I used to see him going out in the late afternoon or early evening. Then he would be wearing a chequered sports shirt without a tie, and, under his arm, a briefcase similar to his morning one, only black.

At the end of the summer the outbreak of a fire on the first floor made all the tenants run out into the street half clothed. The firemen were there, busy doing their job. 'It's not serious,' they told us calmly to reassure us.

Mr Young and I found ourselves at the entrance. We greeted each other in the usual way, embarrassed by our reticence.

'It's shocking,' I said.

'Yes.'

'It doesn't seem to be too serious.'

'No.' He looked me in the eye, smiling slightly.

'Are you still in the bank?'

'Yes, of course.'

I thought I detected a shadow of dread on his face. 'Still the same job?' I asked mechanically.

'No,' he said. 'I'm not on the elevator any more. Messenger, I'm a messenger.'

'Then you have the chance to get out, to move around, to go for a walk,' I said after a slight hesitation. A forced laugh followed each of my words.

'No, I never go out.'

'Of course, that's better. You avoid the snow, rain and heat.'

The alarm was over and we returned to our homes. I was on the verge of inviting Mr Young in for coffee or a drink, but he already had his door open. A strong cooking smell filled the air. So he made his own meals too. Did he live alone? I was convinced that he did.

I never heard any sound through the wall separating us. I even wondered if he had a television set. So I was quite astonished when one evening, returning from a film, I heard clamorous, incomprehensible voices coming from my neighbour's place. Were they arguing or were they expressing their joy at being reunited? They were Chinese, there was no doubt of that. Then, all of a sudden—silence.

The following day Mr Young was wearing his fixed smile. Neither of us referred to the incident. After all, it was his home and he had a perfect right to entertain his friends.

'Do you speak Chinese?' I asked him several weeks later when we were going up to our floor together.

'Yes, of course,' he replied.

In November a colleague from the office took me along to a lecture given at the university by Malcolm Muggeridge, the British writer. To my surprise, I saw Mr Young sitting in the first row with a notebook on his knee and a pencil in his hand, taking notes.

Several weeks later, at a meeting on the government's urban policy, I saw him again, with his notebook and pencil. We nodded to each other. Mr Young was engrossed in his work and I didn't dare disturb him.

That evening I heard a female voice through the partition. I couldn't determine whether she was laughing or crying.

I saw Mr Young again two weeks before the election, at the meeting for the member of parliament for our riding. He was carefully taking down our representative's words. I meant to meet him when it was over, but when the time came he had disappeared into the crowd.

The following Monday I found a notice in my mailbox for a meeting. A well-known lecturer from the United States was to speak on pollution. Spontaneously, I rang my neighbour's bell. He was already wearing his chequered shirt and he greeted me without surprise. I showed him the notice.

'Yes, I know, I received one too.'

'We could go together if you like,' I said.

'No, I'm sorry but I've decided to go to a feminist meeting. If it's over early enough, I will meet you there.'

'Oh, don't bother. I think I'll just spend a quiet evening at home.'

Two or three months later, when I met Mr Young at the entrance to the building, I realized that I hadn't even noticed his absence. 'You disappeared,' I said, putting on a show of good humour.

'I've been here all along,' he said.

'Oh!' I was somewhat disconcerted. 'I haven't seen you.'

At the end of the winter I took two weeks' vacation. I wondered if Mr Young hadn't been away as well. When I returned there wasn't a sound from his place. But that was only normal.

A week later I saw him climbing the stairs. 'I was away on vacation,' I said.

He looked at me impassively, nodding his approval.

'How about you?' I asked.

'I've been sick. I only went back to work yesterday.'

'What was the matter?'

'Nothing in particular. It must have been fatigue.'

'Did you see a doctor, at least?'

'Yes, but it was no use. He didn't know either. He said to wait.'

I was about to answer but he was already inside his apartment, closing the door while nodding to me.

For five or six years we greeted each other. Mr Young left each morning with his brown briefcase and white shirt, and each evening with the black briefcase and chequered shirt. We had tacitly agreed to stick to the customary trivialities. I was always glad to see him on the stairs. Life was following its immutable course. The embarrassment had vanished from our relationship. We were neighbours, perfectly courteous at all times.

One Saturday afternoon Mr Young rang my doorbell. 'May I come in?' he asked casually. He was already in the hall.

'Of course.'

He sat down on a chair in the living-room. 'Can I get you some coffee, a glass of wine or some cognac perhaps?'

'No, thank you, but I'll take tea if you have it.'

'Yes, of course.'

I busied myself in the kitchen, avoiding asking myself any questions.

'I have come to say good-bye,' he said, slowly placing his cup into the saucer.

'Good-bye? You're going away?'

'Yes, I'm leaving Canada.'

'For long? A holiday perhaps?'

'No, permanently. I'm going home to China, to Peking.'

'So you're leaving Canada,' I stammered.

'Yes.'

'You made the decision just like that, all of a sudden?'

'No,' he smiled, 'I decided to return home twenty years ago. When we left China I was very young, a child. My father said to me, "We are leaving, but who knows, perhaps you will return." We spent fifteen years in England. I left London when my father died. My father always sought out the most precious thing a country can offer—knowledge. "Never cease to pursue it," he told me. "Learn, never stop learning. There's always more to learn." '

'So you always knew you'd leave,' I said, disappointed.

'The trip is a long one and very expensive. I didn't have much of a job here and it took a long time to put enough money aside. I need a little money to live on over there.'

'What will you do?' I asked with a touch of irritation. I had a vague feeling he had deceived me.

'I have accumulated notes during my twenty-three-year stay in Canada. I haven't missed a single conference, meeting or lecture. My treasure is a large suitcase full of notes. I didn't always understand the lectures but I recorded them. I knew that one day I would have ample leisure time. I have often been told that Peking has the same climate as Montréal, but less snow and less cold in the winter. I want to see it again. I want to smell the odours my father used to talk about. I must find out for myself. Someone told me the sky is the same colour as it is here, but I don't believe it. You can never know the colour of the sky from far away . . .'

As he spoke endlessly, I watched his thin face, the tiny eyes lost in colourless cheekbones. His intonation didn't change, there was no emotion. I followed his high-pitched voice like a sound in the distance, a taut thread that suddenly becomes loose and falls to dust.

'Don't you like Canada?' I asked.

'Oh, yes. Canada is a marvellous country, and what a mine of knowledge! Never a night without a lecture or a meeting. I've kept everything. I'm taking all my notes with me. I'll need ten or fifteen years in which to consult them, to put them in order, to assimilate them and to absorb this treasure. It's all there in my suitcase.'

'I will miss having you next door.'

'And I will miss you. You have been an excellent neighbour.'

Translated by Judith Madley

HUBERT AQUIN

Back On April Eleventh

When your letter came I was reading a Mickey Spillane. I'd already been interrupted twice, and was having trouble with the plot. There was this man Gardner, who for some reason always carted around the photo of a certain corpse. It's true I was reading to kill time. Now I'm not so interested in killing time.

It seems you have no idea of what's been going on this winter. Perhaps you're afflicted with a strange intermittent amnesia that wipes out me, my work, our apartment, the brown record-player . . . I assure you I can't so easily forget this season I've passed without you, these long, snowy months with you so far away. When you left the first snow had just fallen on Montréal. It blocked the sidewalks, obscured the houses, and laid down great pale counterpanes in the heart of the city.

The evening you left—on my way back from Dorval—I drove aimlessly through the slippery empty streets. Each time the car went into a skid I had the feeling of going on an endless voyage. The Mustang was transformed into a rudderless ship. I drove for a long time without the slightest accident, not even a bump. It was dangerous driving, I know. Punishable by law. But that night even the law had become a mere ghost of itself, as had the city and this damned mountain that we've tramped so often. So much whiteness made a strong impression on me. I remember feeling a kind of anguish.

You, my love, probably think I'm exaggerating as usual and that I get some kind of satisfaction out of establishing these connections between your leaving and my states of mind. You may think I'm putting things together in retrospect in such a way as to explain what happened after that first fall of cerusian white.

But you're wrong: I'm doing nothing of the kind. That night, I tell you, the night you left, I skidded and slipped on that livid snow, fit to break your heart. It was myself I lost control of each time the Mustang slid softly into the abyss of memory. Winter since then has armed our city with many coats of melting mail, and here I am already on the verge of a burnt-ivory spring . . .

Someone really has to tell you, my love, that I tried twice to take my life in the course of this dark winter.

Yes, it's the truth. I'm telling you this without passion, with no bitterness or depths of melancholy. I'm a little disappointed at having bungled it; I feel like a failure, that's all. But now I'm bored. I've fizzled out under the ice. I'm finished.

Have you, my love, changed since last November? Do you still wear your hair long? Have you aged since I saw you last? How do you feel about all this snow that's fallen on me, drifting me in? I suppose a young woman of twenty-five has other souvenirs of her travels besides these discoloured postcards I've pinned to the walls of our apartment?

You've met women . . . or men; you've met perhaps one man and . . . he seemed more charming, more handsome, more 'liberating' than I could ever be. Of course, as I say that, I know that to liberate oneself from another person one has only to be unfaithful. In this case you were right to fly off to Amsterdam to escape my black moods; you were right to turn our liaison into a more relative thing, the kind that other people have, any old love affair, any shabby business of that kind . . .

But that's all nonsense. I'm not really exaggerating, I'm just letting myself go, my love, letting myself drift. A little like the way I drove the Mustang that night last November. I'm in distress, swamped by dark thoughts. And it's no use telling myself that my imagination's gone wild, that I'm crazy to tell you these things, for I feel that this wave of sadness is submerging both of us and condemning me to total desolation. I can still see the snowy streets and me driving through them with no rhyme or reason, as if that aimless motion could magically make up for losing you. But you know, I already had a sedimentary confused desire to die, that very evening.

While I was working out the discords of my loneliness at the steering wheel of the Mustang, you were already miles high in a DC-8 above the North Atlantic. And a few hours later your plane would land gently on the icy runway of Schipol—after a few leisurely manoeuvres over the still plains of the Zuider Zee. By then I would be back in our apartment, reading a Simenon—*The Nahour Affair*—set partly in a Paris blanketed in snow (a rare occurrence), but also in that very city of Amsterdam where you had just arrived. I went to sleep in the small hours of the morning, clutching that bit of reality that somehow reconnected me to you.

The next day was the beginning of my irreversible winter. I tried to act as if nothing had changed and went to my office at the Agency (Place Ville Marie) at about eleven. I got through the day's work one way or another. While I was supposed to be at lunch I went instead to the ground-floor pharmacy. I asked for phenobarbital. The druggist told me, with a big stupid grin, that it called for a prescription. I left the building in a huff, realizing, however, that this needed a little thought.

I had to have a prescription, by whatever means, and

information about brand-names and doses. And I needed at least some knowledge of the various barbiturate compounds.

With this drug very much on my mind I went next day or the day after to the McGill medical bookstore. Here were the shelves dealing with pharmacology. I was looking for a trickle and found myself confronted by the sea. I was overcome, submerged, astonished. I made a choice and left the store with two books under my arm: the *Shorter Therapeutics and Pharmacology*, and the *International Vade Mecum* (a complete listing of products now on the market).

That night, alone with my ghosts, I got at the books. To hell with Mickey Spillane, I had better things to read: for example this superbook (the *Vade Mecum*) which has the most delicious recipes going! Your appetite, your tensions, your depressions—they are all at the command of a few grams of drugs sagely administered. And according to this book of magic potions, life itself can be suppressed if only one knows how to go about it. I was passionately engrossed by this flood of pertinent information, but I still had my problem of how to get a prescription. Or rather, how to forge one that wouldn't turn into a passport to prison. A major problem.

His name was in the phone book: Olivier, J. R., internist. I dialled his number. His secretary asked what would be the best time of day for an appointment and specified that it would be about a month as the doctor was very busy. I answered her with a daring that still surprises me.

'It's urgent.'

'What is it you have?' asked the secretary.

'A duodenal ulcer.'

'How do you know?'

'Well, I've consulted several doctors and they strongly advised me to see Doctor O.'

'Tomorrow at eleven,' she suggested, struck by my argument. 'Will that be convenient?'

'Of course,' I replied.

I spent forty-five minutes in the waiting-room with the secretary I'd phoned the day before. I flipped through the magazines on the table searching for subjects of conversation to use on this doctor friend I hadn't seen for so long.

He appeared in the doorway and his secretary murmured my name. I raised my gloomy gaze to greet this smiling friend. He ushered me into his overstuffed office.

After the usual halting exchange of memories from college and university days I took a deep breath and, talking directly to Olivier, J. R., I told him straight out that I was having trouble sleeping. He burst into laughter, while I crouched deeper in the armchair he kept for patients.

'You're living it up too much, old boy,' he said, smiling.

Just then his intercom blinked. Olivier lifted the phone.

'What is it?' he asked his secretary.

(I had been hoping for something like this.)

'Just a second. I have something to sign. You know how it is. They're making bureaucrats out of us.'

He got up and went out to the reception room, carefully closing the door. At once I spied on his hand-rest the prescription pad with his letterhead. I quickly tore off a number of sheets and stuck them in the left inside pocket of my jacket. I was trembling, dripping with sweat.

'Well, bring me up to date,' said Olivier, coming back. 'Is she running around on you?'

He obviously found his own humour as irresistible as I found it offensive and our chat didn't get much farther. We fell silent and Olivier took his pen. Before starting to write on his prescription pad he looked up at me.

'What was it, now? You wanted some barbiturates to get you to sleep?'

'Yes,' I said.

'Okay, here's some stuff that'll knock out a horse.' He tore off the sheet and held it out to me.

'Thanks, thank you very much.' I suppose I was a bit emotional.

'I've put *non repetatur* at the bottom for these pills have a tendency to be habit-forming. If you really need more after a couple of weeks come and see me again.'

I folded the prescription without even searching out the *non repetatur*, an expression I had learned only a couple of days before. The intercom blinked again. Olivier, annoyed, picked up his phone but I paid no attention. I was already far away. Afterwards Olivier started telling me how his wife complained—or so he said—that she never got to see him any more.

'I'm working too hard,' he said, hand on brow. 'I probably need a holiday, but there it is. My wife's the one who's off to Europe. And it's only a month or so since she did the Greek Islands.'

In my mind I saw you in the streets of Breda and The Hague. I imagined your walks in Scheveningen, your visits to the Maurithuis. I wasn't sure any more just where in Europe you were: at the Hook of Holland, the flying isle of Vlieland, or the seaside suburb of Leiden at Kalwijk aan Zee . . .

I was out again on the chilly street. The sky was dark and lowering. Black clouds scudded by a rooftop level, presaging another snowstorm. Let the snow come to beautify this death-landscape, where I drove in a Mustang while you moved in the clear celestial spaces of the painters of the Dutch school . . .

Back in our apartment I analyzed the prescription I had obtained by trickery. Twelve capsules of sodium amobarbitol. I had no intention of remaining the possessor of a non-repeatable number of pills and began practising Olivier's handwriting. On ordinary paper. I had stolen ten sheets of his letterhead but that precious paper must not be wasted.

In two or three hours I'd managed four good prescriptions. I fell asleep on the strength of my success.

It took me some days to accumulate a *quoad vitam* dose with the help of my forged scribbles. But I wasn't satisfied with the *quoad vitam* dose indicated in the *Vade Mecum*. I went on accumulating the little sky-blue capsules, each with its three-letter stamp—SK&F. There were nights when I slept not at all rather than dip into my stock of precious sodic torpedoes.

Quite a few days passed this way. Strange days. Knowing that I had my stock of death in hand I felt sure of myself and almost in harmony with life. I knew that I was going to die and at that moment it would have been upsetting to receive a letter from you, my love, for I had come too close to the end of living.

When your letter came on November sixteenth it in no way disturbed this harmony, as I had feared it might. After reading it I still wanted to end my life by using, some evening, my surprising accumulation of sodium amobarbital. You'd written in haste (I could tell by your hand) from the Amstel Hotel, but the postmark said Utrecht. So you'd mailed it from there! What were you doing in Utrecht? How had you gone from Amsterdam to that little town where the treaty was signed ratifying the conquest of French Canada? Symbol of the death of a nation, Utrecht became a premonitory symbol of my own death. Had you gone with someone? A European colleague, as you usually describe the men you meet on your travels? Are there many interior decorators in Utrecht? Or perhaps I should ask if they are friendly and charming. I imagined you sitting in the car of a decorator colleague, lunching on the way and perhaps spending the night in Utrecht. I grew weary of calling back so many memories of you, your charm, your beauty, your hot body in my arms. I tore up your letter to put an end to my despair.

By the twenty-eighth of November I'd heard nothing more from you. My days grew shorter and emptier, my nights longer and more sleepless. They finally seemed barely to be interrupted by my days and I was exhausted. Recurrent insomnia had broken my resistance. I was destroyed, hopeless, without the slightest will to organize what was left of my life.

For me an endless night was about to begin, the unique, final, ultimate night. I'd at last decided to put an arbitrary end to my long hesitation, a period to our disordered history; decided, also, no longer to depend on your intermittent grace, which had been cruel only in that I had suffered from it.

That day I made a few phone calls to say that I was not available and spent my time tidying the apartment. When it was evening I took a very hot bath copiously perfumed from the bottle of Seaqua. I soaked for a long time in that benefi-cent water. Then I put on my burnt-orange bathing trunks and piled a few records on our playback: Ray Charles, Feliciano, Nana Mouskouri. I sprawled on our scarlet sofa, a glass of Chivas Regal in my hand, almost naked, fascinated by the total void that was waiting for me. I put Nana Mouskouri on several times. Then I finally made up my mind and swallowed my little sky-blue capsules four at a time, washing them down with great gulps of Chivas Regal. At the end I took more Scotch to help me absorb the lot. I put the nearly empty bottle on the rug just beside the couch. Still quite lucid, I turned on the radio (without getting up) so that the neighbours would not be alerted by the heavy breathing which, according to my medical sources, would begin as soon as I dropped into my coma.

To tell you the truth I wasn't sad but rather impressed, like someone about to start a long, very long, voyage. I thought of you, but faintly, oh, so faintly. You were moving around in the distance, in a funereal fog. I could still see the rich colours of your dresses and bathrobes. I saw you enter the apartment like a ghost and leave it in slow motion, but eternally in mirror perspective leading to infinity. The deeper I slipped into my comatose feast the less you looked my way, or rather the less I was conscious of you. Melancholy had no grip on me, nor fear. In fact I was blanketed in the solemnity of my solitude. Then, afterwards, obliteration became less complex and I became mortuary but not yet dead, left rocking in a total void.

And now, you ask, how are you managing to write this letter from beyond the tomb?

Well, here's your answer. I failed! The only damage I received in this suicide attempt resulted from the coma that lasted several hours. I was not in the best condition. My failure—even if I had no other devastating clues—would be proof enough of my perfect weakness, that diffuse infirmity that cannot be classified by science but which allows me to ruin everything I touch, always, without exception.

I woke up alive, as it were, in a white ward of the Royal Victoria, surrounded by a network of intravenous tubes that pinned me to the bed and ringed by a contingent of nurses. My lips felt frozen and dried and I remember that one of the nurses sponged my lips from time to time with an anti-herpetic solution.

Outside it was snowing, just as it had been on the day you left. The great white flakes fell slowly and I became aware that the very fact of seeing them silently falling was irrefutable proof that I was still, and horridly, alive. My return to a more articulated consciousness was painful, and took (to my relief) an infinity. As soon as I reached that threshold of consciousness I began to imagine you in the Netherlands or somewhere in Europe. Was there snow in Holland? And did you need your high suede boots that we shopped for together a few days before you left?

Suddenly I feel a great fatigue: these thoughts, returning in all their disorder, are taking me back to my stagnant point again . . .

It was really quite ironic that your telegram from Bruges should have become the means of your tardy (and involuntary) intervention on behalf of my poisoned body. I suppose the message was phoned first. But I didn't hear the ring and Western Union simply delivered the typed message to my address. The caretaker, who has no key to the letter boxes in our building, felt the call of duty and decided to bring me the envelope himself. There is something urgent about telegrams, you can't just leave them lying around. People can't imagine a harmless telegram that might read: HAPPY BIRTHDAY. WEATHER MARVELLOUS. KISSES. And yet that's exactly what was written in that telegram from Bruges.

I suppose the caretaker rapped a few times on our door. He probably couldn't see how I'd be out when the radio was blasting away. Finally, his curiosity must have got the better of him. He opened the door with his pass-key and stepped in to leave the envelope on the Louis XV table under the hall mirror. It's easy to imagine the rest: from the door he saw that I was there, he noted my corpse-like face, etc. Then, in a panic, he phoned the Montréal Police who transported me—no doubt at breakneck speed—to the emergency ward of the Royal Victoria. I spent several days under an oxygen tent. I even underwent a tracheotomy. That, in case the term means nothing to you, involves an incision in the trachea, followed by the insertion of a tracheal drain.

I must tell you everything, my love. I'm alive, therefore I am cured. The only traces are an immense scar on my neck and a general debility. While I was surviving one way or another in Montréal, you were continuing your tour of Europe. You saw other cities, Brussels, Charleroi, Amiens, Lille, Roubaix, Paris . . . Bruges had been just a stopover where you perhaps had dinner with a stranger, but no one hangs around in Bruges when the continent is waiting. Though God knows Bruges is a privileged place, an amorous sanctuary, a fortress that has given up a little terra firma to the insistent North Sea. I feel a soft spot for that half-dead city which you left with no special feeling. I stayed on in Bruges after you left, immured beneath its old and crumbling quays, for that was where you wished me (by telegram) a happy birthday.

There is no end to this winter. I don't know how many blizzards I watched from my hospital window. Around the fifteenth of December some doctor decided I should go home, that I was—so to speak—cured. Easy to say! Can one be cured of having wanted to die? When the ambulance attendants took me up to the apartment I saw myself in a mirror. I thought I would collapse. As a precaution I lay down on the couch where I had almost ended my days in November. Nothing had changed since then, but there was a thin film of dust on our furniture and the photos of you. The sky, lowering and dark, looked like more snow. I felt like a ghost. My clothes hung loose on me and my skin had the colour of a corpse. The sleepless nights again took up their death march but I no longer had my reserve of suicide-blue amobarbital pills. And I'd used up all my blank prescription forms. I couldn't sleep. I stared at the ceiling or at the white snowflakes piling up on our balcony. I imagined you at Rome or Civitavecchia or in the outskirts of Verona, completely surrendered to the intense experience of Europe.

From my calendar I knew that you were coming back to Montréal on April eleventh, on board the *Maasdam*. If I went to meet you that day at the docks of the Holland-American Line I would be in an emotional state. Too emotional, unable to tell you about what I did in November or about my disintegration since. Of course you'd give me a great hug and tell me all about those marvels, the fascinating ruins in Bruges, the baths of Caracalla, the Roman arches of triumph: the Arch of Tiberius, of Constantine, of Trajan, and so on. And all through your euphoric monologue I'd feel the knot at my throat.

It's for that reason—and all sorts of others, all somehow related to cowardice—that I'm writing you this letter, my love. I'll soon finish it and address it to Amsterdam, from which the *Maasdam* sails, so that you can read it during the crossing. That way you'll know that I bungled my first suicide attempt in November.

You'll understand that if I say 'first' it means there'll be a second.

Don't you see that my hand is trembling? That my writing is beginning to scrawl? I'm already shaky. The spaces between each word, my love, are merely the symbols of the void that is beginning to accept me. I have ten more lucid minutes, but I've already changed: my mind is slipping, my hand wanders, the apartment, with every light turned on, grows dark where I look. I can barely see the falling snow but what I do see is like blots of ink. My love, I'm shivering with cold. The snow is falling somehow within me, my last snowfall. In a few seconds, I'll no longer exist, I will move no more. And I'm so sorry but I won't be at the dock on April eleventh. After these last words I shall crawl to the bath, which has been standing full for nearly an hour. There, I hope, they will find me, drowned. Before the eleventh of April next.

Translated by Alan Brown

LOUISE MAHEUX-FORCIER

The Carnation

At the end of every month, the old woman's son sweetened the account generously enough to ensure that Roger would always extend a deferential welcome to that anachronistic customer, who ate like a bird but demanded just for herself the nicest table for three, at the back of the restaurant.

Punctually and without fail Madame Anaïs would appear at the stroke of noon, when the owner opened the door, and again at half past six, arriving with Mimi, the little flower-seller whose job it was to replace, at the first sign of wilting, the beautiful red carnation that brightened every table.

Kissing Anaïs's hand, Roger would relieve her of her cane and, in winter, the innumerable layers of furs that made her resemble an onion. With the care of a boatman surrounded by reefs, he would then steer her to her appointed place, where, after helping her to squeeze into the seat, he would light the little lantern, shift the carnation to set it off, and arrange the menu to suit her. Nearly blind, nearly deaf, and intentionally mute, the old woman would signal approval with a nod of her head, enhanced by a quivering feather, and a wag of her turned-up chin as it settled itself on top of a cascade of additional chins, forming a ruffle.

Anaïs was nearing the end of her life and didn't have much appetite any more, but she had not lost the exquisite manners of her day; not for the world would she have refused food so graciously offered, even if her dear one-and-only-always-

216

travelling-bachelor-son had entrusted the trouble of cooking it to strangers.

But truly, that evening Anaïs had no appetite left at all! Every spoonful of soup came to a standstill at the first landing of her throat, and it was only with great effort that she managed to tip the little pool of liquid into the next basin.

Anaïs soon saw that she should not keep trying. In fact, she saw that a great blessing had been granted her, that suddenly she had been freed from one more form of bondage. Having all but taken leave of the need for sounds and colours, at last she was finished with food!

Still, so as not to offend anyone, even her son, she accepted the steak and potatoes; but stealing a peak around her, she furtively dropped every mouthful into her lap and folded a corner of her napkin over it. She did the same with the bread and the raspberries, after which she slipped the messy little bundle into her purse and pretended to hunt for . . . the very thing she was hiding.

Most distressed, Roger ceremoniously scolded the waitress, demanded the missing article, and ordered Madame Anaïs's herbal tea.

It was then that the old woman felt a curious temptation . . . like the cravings she'd had long ago, when she was pregnant . . . in those days the object of her desire was never to be found, but now . . . now . . .

Standing up in its vase, swaying in the lamplight, with all its lacy ruffles sparkling, the red carnation . . . Anaïs reached out her hand, drew the flower to her nose, and took a long deep whiff; then, very daintily, her face radiant and her teeth at the ready, she began tackling it from the outer fringe, the way one does with an artichoke . . .

When she laid the heart on the table, she was vaguely aware of Roger bending over her . . .

Then, in a voice that deafness made both thunderous and sepulchral, and that out of courtesy she inflicted on others as rarely as possible, Anaïs told him: 'I must have white carnations tomorrow . . . Will you ask Mimi? . . . White carnations . . . The red are a little too spicy . . . You understand, Roger? Before I start pushing up the daisies, I want to acquire a taste for them!'

And at that moment, with the astonished staff and delighted patrons all looking on, Madame Anaïs decided to leave this earth, in grand style, choking on her own laughter as it cascaded down the tiers of her multiple chins, while on top of her head the feather tossed and fluttered for the last time.

Translated by Sally Livingston

ANTONINE MAILLET

Two Saints

I often used to go around to Sarah's to get my fortune read; not so much to learn about my own life as about hers. For this Sarah was one of your fortune-tellers who likes to chat and between club and diamond spin you a yarn and drop an opinion or two and rummage around in family history. She knew your Great-Uncle Jaddus, she did, the one who had the one girl and then eleven boys . . . eleven boys, Great God yes, one on top of another. Ah! they really knew how to do things in those days! And she knew the old sorcerer from Rivière à Hache, the one who could just as well burn you a church right down to the ground as go bury himself stark naked in the middle of a field of wild mustard not a hundred feet from the graveyard. Ah yes, they were something else again, that race of devils was, and you can only hope that on the Other Side there'll be some kind of a Good Lord to look after them . . . And then she knew the Sagouine young, too.

I was afraid Sarah would start talking about something else as she sat there shuffling the cards, so I pounced on the ace of spades when it dropped all hot from her fondling fingers.

'So you knew the Sagouine young, did you?'

'Knew her young and knew her old, aye, and then too the wee bit in between when a person's, as you might say, astraddle life like a cow's back.'

And Sarah let spurt from her throat and eyes that big laugh she got from her father who held it himself from a line of ancestors who reached this land jumping across the ice-floes in the bay. Was it the thought of a Sagouine astride a cow's back that set off her laughter, or was she already thinking of something else?

'I knew the Sagouine at the time of her squabble with La Sainte,' she says to me. 'And that was something, that was. Too bad you missed that.'

The old witch was making my mouth water. To think I'd lived so close by and missed it all.

But little by little I got the whole story or what was left of it as Sarah unravelled her ragged memories.

Once a week back in those prosperous times the Sagouine used to open up her stall of old rags and hand-me-down clothes which she sold at bargain prices, though her customers bargained for them just the same, for the pleasure of it. Because it would have been an insult to everyone, and to the Sagouine in particular, to step up and pay cash without bartering, like the bigwigs. No, where the Sagouine comes from you call each other names and haggle and it's all part of the business.

You haggled over the prices but also over the quality of the goods, though nobody was the least in the dark as to where they came from. They could have told you with their eyes shut that was the banker's shirt or the doctor's coat on the back of Henri Big-Belly or Francis Motté.

But don't you go thinking that the Sagouine was a thief. No, she was a beggar. Yes, she begged, as is the right of any poor slave of the Good Lord who never got more out of belonging to the Church than three drops of water at baptism and a slap at confirmation. It was all to the honour of her bump of business acumen then if, from the fruits of her begging on behalf of the shivering poor of the parish, she managed to mount a small trade that allowed her to live with respect and dignity.

That's about how the Sagouine saw things anyway, and the way La Sainte began to see them too one fine day without letting on to anyone.

The entry of La Sainte on the rag market was the hardest blow the Sagouine ever received in her life. Up till then the Catounes and Pitounes of the place had gladly disputed with the Sagouine another commercial activity which on occasion, by necessity, she also practised. But the Sagouine was of an age to understand that in that particular trade there was room for a little competition. Whereas in business, the success of the one is the bankruptcy of the other. That much the Sagouine knew. And it wasn't long before the facts began to bear this out.

Day by day she saw La Sainte adding more and more orange crates to her stand and filling them up with bundles of old clothes. And she was forced to watch, powerless, as business boomed for this brazen upstart who didn't even deign to begin at the bottom of the ladder like everyone else with socks and underwear.

No, right off the bat the hussy was dealing in coats and dresses as if to the manner born. And next breath making so bold as to move right into hats! Yes Ma'am, hats, if you please! And no one there but could recognize the feathers of Dominique's wife's bonnet and the vicar's fur hat. And O Sweet Holy Mother of God! A fox! A fox piece, I tell you! If that isn't a shame to stoop to selling foxes to the poor likes of us who haven't ever even slept in a feather bed yet. A fox! The Sagouine choked on it. It was just too much this time, really too much. And she closed up shop and went down to the shore to mull things over.

Had to find a way to put that big cow back in her place. But the Sagouine saw straight away that it wouldn't be easy. How to get under the skin of a woman who had sworn off all the sins of the flesh for so long? She didn't drink, the old bat, didn't smoke, or dance, or go gallivanting around either, naturally, saint that she was. La Sainte? Phooey! The Sagouine didn't have much book learning but she wasn't born yesterday either, and she judged there was plenty of grimacing under that guise of saintliness. Prissy stuck-up plaster saint paddling in holy water, the Sagouine exclaimed with a roar of laughter.

Then she sobered up. A saint who goes around stealing other folks' business deserves the same treatment . . . But how do you set about stealing somebody's saintliness? Sitting there, feet buried in the sand and head bowed with heavy thoughts, the Sagouine lifted her eyes and saw a heron pass by with his long beak stuck onto his long neck. Along he strode, disdainful and superb, waggling his precious behind with the dignified air of someone on their way to sing vespers. The Sagouine contemplated this shore-bird an instant, then leaping up and yanking her feet out of the sand, let out a tremendous 'Hah!' and lit out for the church.

You might have assumed that the Sagouine's first steps in the paths of sanctity would be difficult and gauche. That would be to misjudge a woman who from force of circumstance had been obliged to change her profession at least seven or eight times in her life. And besides, churches were something she knew a little about after all. For years now she had scrubbed out the sisters' chapel and the floor of the parish hall.

So she took to her new *métier* with the same flair as to the others, throwing herself into it heart and soul, belly and guts. As she used to say, either you're a saint or you're not, and the Sagouine was never one to do things by halves. She fitted herself out with a Sunday missal, two hymn books, and the usual array of medals, rosaries and scapulars guaranteed to ward off sickness, bad weather and unrepentant death. She gave up smoking, ceased to chew, quit swearing—yes by the Dear Lord Jesus Christ she did—and even abstained from sounding off from door to door about the conduct of her worst enemy, La Sainte. It was the most sudden and total metamorphosis ever seen on this stretch of coast since the time of the great rains.

It was La Sainte who was the most amazed. The most outraged. For here was someone filching the only thing that was truly hers, stealing her paradise, from her who had renounced the things of this world. It was an insult to God and his saints and a rank injustice to someone who had never missed a First Friday or Sunday Vespers or Public Prayers, Prayers with three rosaries one after the other, interspersed with intentions that La Sainte improvised as the spirit moved her for the dying, the sinners and the renegades of the parish. This time she'd cook up a prayer there'd be no mistaking for the intention of those pushy barbarians who figure they can take over other people's paradises just like that. She'd put that rag-seller back in her place, she would!

. . . But poor La Sainte didn't have a chance to put anyone in their place since her own, there in the front pew as prayer leader, had already been taken. Though she couldn't believe her eyes she was forced to admit that it was really the Sagouine up there at the lectern announcing the intention for the first decade of the rosary: 'Let us pray,' she declaimed, 'that the men of this parish heretofore see fit to do their duty. Our Father who art in Heaven . . .'

So that's how the Sagouine got her business back, for La Sainte understood that she would have to choose between earth and heaven. She chose heaven and left the earth to the

Sagouine who, the next day, sold her medals and her scapular along with her socks and coats and underwear.

And that's the story Sarah told me in bits and pieces as she ran her long fingers between heart and spade, laughing her big white-toothed laugh and shuffling her memories with the deck.

Translated by Philip Stratford

CLAUDE JASMIN

Lulu the Tailor

The least thing makes him blush. He's painfully shy. Like a young girl. His friends call him Lulu. Lulu is talented. Very. Everybody likes him. He's charming. And when there are no girls around he can be a lot of fun. With his co-workers, that is. If a stranger happens along while he's joking and fooling around—it doesn't matter if it's only someone from the next department—he clams up right away, cuts short his little act and withdraws into the depths of that shyness of his.

Lulu has a heart of gold too. He'll often bail out a friend who's hard up. But whenever a girl comes on the scene it's game over. It's not that Lulu hates women, he just finds them strange, mysterious. Doesn't know what to say or do. People inevitably make fun of him. They introduce terrific-looking women to him. Play tricks on him. Set him up with fictitious dates. Take out magazine subscriptions in his name. And lend him books like *How to Overcome Your Shyness*, *How to Talk to Women*, *How to Become a Don Juan*, *The Secrets of Seduction*. They recommend hare-brained schemes and zany products: miracle after-shave, trick cigars. Lulu is swamped by his friends' good intentions.

But Lulu has a secret. These days the routine of practical jokes and dirty tricks doesn't bother him a bit. He has his secret: a girl. A beautiful girl. He's seen her every day for a week and a half. He sees her, but he doesn't really talk to her. They wave to each other, chat in sign language. She lives in the building opposite, on the other side of Clark, a short side-street.

She's rather odd. A flirt. She comes and goes unpredictably. Lucien has been watching her for ten days, since the first of May. He arrives early in the morning at the fourth floor cutting-rooms of the Joseph Gaugstein Company, where he works as a tailor and—by special arrangement—a dress designer. 'Special arrangement' because he's not really a designer, it's just that occasionally they let him do rough sketches of styles that the two designers then alter and improve.

Lucien is imaginative. He has given his neighbour a thousand charms, decked her out in all the virtues. For a week now he's been arriving at seven, an hour before the workrooms open. The watchman was surprised. 'Extra work,' muttered Lucien as he climbed the stairs. He hurried up to spend an hour with his nose pressed to the windowpane, waiting and watching for the paragon next door.

By now they exchange little pleasantries: 'Nice day!' 'Lousy weather!', 'I'm tired', 'Did you sleep well?', 'I'm going to get a bite to eat', 'I think I'll read for a while', 'Have you got a car?'. Gradually these exchanges between the two windows have become more familiar, more romantic: 'How old are you?', 'I like your outfit', 'Is anything wrong?', 'Where were you yesterday?'

He didn't see her yesterday. She didn't show up all day. Lulu went home feeling sick at heart. Maybe she was ill. She might be sick in bed for a few days. What if he couldn't see her for a whole month? It made his heart ache to think of not being able to see her through the window, primping away, making up her face, endlessly combing her long blond and—to him—marvellous hair. Confined to her bed, not even able to drag herself to the window to tell him she was sick or ask his help. Because she obviously lived alone. He had never noticed anyone else wandering around her apartment, or even just passing through. Seriously ill? Dead, maybe? He couldn't finish his soup at Murray's restaurant for thinking the worst, imagining a catastrophe. Even though he was wide awake he had a brief nightmare: after days of fruitless watching, he climbed the stairs to his lovely neighbour's apartment, knocked at one of the doors, and tried to compose himself. No answer! He threw his shoulder against the door and broke it open to find her stretched out on the white carpet in her tiny living-room, mortally wounded, her blood draining away and the carpet hideously stained with red.

Poor Lulu. He's been sleeping badly. And this morning at six o'clock, here he is, keeping his eye peeled for his unknown lady-love. He doesn't even know her name. Her name! Why didn't he think of that before? He might be able to find her number in the phone book. Now it's too late. It's eight o'clock, the others are arriving, and there's still no sign of her. Lucien paces up and down in the little workroom where he cuts out the patterns. He hasn't been doing good work for ten days. Since yesterday he's done nothing at all. He just stares at the window opposite. But the curtain doesn't move, and there's not so much as a silhouette to reassure him and relieve his anxiety. Could she have moved? No, she would have let him know in some way.

All of a sudden, at exactly twelve minutes past eight, his moment of relief comes. There she is. She's there! And in a stunning filmy negligée. Lucien grins from ear to ear. He plants himself at the window. He reaches out as if to touch her, feels that he actually is touching her, caressing her. She seems different somehow; yes, she's dyed her hair. Her hair is red. Why? Lucien loved the silky blond hair she had before. She smiles at him. He places his hand over his heart. She shows him her suitcase. Has she been away? To visit her family maybe? For the first time he looks at her without feeling shy. He was so frightened. She seems to be wearing a shade too much makeup. He'll mention it to her. He supposes she hasn't been very well brought up, hasn't had much education. He did notice the rather ungainly way she had of sitting on the window ledge, with her knees up, spread out like a tomboy. Lucien can see himself gently taking her in hand, bringing her his Bach and Mozart records, his rare books of poems by de Musset and Verlaine; he can help her. It occurs to him that he must do this before something else happens to interfere. In large letters he writes on the side of a carton: 'What is your phone number please?' She reads, then smiles in the most winning, childlike manner. She disappears. Isn't she coming back? Has he gone too far, too soon? Is she put off by his eagerness? At times she has seemed indifferent to his overtures, to the little greetings and bits of sign language that he always initiates. Maybe she isn't free, maybe she's unable to go beyond a mere 'hello', a few harmless waves, an inconsequential flirtation. That's it; she probably has a man in her life.

At last she returns. She must have gone to look for a coloured pencil, because her number is written in huge figures on one of the classified pages of a newspaper. Lucien takes it down and thanks her. Again she disappears. Has she gone to the phone? Or does she regret her boldness? He doesn't dare call her right away. He doesn't want to rush her. But he's happy, oh so happy—ever since twelve past eight. Almost too happy. He couldn't be more so. He dials, practically trembling. He hears the phone ringing. It's as if he were actually entering her apartment. That strikes him as being very funny. He has finally cracked that shell of old red bricks, broken through the wall of glass. He'll recognize her voice.

'Is that you, my nice neighbour from across the way?'

He doesn't answer immediately. He's slightly unnerved by the kittenish tone and the faintly vulgar accent of his 'vision of loveliness'. He tells himself that reality is always like this, a bit brutal, a bit shocking, a bit of a letdown. Somewhat taken aback he says, 'Yes, it's me. What's your name?' He waits with his heart in his mouth to hear the touch of coarseness in her voice, the voice, he says to himself, of a girl who's had a hard life, who most likely works as a waitress in a Montréal night club. Isn't she always home during the day?

'My name is Pierrette. Come over to my place tonight after work. I have something to show you—you'll like it.' And she hangs up. He doesn't call back. He would have liked so much to tell her his name and explain himself, make her understand why he has been so forward. He's had her on his mind for so long; ten days and nights. When he goes to the window there's no longer anything to see. And he has no way of knowing whether she's gone out, or what time she'll return, because the front door of her apartment building is on Pine Avenue.

Now poor Lucien is afraid. He's not quite so anxious for five o'clock to come. He won't go. It's a trap. She only wanted to find out what kind of fellow he was. If he does go, she won't answer the door. No. He won't go. He realizes that he doesn't even know her apartment number. Tomorrow morning at eight o'clock he'll make up some story in case she questions him from across the way.

Across the way . . . It dawns on Lucien that he enjoyed the adventure thoroughly as long as there was no risk, as long as he was protected by the brick walls, one red and one yellow. With Clark Street between them he could dream to his heart's content, invent situations, impressions, feelings, and interpret in any way he liked the smallest gesture or glance from his inaccessible lady-love.

But that doesn't make sense. He'll have to go. Sooner or later he'll have to get to know this girl. After all, he's twenty-three years old. All right, he'll go. It's crucial for him to lay to rest, once and for all, this obsessive fear of girls. It's bizarre, this irrational fear that provokes so many gibes from the guys in his neighbourhood, allows his family to make fun of him, and brings out the gross sarcasm of his beastly, drunken father. It's time he seduced a woman.

The thought suddenly makes him feel ashamed. What's the matter with him? Can it be that he's just like the rest of the boys from his neighbourhood in the north end—a crass, boorish clod, always bragging about sex? No! Hey, there's the lovely red-haired Pierrette, with a great big lollipop in her mouth! A child, that's what she is. Lulu pictures a sort of backward country girl, playing at being citified but really a figure of fun in that nightclub where they exploit her. Her goofy smile and the giant lollipop give him new courage. 'I've got to help her,' Lucien tells himself. On the end of a box he writes, 'The apartment number?' And she writes on the windowpane with a lipstick, '38'. Then, she takes her lipstick and changes the numbers into two little red hearts! 'A kid, a real little kid,' Lulu says to himself.

How he has wavered! He's had second thoughts all afternoon. He hasn't seen her at the window again. He figures she must be cleaning her apartment; everything will be spotless; she may even have gone out to get some little tidbit, a treat to mark the beginning of a long love affair.

Still, he's been uneasy. The first thing he does is go to the High 'n' Dry bar next door. He gulps down two shots of brandy, one right after the other. A man like Lucien needs courage before he can visit a girl in her own apartment, even if she's only an overgrown kid who sucks lollipops and writes on the window with lipstick. At last he's ready. Slowly he climbs the stairs of the Riviera Apartments. On the third floor he finds numbers 34, 35, 36, 37. Oh my God! There it is. He listens at the door. Silence. He wishes it would open without his having to ring. His damned shyness. He pushes the bell and it sounds like a gun going off in a church.

She comes to the door. She's wearing the same negligée

that she had on this morning. But she's blond again! Lucien gives up trying to understand. All he can manage is to go inside, as she's asked him to, without falling on his face. He's so awkward with strangers. He feels hot and cold. She seems to be far too tall for him; either that or he's shrunk. He feels like a fool. He stammers, 'Hello', and the inane sound of it appals him. She'll think he's some kind of child-ish innocent. 'And that's what I am,' he says to himself. She walks ahead of him, conspicuously swaying her hips. Lucien isn't sure whether he finds this ridiculous or delightfully gauche. 'She's acting, she's playing a role for me,' he thinks, 'to amuse me—no, to make me feel at ease.' She invites him to sit on the sofa. But Lucien goes at once to the window. He smiles at the sight of 'his window' on the fourth floor of the Gaugstein building. She comes up to him and puts her arm around his neck. Clumsily, a bit brusquely, he breaks away. He wants to excuse himself and leave, right now. She's already seated, squatting comically with her knees in the air on one of the lemon-yellow sofa cushions. Either she's crazy or she's a tease, a real tramp, thinks Lucien, feeling disap-pointed and heartened at the same time. She rolls her eyes and lights a cigarette, simpering like an actress in a TV commercial. This is definitely not artless. Lulu gapes at her. Still smiling, she offers him her cigarette. 'I don't smoke, thank you,' says Lucien, who is smiling too.

'I'm going to show you the surprise!'

The amazing Pierrette goes into the next room and emerges instantly with a blue box. Lucien recognizes the cut of an outfit he designed for Gaugstein.

'You're pleased. They told me it was one of your designs. It fits me like a glove. You'll soon see.'

And Pierrette lolls full length on the sofa, like a playful kitten.

'Come and sit beside me, Lulu.'

'She knows what they call me,' says Lucien to himself.

All the time he was planning his approach she was making her own little investigation. This is one very crafty girl. And that's just fine, he thinks, it makes things easier. Because this is not easy for him, his first contact with a girl, one he has admired and secretly fallen in love with. 'Good heavens, no!' he splutters.

He sits on an ottoman at her feet, looking sheepish in spite of himself. He thinks again about her hair. Maybe it had something to do with the sunlight through the window, her hair looking red this morning. He doesn't dare bring it up, but she says: 'Do you like me better as a redhead or as a blonde, Lulu?'

'Uhhh . . . I don't know. I don't know. How do you do it?'

'I have another wig, the red one, in the other room. Do you want to see it?' She points to the room she went into a moment ago.

'No. I like the blond one best. That's the way I've always seen you.'

Strange girl, to look at him like that, always rolling her eyes like a mechanical doll. Strange too, that rough voice in a girl who seems barely twenty. And Lucien quite naïvely peers at her and sees, actually makes bold to see, that under her flimsy nightdress Pierrette has no breasts. And then he notices, abruptly, that her arms and legs are unusually muscular, like a boy's.

He gets up suddenly. He's afraid to understand. He sees better, oh, better and better, that the garish makeup hides the features of . . . a boy? He puts out his hand and she pulls him towards her. He loses his balance and falls—right on top of her! She laughs, and her laughter sounds even more coarse and rough. Masculine. Lulu grabs her beautiful blond hair and she lets out a little screech, holding on to him fiercely and locking her legs around his.

'Do you want to see my real hair, dear boy?'

Then she loosens some hairpins and shows him her short, dark hair, very much like his own. Lucien is drenched with sweat. He feels like screaming, but at the same time he experiences a lovely warmth that is quite simply the effect of being held in someone's arms. 'If it were the devil himself,' he thinks, 'it feels so good to be in someone's arms.'

He struggles and manages to get free. She is no longer laughing. Neither is he. They look at each other; she, sprawled out with her legs apart, the wig in her hand, biting her lip; and he, standing between her knees, not knowing any more whether he should throw himself on this strange, warm, throbbing body, or run away and never come back.

He quickly decides to flee. But, at the end of the hall, he turns back. He sees this circus apparition leaning in his doorway, waving his fingers, tentatively. Lucien waves back. On the stairs, he weeps, because he knows now, poor Lucien, that he will come back here and that he will stay a long time. He knows it. His aching body reminds him every slow step of the way down.

Translated by Patricia Sillers

ROCH CARRIER

What Language Do Bears Speak?

Following our own morning ritual, to which we submitted with more conviction than to the one of saying our prayers when we jumped out of bed, we ran to the windows and lingered there, silent and contemplative, for long moments. Meanwhile, in the kitchen, our mother was becoming impatient, for we were late. She was always afraid we'd be late . . . Life was there all around us and above us, vibrant and luminous, filled with trees; it offered us fields of daisies and it led to hills that concealed great mysteries.

The story of that morning begins with some posters. During the night, posters had been put up on the wooden poles that supported the hydro wires.

'Posters! They've put up posters!'

Did they announce that hairy wrestlers were coming? Far West singers? Strong men who could carry horses on their shoulders? Comic artists who had 'made all America collapse with laughter'? An international tap-dance champion? A sword swallower? Posters! Perhaps we'd be allowed to go and see a play on the stage of the parish hall—if the curé declared from the pulpit that the play wasn't immoral and if we were resourceful enough to earn the money for a ticket. Posters! The artists in the photographs would gradually come down from the posters until they inhabited our dreams, haunted our games and accompanied us, invisible, on our expeditions.

'There's posters up!'

We weren't allowed to run to the posters and, trembling, read their marvellous messages; it was contrary to maternal law to set foot outside before we had washed and combed our hair. After submitting to this painful obligation we were able to learn that we would see, in flesh and blood, the unsurpassable Dr Schultz, former hunter in Africa, former director of zoos in the countries of Europe, former lion-tamer, former elephant-hunter and former free-style wrestling champion in Germany, Austria and the United Kingdom, in an unbelievable, unsurpassable show—'almost unimaginable'. Dr Schultz would present dogs that could balance on balls, rabbit-clowns, educated monkeys, hens that could add and subtract; in addition, Dr Schultz would brave a savage bear in an uneven wrestling match 'between the fierce forces of nature and the cunning of human intelligence, of which the outcome might be fatal for one of the protagonists'.

We had seen bears before, but dead ones, with mouths bleeding, teeth gleaming. Hunters liked to tell how their victims had appeared to them: '. . . standing up, practically walking like a man, but a big man, hairy like a bear; and then it came at me roaring like thunder when it's far away behind the sky, with claws like knives at the end of his paws, and then when I fired it didn't move any more than if a mosquito'd got into its fur. Wasn't till the tenth bullet that I saw him fall down . . .' Loggers, too, had spotted bears and some, so they said, had been so frightened their hair had turned white.

Dr Schultz was going to risk his life before our eyes by pitting himself against this merciless beast. We would see with our own eyes, alive before us, not only a bear but a man fighting a bear. We'd see all of that!

A voice that reached the entire village, a voice that was magnified by loudspeakers, announced that the great day had arrived: 'At last you can see, in person, the unsurpassable

Dr Schultz, the man with the most scars in the world, and his bear—a bear that gets fiercer and fiercer as the season for love comes closer!'

We saw an old yellow bus drive up, covered with stars painted in red, pulling a trailer on whose sides we could read: DR SCHULTZ AND ASSOCIATES UNIVERSAL WONDER CIRCUS LTD. The whole thing was covered with iron bars that were tangled and crossed and knotted and padlocked. A net of clinking chains added to the security. Between messages, crackling music made curtains open at the windows and drew the children outdoors. Then the magical procession entered the lot where we played ball in the summer. The motor growled, the bus moved forward, back, hesitated. At last it found its place and the motor was silent. A man got out of the bus. He stood on the running-board; twenty or thirty children had followed the circus. He considered us with a smile.

'Hi, kids,' he said.

He added something else, words in the same language, which we'd never heard before.

'Either he's talking bear,' said my friend Lapin, 'or he's talking English.'

'If we can't understand him,' I concluded, 'it must be English.'

The man on the running-board was still talking; in his strange language he seemed to be asking questions. Not understanding, we listened, stupefied to see Dr Schultz in person, alive, come down from the posters.

'We talk French here,' one of us shouted.

Smiling again, Dr Schultz said something else we didn't understand.

'We should go get Monsieur Rancourt,' I suggested.

Monsieur Rancourt had gone to Europe to fight in the First World War and he'd had to learn English so he could

follow the soldiers in his army. I ran to get Monsieur Rancourt. Panting behind his big belly, he hurried as fast as he
could. He was looking forward to speaking this language.
He hadn't spoken it for so many years he wasn't sure, he
told me, that he could remember it. As soon as he saw the
man from the circus he told me: 'I'm gonna try to tell him
hello in English.'

'Good day sir! How you like it here today?' ('I remember!'
Monsieur Rancourt rejoiced, shouting with delight. 'I didn't
forget!')

Dr Schultz moved towards Monsieur Rancourt, holding
out his hand. A hand wearing a leather glove, in the middle
of summer.

'It's because of the bear bites,' my friend Lapin explained
to me.

'Apparently the *Anglais* can't take the cold,' said one of
our friends whose mother's sister had a cousin who worked
in an *Anglais* house in Ontario.

The man from the circus and Monsieur Rancourt were
talking like two old friends meeting after a number of years.
They even laughed. In English, Monsieur Rancourt laughed
in a special way, 'a real English laugh', we judged, whispering. In French, Monsieur Rancourt never laughed; he was
surly. We listened to them, mouths agape. This English
language which we'd heard on the radio, in the spaces between
the French stations when we turned the tuning knob, we
were hearing now for real, in life, in our village, spoken by
two men standing in the sun. I made an observation: instead
of speaking normally, as in French, instead of spitting the
words outside their lips, the two men were swallowing them.
My friend Lapin had noticed the same thing, for he said:

'Sounds like they're choking.'

Suddenly something was overturned in the trailer; we could
hear chains clinking, a bump swelled out the canvas cover-

ing and we saw a black ball burst out—the head of a bear.

Dr Schultz and Monsieur Rancourt had rolled up their shirt-sleeves and they were comparing tattoos.

'The bear's loose!'

The animal ran out on the canvas, came down from the roof of the bus and jumped to the ground. How could we tell that to Dr Schultz who didn't understand our language, whose back was turned to the trailer and who was completely absorbed in his conversation?

'Monsieur Rancourt!' I shouted. 'The bear's running away!'

There was no need to translate. The man from the circus had understood. Waving a revolver, he sped towards the bear, which was fleeing into a neighbouring field. He shouted, pleaded, threatened.

'What's he saying?' we asked Monsieur Rancourt.

'Words that English children don't learn till they're men.'

'He must be saying the same words my father says when a cow jumps over the fence. They aren't nice.'

Dr Schultz, whom we had seen disappear into the oats, came back after a long moment and spoke to Monsieur Rancourt, who ran to the village. The men who were gathered at the general store rushed off to find other men; they took out traps, rifles, ropes. While the mothers gathered up their children who were scattered over the village, the men set out, directed by fat Monsieur Rancourt. Because of his experience in the war, he took charge of the round-up. Dr Schultz had confided to him, we learned later:

'That bear's more important than my own wife.'

They mustn't kill it, then, but bring it back alive.

The show was to begin in the early afternoon. Dr Schultz, who had gone with the men into the forest, came back muttering; we guessed that he was unhappy. At his trailer he opened the padlock, unfastened the crossed iron bars, pulled out the pegs and undid the chains. We saw him transform his trailer into a stage, with the help of a system of pulleys, ropes and tripods. Suddenly we were working with the circus man: we carried boxes, held out ropes, unrolled canvas, stuck pickets in the ground, lined up chairs. Dr Schultz directed our labours. Small, over-excited men that we were, we had forgotten he was speaking a language we didn't understand.

A piece of unrolled canvas suspended from a rope, which was held in place by stakes, formed a circular enclosure. It resembled a tent without a roof; we had built it. We were proud; would we, as long as we lived, ever have another day as beautiful as this one? From now on we were part of the circus.

At last it was time for the show. The music cried out as far as the horizon. In the stands there were mostly women: the men were still pursuing the lost bear.

In gleaming leather boots, in a costume sparkling with gilt braid, Dr Schultz walked out on the stage. He said a few words and the crowd applauded fervently; the spectators no doubt considered it a mark of prowess to speak with such ease a language of which they couldn't utter a single word.

He opened a cage and a dozen rabbits came out. On the back of each he hung a number. At the other end of the platform was a board with holes cut out of it. Above each hole, a number. The man from the circus gave an order and the rabbits ran to the holes that bore their numbers. Unbelievable, wasn't it? We all raised rabbits, but our animals had never learned anything more intelligent than how to chew clover. Our hands were burning, so much had we applauded our friend Dr Schultz. Next came the trained dogs' act: one danced a waltz; another rode around a track on a bicycle while his twin played a drum. We applauded our great friend hard enough to break our metacarpals.

The acrobatic chimpanzee's act had scarcely begun when a great uproar drowned the music from the loudspeakers. The canvas wall shook, it opened, and we saw the captured bear come in. The men from the village were returning it to its master, roaring, furious, screaming, clawing, kicking, gasping, famished. The men from the village, accustomed to recalcitrant bulls and horses, were leading it with strong authority; they had passed ropes around its neck and paws so the furious animal had to obey. Monsieur Rancourt was speaking French and English all at once.

When he saw his bear, Dr Schultz let out a cry that Monsieur Rancourt didn't translate. The men's hands dropped the ropes: the bear was free. He didn't notice immediately. We heard his harsh breathing, and his master's too. The hour had come: we were going to see the greatest circus attraction in the Americas, we were going to see with our own eyes the famous Dr Schultz, our friend, wrestle a giant black bear.

No longer feeling the ropes burning its neck, no longer submitting to the strength of the men who were tearing it apart, the bear stood up, spread its arms and shot forward with a roar. The bear struck Dr Schultz like a mountain that might have rolled onto him. The bear and our friend tumbled off the stage. There was a ripple of applause; all the men together would never have succeeded in mustering half the daring of Dr Schultz. The bear got up again, trampled on the great tamer of wild beasts and dived into the canvas enclosure, tearing it with one swipe of its claws before disappearing.

Dr Schultz had lost his jacket and trousers. His body was streaked with red scratches. He was weeping.

'If I understand right,' said Monsieur Rancourt, 'he's telling us that the bear wasn't *his* bear . . .'

'It isn't *his* bear . . .'

The men shook and spluttered with laughter as they did

at the general store when one of them told a funny story.

The men laughed so hard that Monsieur Rancourt could no longer hear Dr Schultz's moans as he lay bleeding on the platform. The undertaker apologized for the misunderstanding.

'That bear was a bear that talked English, though, because I didn't understand a single word he said.'

Translated by Sheila Fischman

MARIE-CLAIRE BLAIS

An Act of Pity

The curé of Vallée d'Or had been well aware of his growing self-satisfaction, born of long ambition and pride, piously maintained. Did he not feel a thrill of secret pleasure when, dispensing his stern compassion, he saw the humble gratitude of his poor parishioners turning into murmurs of praise? 'M'sieur le curé is the best man on earth! Nobody's ever had a curé like him, not in a hundred years!' That morning, however, walking to the Sansfaçons' he knew that death waited there on the hill; that he was going not to amuse Maria, or to tell stories that would make her sit up and laugh in her feverish bed, but to bless her one last time while closing her eyes. With this thought a feeling of weariness came over him; he was beginning to realize that even the appearance of saintliness—the glowing reputation he enjoyed in the village—meant nothing, because he was unworthy of it; because in the five years of his ministry compassion had never truly entered his heart. Yes, he had loved God with a fervour that satisfied his cool priestly pride, but he had never been able to approach people naturally, without feeling disgust. He thought of Maria's frail life fading out in a dirty bed, like so many others carried off by consumption in the village, and shuddered again with disgust. 'But it's too late,' he thought, 'I've loved their false image of me for too long.' How often had he feigned charity, compassion, even love, denying the horrible nausea he instinctively felt at the sight of the weakness around him? How often had he steeled himself to do good works so that he could later revel in the words, 'Our curé is Jesus on earth'?

But this sweet superiority had required sacrifices. He had not lived in the well-fed comfort many of his colleagues in neighbouring villages had. He would never have more than a roof over his head. Yet it seemed to him that his penury gave rise to excessive self-esteem, a kind of pleasure in austerity and abstinence that he would have been quick to condemn had he not craved it. At the poor tables of his parish he had gone without bread, thinking all the while of the meal that awaited him in the evening, and though sharing the hungry silence, he did so thinking chiefly of himself, of the saintly image others had of him; he would not let himself be moved by the misery of the hovels he visited.

Dead fields, a village crushed by drought under a burning sky, children who came begging like dogs the moment he appeared—was this poor thing the empire he'd dreamed of? Yet the only request he shrank from was the one he could not fulfil: pity he always withheld. 'Is it my fault if a wall of ice has risen between them and me? If the distance of privilege comes between us?' No, it was more than that, he thought, more than the distance created by his uneasy disgust: he despised them. Those downtrodden women and ageless men, resigned to the early death of their sons as to the ravages of the seasons, inspired no compassion in him.

'Ah, we've had bad luck this year, M'sieur le curé.' But he knew that they were a beaten people. He walked on slowly, weighed down by his thoughts. 'They're already dead; there's no fight left in them. And they've never pitied me. They've burdened me with their trust, and worse, their ignorance; they've exposed their wretchedness to me without even wanting to be helped.'

'Bonjour, M'sieur le curé. Going to see the little Sansfaçon, eh? They go fast on that side of the village; it's contagious. Looks like the Letourneau baby's dying too.' Tournemule began to laugh. 'No sooner born than dead, eh? Come and see us, M'sieur le curé, my old mother wants your blessing before she goes to heaven.'

'I'll come tomorrow,' said the curé, curbing his anger as it struck him that this beautiful countryside—he was looking at the sea shimmering in the distance, across from the scorched fields and barren trees—this beautiful place created by God, with its promise of serenity and happiness, held nothing but sorrow and decay. 'Go home, Tournemule, don't leave your mother alone. Tell her I'll come tomorrow.'

But Tournemule's grizzled hands clung to the priest's cassock.

'What do you want?' he asked.

Tournemule didn't know. A look, one miserable caress? The curé bent his head towards the blind man's face but was careful not to touch him, nor to meet the bruised eyes under the heavy bewildered lids. 'You're not a child any more, Tournemule. Go on, go home.'

His voice had been firm but resonant with a counterfeit charity that reassured the humble Tournemule, locked in a cage of shadows that echoed still with the sickly cries of his mother . . . 'Tournemule, where are you? Tournemule? He's gone and left me all alone! Tournemule!'

'You see, M'sieur le curé, the poor woman's always calling me, day and night. I can't get any peace; she never stops howling my name.'

'Have pity,' the curé said coldly, aware of the contempt that crept into his voice. And he moved away, as Tournemule stood stifling queer mutterings with his hand.

The curé stopped for a moment outside the Sansfaçons' door before knocking. The depths of pain and mourning that the houses of Vallée d'Or revealed shook him with anguish. A distant cloud hung motionless in the dull blue sky: the air was so hot he could hardly breathe. A swarm of flies buzzed around a pile of refuse in the yard. 'Not a flower, not a bird, nothing but drought and death . . .'

'What are you doing, M'sieur le curé, standing there in this heat?' cried a woman's voice. 'Quick, come and give her the last rites, she's lost a lot of blood . . .'

Now he could not escape. The woman drew him into the house. Without raising his eyes, he walked towards Maria's bed, brushing aside the sour-smelling children in his way, breathing the odour of the beaten, the forsaken.

'The doctor hasn't come?' asked the priest.

'No need for the doctor,' said the mother, 'she's going to die.'

'They're dying like flies,' said the husband, rocking one of the children in his lap. 'I don't understand what happens to them in the summer, you'd think they were smothering . . .'

'It's the sun,' the mother said sadly.

She sat on the edge of the bed, stroking the child's hair and waving away the flies.

'Maria, your friend's come to see you. M'sieur le curé is here. Don't sulk like that, open your eyes . . .'

The mother went on in her weary, impatient voice: 'She used to be an angel, M'sieur le curé, and then all of a sudden she changed. Now she's so stubborn she'd try the patience of a saint—Maria, do you hear me?'

'Do you hear your mother?' the husband asked, but in a sad, tender tone that surprised the priest. 'Don't you hear your mother, Maria?'

The priest made a gesture begging for silence. Approaching the child he tried to touch her hand, but she quickly drew it away. 'She doesn't love me any more,' he thought. 'She knows all about my struggle; she knows the hardness of my heart as well as God does.' Frightened by Maria's silence, and the fierce glare she suddenly shot him, he asked her a question he immediately regretted: 'Does it hurt very much, Maria?'

She bit her lip and did not answer. For a moment she seemed to forget that the priest was there, as she watched an idle ray of light flickering over the bed.

'You remember,' he said, 'when we were friends . . .'

No, she didn't remember. If he was her friend, how could he let her die like this? How could he give his blessing to the torments she had to bear?

'Maybe she's afraid of going to hell,' said the mother.

'May God protect you,' said the priest, sparing of his words of consolation because he knew there was nothing more he could do but entrust Maria to God. It was too late. Or perhaps too soon: the time for compassion had not come. 'How many children's ghosts inhabit this sickening limbo? They haunt me, although I've never loved them.' He stared at Maria, lost in the dream-like obstinacy of the gaze that rested on him, unaware that the patient had ceased to live several moments before; lost in his unawareness, in a bitter indifference where a cry of torment could no longer reach him . . .

'Maria, Maria,' the mother said quietly.

'Don't you hear your mother any more?' said the father from the end of the room.

At the sound of his deep, imploring voice the child on his knee began to cry; the father slapped the baby and it stopped. But then another child with yellow hair started crying. The father gave a weary look but said nothing.

'She's dead,' said the mother.

The children approached the bed. The familiar sight did not frighten them. They all looked at the thin trickle of blood running from Maria's silent mouth. 'Degenerate from the start,' the priest thought sadly, 'carriers of vermin, disease, corruption . . .' But they pressed around him, their hungry eyes pleading:

'Don't leave, M'sieur le curé!'

Suddenly he recalled a bad dream. It was Sunday morning, the moment of Communion. A crowd of the faithful knelt before him, waiting to receive the host; they were opening their mouths so wide he was revolted, for as he bent over the miserable faces presented to him he could see festering sores deep in their throats. Hardly had he placed the host on the tongue of one old woman from Vallée d'Or than she bared her teeth like a raging animal. 'They're eating me alive,' he thought, 'they're devouring me.' He woke from the dream numb with dread and fear. In it he recognized all the signs of his weakness. It was not God that he was obliged to feed them with, but himself. And he was not giving himself. Yet they devoured him in his sleep. He must one day consent to lose himself in the misery of his people ('My people?' he thought, 'why mine? They're stranger to me than I am to myself'); to disappear so completely into their wretchedness that he would cease to exist ('But such compassion would be suicide, and I want to live').

Leaving Maria's house he could still hear the mother sobbing softly. Oh, to get back to the coolness of his church, to abandon himself to solitude . . . It was too hot to pray, too hot to live. Again he felt a sudden, fierce thirst; water was scarce in that burnt-out region. And it occurred to him that his own drought was more than just his refusal to suffer: his life was a desert. Was he not forsaken by everyone, even God? Like his church, he was uninhabited, living in an austere detachment that nothing could disturb. Christ dying on the cross stood for this same unjust suffering. He stared at the cross as he had at Maria's face a few hours before: 'When will this torture end?'

He would have liked to turn his back, as firmly as in his

youth when he had renounced joy and happiness, and walk away; to leave behind forever all the miseries he had seen and never been able to relieve. The failure of saintliness was the failure of happiness as well. He no longer liked the man he had been, clothed in so many trappings of goodness, fed with so many illusions that in the end he had deceived himself more than anyone. 'If only the children of Vallée d'Or were true children of God, not children of his shame and humiliation . . .'

Shutting his eyes, he had a vision of Maria running towards him.

'Why are your knees bleeding again, Maria?'

'Mama says I'm so weak I can't run without falling down . . . Wait up, M'sieur le curé! Don't walk so fast!'

She was calling him but he refused to hear. 'The stigmata of childhood in Vallée d'Or,' he thought. 'I've never been able to look at them without wanting to run away . . . But is it my fault that you can't touch a child in this village without wanting to vomit?'

Their misery stuck to you, their smell, their hunger penetrated you. 'How do you expect me to love them, Lord, you who made them so deprived and so humble?' Might he still, in a burst of vanity, have the courage to lie? To hear those words, 'Our curé is a saint.' He was capable of playing the martyr. But a strange weariness had overtaken him since Maria's death . . .

How many times had he driven Maria away when she waited for him in the evening at the church door? 'Go on, Maria, I want to be alone, and here you are chattering like a little bird.'

'I've got things to tell you.'

'You can tell me tomorrow.'

But he knew that she would not be there tomorrow. He had noticed before, during catechism, how pale Maria's face was when she spat blood. But so many children coughed and spat blood in Vallée d'Or! Their hacking coughs harassed him in his sleep, broke the silence of his dreams.

'You mustn't spit on the ground, Maria, take my hand-kerchief.' He had wanted to add, 'That's all I can ever give you in your brief life.'

They died on their feet in Vallée d'Or. Only when the final agony began would Maria gain a place in her mother's bed.

'Maria used to talk to me in the evening, but what was she saying? I wasn't listening; I remember that the sound of her voice pained me. I couldn't look at her without feeling guilty.'

'M'sieur le curé, M'sieur le curé . . .'

That night other children called to him, but Maria was not among them. He had let her die inadvertently, by neglect.

The priest was suffocating in his room. The day was too long, the sun sinking slowly over the barren fields. Motionless at the window, he forgot to eat the meagre meal of bread and vegetables waiting on the table. He had been so overcome with loathing during the past few days that the bread on the table reminded him of the rotting flesh of Vallée d'Or. All around him, the same nakedness, the same drought reflected his inner turmoil. 'Lord, let me possess nothing but spiritual zeal, spare me all satisfaction . . .'—thus he had prayed in the humility of his youth. He looked at the iron bed against the white wall, the crucifix, the shabby table, and realized he had been living not in simplicity, but in avarice. 'Yes, I have lived this way because I dreaded the gaze of the things one possesses. Or rather, I dreaded being possessed by them.' Despising poverty, he had enjoyed its privileges, the honour that went with it. 'Those pious words that flowed so readily from the lips of the dying . . .'

'M'sieur le curé, our saviour!'

'M'sieur le curé, it's me, Tournemule!'

'What is it this time?' asked the priest as he opened his

door to the blind man, who was shaking with laughter.

'It's my mother, M'sieur le curé, she's asking for you, she's afraid she won't last the night.'

'She's always afraid of death at the end of the day. Tell her I'll come tomorrow.'

'But the more frightened she gets, the more she curses—like a devil, M'sieur le curé. Look how I'm shaking.'

'It's you who's afraid, Tournemule. Why lie about it?' Then, seeing the half-eaten bread on the table, 'Take this piece of bread, Tournemule, I have no appetite tonight.' A few minutes later he was walking ahead of Tournemule along the dusty road. The heat persisted, but night would come soon.

'My child, my child,' he said to the old woman raving in her dismal bed. 'It's late, it's time to repent.' But Tournemule's mother shrieked with anger, 'I'm thirsty, I don't want to die . . .' Suddenly her delirium shattered into a strange hilarity, a wild, almost criminal glee.

'You're mad,' said the priest. 'Be still.'

But she kept up her wild harangue: 'Tournemule tried to kill me, yes he did, once with a pick-axe, and another time with a hatchet. Tell the truth, Tournemule! Oh, I don't like him, that Tournemule, I should've put out his eyes, like a kitten!'

'She's thirsty,' said the priest. 'Give her a drink.'

With trembling hands Tournemule helped his mother to drink, then dipped one hand in the pail and gently stroked the old woman's cheeks and forehead with water.

'Poor mother, don't be afraid, I want to make you feel better.'

Perhaps remembering a long-forgotten habit, she touched his eyes as if he were a little child.

'I'm telling you, he tried to kill me, M'sieur le curé, this wicked creature. He tried to chop off my head, yes he did. Tell the curé the truth, Tournemule!'

'The time for hatred is past,' said the priest. 'Terrible hardships and misfortunes have brought you together. And who knows, maybe there's still a spark of affection left under the ashes . . . You must think of that now, only that . . .'
'Hypocrite,' he thought, 'I'm saying words I don't feel; perhaps I've never felt them, except today, facing Maria and her harsh dignity.'

The old woman died at dawn, accusing her son with blithe indecency, and giving way at last in a slow whirl of madness, mournful and broken.

That night he had a dream. He was purifying himself of his sins by setting fire to his church. But God demanded still more from him. He must become like the littlest child in Vallée d'Or; he must leave the priesthood and depart at last from the world of religious appearances in which he had been living; naked as a beggar in rags, sick and exhausted, he must take to the road and beg—not for the bread that no longer sustained his soul, but for the freshness, the truth, of one single act of pity.

'Tournemule, where are you going? I need you, or someone, anyone who can teach me poverty.' But Tournemule was pushing a black cart ahead of him. He could not see his face, only the thin shoulders twitching nervously.

'Look at me, Tournemule.'

'Too late, M'sieur le curé, night is falling and I must bury my poor old mother.'

He was singing like a drunkard:

> *Three cheers for mother hurray*
> *She goes to her grave today*
> *Three cheers for mother hurray*
> *The hatchet Tournemule Tournemule*
> *I've dreamed a long time . . .*

But the words of the song died away in the hot air. Soon Tournemule's whole silhouette vanished into the bushes. The priest knelt to pray, but not a word of gratitude to God came to his lips. He saw Maria walking towards him as she used to do. But this time it was she who offered bread to him. He wanted to speak to her, to keep her near him for a moment, for he had never felt so lost, so lonely, but Maria had already fled. He bit into the stale, tasteless bread, and as he ate, icy blood began to drip from between his fingers . . .

He woke up weeping, and told himself that the cowardly tears of his indifference were flowing at last. The release of his shame made him feel better, and for a moment he thought that before long he would be cured of his lack of compassion, that he could accomplish great things in Vallée d'Or. 'Yes, the people of Vallée d'Or will be proud of their curé.' But this arrogant thought plunged him again into melancholy, and he wept with sincere repentance. So he was still in love with that image of himself? That nothingness? Was that all he loved?

'Eat, eat this bread,' the voice in his dream had said.

And was this food bringing not life, but death? Recognizing his weakness was a miraculous awakening of consiousness—but would it keep him from lying, from concealing the hardness of his heart?

'I know that tomorrow again I'll say, "Tell me the truth, Tournemule", demanding virtues from him that I don't have myself. I'll go to Maria's mother and comfort her without love . . . I . . .'

But did God have pity? What did anyone know of that invisible compassion that expressed itself so rarely, so remotely? 'I know that God's compassion is a symbol. But if it were always there before me, a fervent, living example, I would not be able to go on committing the sin of injustice a hundred times a day.'

Sitting on the edge of his bed, he looked at his clean white hands.

'My hands will never be grey and withered like Tournemule's. I will never spit blood like Maria. God protects me too much!' Gradually he became indifferent to his own tears. It was hot in the room; flies stuck to the window. Dawn was coming up suffocating, the same as yesterday. And if the priest was suddenly stirred by a vague feeling of compassion, it was perhaps too late. No one was there to receive it.

Translated by Sally Livingston

MICHEL TREMBLAY

The Devil and the Mushroom

He was a big devil of a devil. Like all devils, he had a tail. A funny sort of tail. A devil's tail, a long tail that dragged on the ground. And ended in an arrowhead. In short, he was a big devil of a devil with a tail.

He was walking along the road and all the girls he met ran away holding their skirts. When they got home they cried: 'I've seen the Devil! The Devil is there, I saw him! I tell you, it's true!'

And the devil continued on his way. Looked at them running away and smiled.

He came to an inn. 'Something to drink,' cried the devil. He was given something to drink. The innkeeper was scared. 'Are you afraid of the Devil?' asked the devil. 'Yes,' replied the innkeeper timidly and the devil laughed. 'Your wine is good, innkeeper, I shall come back.' The innkeeper lowered his head as he wiped his hands on his innkeeper's apron. White. But dirty. With traces of sauces, of meats, of vegetables just pulled out of the ground, and of coal too, because the ovens have to be lit in the morning. 'This once,' thought the innkeeper, 'I should have preferred my wine to be less good.' And the devil, who read thoughts like all devils, laughed louder still and even slapped his thighs.

But someone had entered the inn and the devil fell silent. It was a boy. A young boy with a beautiful face. 'Where's that roll of drums coming from that I can hear?' asked the devil. 'I don't know,' replied the boy. 'This roll of drums has gone with me wherever I go ever since I was born and I don't know where it comes from. It's always like that. It's always with me.' The devil went up to the boy and sat down beside him on a bench. 'Are you a soldier?' asked the devil. That same moment the drumming stopped. 'A soldier? What's that?' asked the boy in his turn. 'What,' cried the devil, 'you don't know what a soldier is?' The innkeeper, who had gone back to his kitchen, returned to the parlour and said: 'I don't know what a soldier is either.'

'Well, come on,' cried the devil, 'come on! A soldier is someone who makes war!'

'War,' said the boy. 'What's that?'

'You don't know what war is?' asked the devil.

'No, that's a word I don't know,' replied the boy.

'That's quite a new word to us,' added the innkeeper.

Then the devil, in a fury, holding his head in his hands, yelled: 'Have I forgotten to invent war?'

In the road outside the inn a little girl was singing:

> *A woman opened the door.*
> *The Devil cried out: 'Die.'*
> *The woman was no more.*
> *Her soul to hell did fly.*

'I want a piece of charcoal,' cried the devil. The innkeeper brought him a piece. 'That's not big enough. I need a big piece of charcoal. I need the biggest piece of charcoal!' Then the innkeeper gave him the biggest piece of charcoal he had. 'That's not big enough yet,' said the devil. The innkeeper replied: 'There isn't a bigger piece. That's the biggest piece. The biggest I have.'

'Very well,' said the devil, annoyed, 'if that's the biggest piece you have . . .'

Then the devil climbed onto the table and made this speech: 'You who don't know what war is, open your ears wide.'

The inn parlour was full to bursting. So full the innkeeper had been forced to seat people on the ceiling. 'Look at this wall,' continued the devil. 'With this wretched piece of charcoal I will show you what war is.' Then, hurling himself at the wall, the devil started drawing furiously. The drawing he made was a drawing of a mushroom. A huge mushroom that covered the wall of the inn. When he had finished, the devil jumped back onto the table and declared: 'There you are. I've drawn you a war. A small war, because my piece of charcoal is too small for me to draw you a big one, a real one.' Everyone went off clapping and there was no one left but the devil, the boy and the innkeeper. 'But it's a mushroom,' said the boy, 'an ordinary mushroom. Do you mean a soldier is someone who grows mushrooms?'

'You don't understand anything,' said the devil, twirling his tail, 'nothing at all. That mushroom isn't an ordinary mushroom. Do you know what a gun is?'

'Yes,' replied the boy.

'Ah, at least there's one thing I didn't forget to invent. That's something. Have you a gun?'

'Yes.'

'Go and fetch it right away. The war can't wait. It's late enough as it is.'

The boy went off to fetch his gun, while the devil drank another bottle of wine (he was a rather drunk devil).

The innkeeper looked at the mushroom on the wall and scratched his head, thinking: 'Such a big mushroom . . . how economical.' And he went back to his kitchen.

The devil wasn't pleased with himself. 'Idiot,' he said, 'idiot, blockhead, numbskull that I am. That's why our affairs are going so badly! I forgot to invent war! Oh, well, they won't lose anything by waiting! I'll cook them up a real honey of a war! The real thing! So they don't know what war is! Devil's honour, they won't take long to learn!

The loveliest little war is going to burst in their faces . . .'

The boy was already back with his gun. When the devil saw the boy's gun, his anger doubled. They called that a gun? Did they take him for an idiot or what? All rusty! All filthy! There were even parts missing! The devil took hold of the gun and twisted it. The boy opened his eyes wide and said: 'Oh!'

The devil went to the fire, took the poker, blew on it and turned it into the finest gun anyone had ever seen. The boy said to the devil: 'Can I touch it?'

'Well, of course,' replied the devil. 'It's yours. I give it to you.' The boy thanked him. 'Don't thank me, that always disappoints me.'

The boy hugged and kissed the gun. He began to dance, holding it in his arms as if it were a woman. 'You love the gun, eh?' said the devil. 'Oh, yes,' replied the boy, dancing. The devil stopped him with a gesture and made him move back to the bench. 'What's the next country called? The country next door to yours?' he asked the boy. The boy seemed very surprised. 'The next country? But there isn't any next country. There's only one country, the world. The world is one country. Mine.' The devil slapped the boy so hard in the face that he spun round twice.

'Did anyone ever see such ignorant people!' roared the devil. 'The world one country? You're all mad. Listen, in order to have a war you need at least two countries. Let's say the village on the other side of the river is another country. An enemy country. And don't you tell me you don't know what the word enemy means or I'll give you another couple of swipes. You hate the people in the other village, you hate them with all your heart, do you understand?'

'But my fiancée . . .'

'Your fiancée too. Her more than the others. You hate them all and you want to kill them.'

The boy sprang to his feet. 'With my gun?' he cried. 'But that's impossible! We only use our guns to kill birds or animals . . .'

'You want to kill them with your gun because that's how the first war has to start. You will be the first soldier.'

'You mean you have to kill people to make war?' said the boy, looking at the mushroom.

'That's right. To make war means to kill people. Lots of people. You'll see what fun it is!'

'What about the mushroom?' asked the boy.

'The mushroom? That will come later. Much later. You may be dead by then.'

'Killed?'

'Probably.'

'In the war?'

'Yes.'

'Then I don't want to be a soldier. Not to make war.'

The devil climbed up onto the table and let out a terrible devil's bellow. 'You'll do what I tell you to do,' he then yelled at the boy.

The innkeeper came out of the kitchen. He was dragging behind him an enormous cauldron. 'I want you to tell me where I can find a mushroom as big as that one on the wall,' he said pointing to the mushroom. 'Go back to your kitchen, you ignorant man!' yelled the devil. 'It's not you that will eat that mushroom, it's the mushroom that will eat you.'

The devil got down off the table, took the boy by the shoulders, made him sit down and said to him: 'You're a man, so I suppose you like fighting . . . No, don't interrupt me, I understand. You never fought, right? If I wasn't damned already you would surely get me damned . . . Listen . . . You wouldn't like to see someone rise up in front of you that you had always disliked . . . There must be someone you're not particularly fond of . . . someone you could frankly hate and with whom you could fight . . . Didn't you ever feel the need to hate? The need to fight?' The boy answered in a low voice: 'Yes, I have felt the need and I'd like to fight with . . .'

'Who, who?' cried the devil.

'My fiancée's brother who opposes our marriage.'

Immediately the door of the inn opened and the fiancée's brother appeared. 'Get going,' the devil whispered in the boy's ear. 'Seize the opportunity. No one will see or hear you. Provoke him . . . say nasty things to him . . . the battle will come by itself.'

The boy rose, went up to his fiancée's brother and said something into his ear. The brother started and looked at the boy with big, questioning eyes. Then the boy spat in his face. The two men went out of the inn while the devil settled down at the window.

At the end of barely two minutes the boy came back into the inn. He was covered in dust and his clothes were spattered with blood. There was a light in the depths of his eyes and he was smiling. 'I've killed him,' he cried, 'I've killed him and I enjoyed seeing him die!'

A brass band invaded the courtyard of the inn. A brass band of devils who were playing tunes that soldiers like.

'Let us follow the band,' said the devil to the boy. 'Let us go to the next village and tell the peasants that you have killed their son. They will get out their guns . . . they'll try to attack you . . . your people will come and defend you. Come on, soldier, the war is waiting for us!'

The brass band, the devil and the soldier went off in the direction of the neighbouring village. And the band played fine tunes, and the devil danced, and the boy laughed . . . Then the soldier multiplied: two soldiers, then four soldiers, then eight, then sixteen, then thirty-two, then sixty-four, then a hundred and twenty-eight, then two hundred and fifty-six, then five hundred and twelve, then a thousand and twenty-four, then two thousand and forty-eight, then four thousand and ninety-six . . . There were curses, insults, then blows, then gunshots; people ran, hid, attacked, defended themselves, killed, fell down, got up, fell down again . . . The guns arrived; all sorts of guns, small ones, medium-sized ones, big ones, less small ones and bigger ones; then cannons, machine-guns, airplanes fitted with weapons, ships fitted with weapons, cars, trains, tractors, buses, fire engines, bicycles, scooters, baby carriages fitted with weapons . . . The struggle grew more and more violent, without ever stopping. It went on and on and on and on.

Then one day, when the sky was clear, the devil made a little sign with his hand and the mushroom appeared.

Translated by Michael Bullock

Biographical Notes

AQUIN, Hubert (1929-77). Born in Montreal, and a graduate of the Université de Montréal, Aquin studied at the Institut d'Études politiques in Paris. After holding various positions at Radio-Canada and the National Film Board, he worked as a stockbroker, later becoming an editor of *Liberté*, which he helped found, and literary director of *Les Éditions la Presse*. He committed suicide on 15 March 1977. Active in radical Québécois politics and an advocate of separatism, he left a collection of political essays and letters, *Points de fuite* (1971), and four novels: *Prochain épisode* (1965; Eng. trans. 1967), *Trou de mémoire* (1968; *Blackout*, 1974), *L'Antiphonaire* (1969; *The Antiphonary*, 1973), and *Neige noire* (1974; *Hamlet's Twin*, 1979). 'Back on April Eleventh', which prefigures Aquin's own death, first appeared in *Liberté* (March 1969).

AUBERT DE GASPÉ, Philippe-Ignace-François (1814-41). Born in Quebec City, Aubert de Gaspé studied at the Séminaire de Nicolet, and became a stenographer and journalist. With the help of his father, the author of *Les Anciens Canadiens*, he wrote the first French-Canadian novel, *L'Influence d'un livre* (1837). He worked as a journalist in Halifax, where he died prematurely at twenty-seven. 'Rose Latulipe', a complete tale taken from chapter five of *L'Influence d'un livre*, may have been largely written by Aubert de Gaspé the elder.

BESSETTE, Gérard (b. 1920). Born in Sainte-Anne-de-Sabrevois, Qué., Bessette received a doctorate from the Université de Montréal and has taught at the University of Saskatchewan, Duquesne University in Pittsburgh, the Royal Military College in Kingston, and Queen's University. Since

1979 he has devoted his time to writing. The author of both poetry and literary criticism, Bessette is best known for his novels, including *La Bagarre* (1958; *The Brawl*, 1978), *Les Pédagogues* (1960), *L'Incubation* (1965; *Incubation*, 1967), *Les Anthropoïdes* (1977), and *Le Semestre* (1979). His short stories, including 'The Mustard Plaster', were collected in *La Garden-party de Christophine* (1980).

BLAIS, Marie-Claire (b. 1939). Born in Quebec City, Blais has pursued a distinguished writing career since her first novel, *La Belle Bête* (1959; *Mad Shadows*, 1960), was published when she was only twenty. She lives in Montreal. Her work includes *Tête blanche* (1960; Eng. trans. 1974), the classic *Une saison dans la vie d'Emmanuel* (1965; *A Season in the Life of Emmanuel*, 1966), *Les Manuscrits de Pauline Archange* (1968; *The Manuscripts of Pauline Archange*, 1969), *Vivre! vivre!* (1969), *Les Apparences* (1970; *Dürer's Angel*, 1976), *L'Insoumise* (1966; *The Fugitive*, 1978), *David Sterne* (1967; Eng. trans. 1973), *Le Loup* (1972; *The Wolf*, 1974), *Une liaison parisienne* (1975; *A Literary Affair*, 1980), *Un joualonais sa joualonie* (1973; published in France as *A coeur joual*, 1974; *St Lawrence Blues*, 1974), *Les Nuits d'underground* (1978; *Nights in the Underground,* 1979), *Le Sourd dans la ville* (1979; *Deaf to the City*, 1980), and *Visions d'Anna* (1982). Blais has also published two collections of poetry, three plays, and several novellas.

CARRIER, Roch (b. 1937). Born in Sainte-Justine-de-Dorchester, Qué., Carrier studied at the Université de Montréal and received his doctorate from the Sorbonne. He has worked as secretary-general of Montreal's Théâtre du Nouveau Monde, and now combines teaching at Le Collège Militaire Royal de Saint-Jean with writing. His novels include *La Guerre, yes sir!* (1968; Eng. trans. 1970), *Floralie, où est-tu?* (1969; *Floralie, Where Are You?*, 1971), and *Le Jardin des délices* (1975; *The Garden of Delights*, 1978). Carrier has also written plays—adaptations of *La Guerre, yes sir!* (1970) and *Floralie* (1973), and *La Céleste Bicyclette* (1980; *The Celestial Bicycle*, 1982)—as well as several collections of short stories and tales, including his first published book, *Jolis deuils* (1964) and *Les Enfants du bonhomme dans la lune* (1979; *The Hockey Sweater and Other Stories*, 1979), from which 'What Language Do Bears Speak?' is taken.

DANTIN, Louis (Eugène Seers, 1865-1945). Eugène Seers, who used the pseudonym 'Louis Dantin', was born at Beauharnois, Canada East (Qué.). During a trip to Europe in 1883 he entered the novitiate of Les Pères du Saint-Sacrement in Brussels; he received a doctorate from the Gregorian University in Rome and was ordained a priest. After a distinguished ecclesiastical career abroad, Seers returned to Montreal and, during a crisis of faith, left the Church. He moved to Boston, married, and worked there as a compositor and typographer. Eventually employed by the Harvard University Press, Seers died in Cambridge, Mass. His work includes such books of literary criticism as the series *Poètes de l'Amérique française* (1928 and 1934); numerous critical essays and prefaces, including one for *Émile Nelligan et son oeuvre* (1903); three volumes of short stories—*La Vie en rêve* (1930), *Contes de Noël* (1936), and *L'Invitée* (1936); over five thousand poems, published after his death as *Poèmes d'outre-tombe* (1962); and a posthumous autobiographical novel, *Les Enfances de Fanny* (1951). 'You're Coughing?' is taken from *La Vie en rêve*.

FERRON, Jacques (b. 1921). Born in Louiseville, Qué., Ferron received his medical degree from Université Laval. After practising medicine on the Gaspé Peninsula, he worked in Montreal and is now a family doctor in Longueuil. Actively involved in politics, Ferron has written plays, including *Les Grands Soleils* (1958); such novels as *La Barbe de François Hertel* (1951), *Cotnoir* (1962; *Doctor Cotnoir*, 1973), *Le Ciel de Québec* (1969), and *Le Saint-Élias* (1972; *The Saint Elias*, 1975); and several collections of legends, fables, and stories, including *Contes du pays incertain* (1962), which was republished in 1968 with *Contes anglais et autres* and *Contes inédits*. A selection of these stories was translated as *Tales from the Uncertain Country* (1972), from which 'Mélie and the Bull' is taken.

FRÉCHETTE, Louis (1838-1908). Born at Hadlow Cove, near Lévis, Qué., Fréchette studied law at Université Laval and helped found two short-lived Liberal newspapers before moving to Chicago, in 1866, where he worked for the Illinois Central Railroad and founded more newspapers. He returned to Lévis in 1871 and was elected to the House of Commons as a Liberal member (1874-8). His marriage to Emma Beaudray, the daughter of a wealthy Montreal family, gave Fréchette the financial freedom to concentrate on his writing. The author of many collections of poetry, including *La Légende d'un peuple* (1887), his major work of historical poems, and *Feuilles volantes* (1890), Fréchette also wrote several plays, including *Papineau* (1880), and political journalism for *La Patrie*, the Montreal Liberal newspaper. His prose works include a collection of short stories, *Christmas in French Canada* (1899), published the following year as *Le Noël au Canada*. 'Tom Cariboo', taken from this collection, is Fréchette's own translation of his story.

GRANDBOIS, Alain (1900–75). Born in Saint-Casimir de Portneuf, Qué., Grandbois studied law at Université Laval before beginning his travels abroad, between the two world wars, in Europe, Russia, Africa, India, China, and Japan. After returning to Canada in 1939, he worked as a lecturer and writer, spending the final years of his life in Quebec City, where he was employed by the Musée de la Province de Québec. One of Québec's finest poets, Grandbois also wrote several biographies of explorers, accounts of his travels, and one collection of short stories, *Avant le chaos* (1945), republished with four additional stories in 1964, from which 'May Blossom' is taken.

HÉBERT, Anne (b. 1916). Born at Sainte-Catherine-de-Fossambault, Qué., she worked (as did her cousin, Hector de Saint-Denys-Garneau) as a writer for the National Film Board in Montreal before moving to Paris, where she now resides. Hébert has produced several collections of poetry, including *Les Songes en équilibre* (1942) and *Le Tombeau des rois* (1953); plays; novels, including *Kamouraska* (1970; Eng. trans. 1974), *Les Enfants du sabbat* (1975; *Children of the Black Sabbath,* 1977) and *Héloïse* (1982; Eng. trans. 1982); and a collection of short stories, *Le Torrent* (1950), which was reissued with four new stories in 1963 and translated in 1967. 'The Torrent' is the title story of this collection.

JASMIN, Claude (b. 1930). Born in Montreal, Jasmin studied at the École des Arts appliqués. He has worked as an actor, art teacher, potter, television designer, and director of the literary and art pages of the *Journal de Montréal*. He has written nine novels, including *Ethel et le terroriste* (1964; *Ethel and the Terrorist*, 1965), *Revoir Ethel* (1976), and *La Sablière* (1979); plays, autobiographical sketches, essays, and social commentaries; and one collection of short stories, *Les Coeurs empaillés* (1967), from which 'Lulu the Tailor' is taken.

KATTAN, Naim (b. 1928). Born in Baghdad, Iraq, Kattan studied at the University of Baghdad and at the Sorbonne before moving to Montreal in 1954. He is now the head of the Canada Council's literary section in Ottawa. A prodigious writer, Kattan has produced books of essays, including *Le Réel et le théâtral* (1970; *Reality and Theatre*, 1972); novels, including the autobiographical *Adieu, Babylone* (1975; *Farewell, Babylon*, 1976), and *Les Fruits arrachés* (1977; *Paris Interlude*, 1979); and several collections of short stories—*Dans le désert* (1974), *La Traversée* (1976), *Le Rivage* (1979), and *Le Sable de l'île* (1981). 'The Neighbour' is the title story of a selection of Kattan's work in translation: *The Neighbour and Other Stories* (1982).

LABERGE, Albert (1877-1960). Born in Beauharnois, Qué., Laberge was drawn to the priesthood but rejected it for the study of law. He began working at Montreal's *La Presse* in 1896, remaining there for thirty-six years as a sports writer and also an art critic. He retired to Châteauguay in 1932 and devoted himself to writing. Laberge's many published books of short stories and sketches include *Visages de la vie et de la mort* (1936), *La Fin du voyage* (1942), *Le Destin des hommes* (1950), and *Le Dernier Souper* (1953). He also wrote the novel *La Scouine* (1918), considered to be Canada's first realistic novel; three volumes of memoirs; art and literary criticism, including *Propos sur nos écrivains* (1954); as well as poetry. *Anthologie d'Albert Laberge* (1963), a selection of his work that includes thirteen short stories, was introduced by Gérard Bessette. 'The Patient' is taken from *Visages de la vie et de la mort*.

LEMAY, Pamphile (1837-1918). Born in Lotbinière, Lower Canada, Lemay enrolled at the seminary of the Université d'Ottawa but withdrew from the priesthood, because of illness, and studied law. He worked as a parliamentary translator and librarian and was a founding member of the Royal Society of Canada. He was a prolific writer, producing several volumes of poetry, including *Les Gouttelettes* (1904); essays; novels, including *Le Pélerin de Sainte-Anne* (1877), *Piconouc le maudit*

(1878), and *L'Affaire sougraine* (1884), one of the first detective novels in Québec; and translations of Longfellow's *Evangeline* and William Kirby's novel *The Golden Dog*. His major prose work was *Contes vrais* (1899), from which 'Blood and Gold' is taken.

LEMELIN, Roger (b. 1919). Born in Quebec City, Lemelin worked at various jobs before joining the staff of Montreal's *La Presse*, where he is now publisher and president. His four novels are *Au pied de la pente douce* (1947; *The Town Below*, 1958), the popular *Les Plouffe* (1948; *The Plouffe Family*, 1950), which served as the basis of the CBC television series and film (1980), *Pierre le magnifique* (1952; *In Quest of Splendour*, 1955), and *Le Crime d'Ovide Plouffe* (1982). He also wrote a book of reminiscences, *La Culotte en or* (1980), and one collection of short stories, *Fantaisies sur les péchés capitaux* (1940), from which 'The Stations of the Cross' is taken.

MAHEUX-FORCIER, Louise (b. 1929). Born in Montreal, Maheux-Forcier studied music in Quebec and Paris before attending the Université de Montréal. In 1959 she turned from a career in music to writing, and has since produced five novels: *Amadou* (1963), *L'Île joyeuse* (1965), *Une forêt pour Zoé* (1969), *Paroles et musiques* (1973), and *Appassionata* (1978). 'The Carnation,' presented here in a new translation, is taken from her collection of short stories *En toutes lettres* (1980: *Letter by Letter*, 1982).

MAILLET, Antonine (b. 1929). Born in Buctouche, N.B., Maillet received a doctorate from Université Laval, where she now teaches. Her novels and stories of Acadian life, past and present, include *Pointe-aux-Coques* (1958), *La Sagouine* (1971; Eng. trans. 1979), a series of interlocking monologues, widely performed in both French and English by Viola Léger; *Don l'Orignal* (1972), and *Pélagie-la-charrette* (1980; *Pelagie: The Return to a Homeland*, 1982). For this novel Maillet won the Prix Goncourt, becoming the first non-French recipient of that award. She has also written plays, including *Évangéline Deusse* (1977), and a travel book, *L'Acadie pour quasiment rien* (1973). 'Two Saints' is taken from a collection of sketches and portraits, *Par derrière chez mon père* (1972).

MARTIN, Claire (b. 1914). Born in Quebec City, Martin worked as a radio announcer for Radio-Canada before turning to a career in writing while living in Ottawa and Europe. She now lives in Quebec City. Martin has published one collection of short stories, *Avec ou sans amour* (1958); novels, including *Doux-amer* (1960) and *Quand j'aurai payé ton visage* (1962); and two widely read memoirs, *Dans un gant de fer* (1965; *In an Iron Glove*, 1973), and *La Joue droite* (1966; *The Right Cheek*, 1975). Since 1972 she has translated English-Canadian books into French, including Margaret Laurence's *The Stone Angel* (*L'Ange de pierre*, 1976). 'The Gift' is taken from *Avec ou sans amour*.

RINGUET (Philippe Panneton, 1895-1960). Philippe Panneton, who used his mother's family name, Ringuet, as his pseudonym, was born in Trois-Rivières, Qué. He received his medical degree from the Université de Montréal, practised medicine in that city, and became a professor in the faculty of medicine of the Université de Montréal in 1935. President of the French-Canadian Academy from 1947 to 1953, he was appointed Ambassador to Portugal in 1956 and died there. His books of fiction include several novels—the classic *Trente arpents* (1938; *Thirty Acres*, 1940), *Fausse monnaie* (1947), and *Le Poids du jour* (1949)—as well as a collection of short stories, *L'Heritage et autres contes* (1946), from which 'The Heritage' is taken.

ROY, Gabrielle (1909-83). Born in Saint-Boniface, Man., Roy studied at the Winnipeg Normal School. She taught in rural Manitoba and travelled in Europe prior to the Second World War, after which she devoted herself to writing. Her novels include the famous *Bonheur d'occasion* (1945; *The Tin Flute*, 1947), *Alexandre Chênevert* (1955; *The Cashier*, 1955), and *La Montagne secrète* (1961; *The Hidden Mountain*, 1962). She also wrote several volumes of linked stories—*La Petite Poule d'eau* (1950; *Where Nests the Water Hen*, 1950), *Rue Deschambault* (1955; *Street of Riches*, 1957), and *La Route d'Altamont* (1966; *The Road Past Altamont*, 1966)—and several collections of short stories and sketches, including *Un jardin au bout du monde* (1975; *Garden in the Wind*, 1977, reissued as *Enchanted Summer*, 1982). A selection of three decades of Roy's non-fiction appeared as *Fragiles lumières de la terre* (1975; *Fragile Lights of Earth*, 1983). 'Ely! Ely! Ely!' was first published in *Liberté*

(May 1979), and later in English in *Canadian Fiction Magazine* (no. 34/35, 1980).

THÉRIAULT, Yves (b. 1915). Born in Quebec City, as a young boy Thériault learned Cree from his father, an Acadian of partly Montagnais Indian ancestry. Thériault has worked as a radio announcer, public-relations officer, and script writer for the National Film Board, and as cultural director for the Department of Indian and Northern Affairs in Ottawa. At present a co-director of a film company, he lives in the Laurentians, west of Joliette, Qué. He is a prolific writer, producing novels, including *La Fille laide* (1950), *Aaron* (1954), and several classics about the Canadian North: *Agaguk* (1958; Eng. trans. 1967), *Ashini* (1960; Eng. trans. 1972), and *N'Tusk* (1968; Eng. trans. 1972); and, over a forty-year period, more than a thousand short stories, most of which are still unpublished. Thériault's collections of stories include *Le Vendeur d'étoiles et autres contes* (1961), *L'Île introuvable* (1968), *Oeuvre de chair* (1975), and *La Femme Anna et autres contes* (1981), from which 'The Whale' is taken.

TREMBLAY, Michel (b. 1942). Born in Montreal, Tremblay studied graphic arts and worked as a linotype operator before his first play, *Le Train* (1964), was produced. Tremblay is the best-known Québécois playwright in Canada and most of his plays have been translated and performed in English. Among them are *Les Belles-soeurs* (1968; Eng. trans. 1974), *Hosanna* (1973; 1974), *Bonjour, là, bonjour* (1974; 1975), and *Sainte Carmen de la Main* (1976; 1981). (Tremblay himself has translated plays by Aristophanes, Paul Zindel, and Tennessee Williams.) As a fiction writer, Tremblay has produced several novels, including *La Grosse Femme d'à côté est enceinte* (1978; *The Fat Woman Next Door is Pregnant*, 1981), and *Thérèse et Pierrette à l'École des Saints-Anges* (1980; *Thérèse and Pierrette at the École des Saints-Anges*, 1982), and a collection of short stories, *Contes pour buveurs attardés* (1966; *Stories for Late Night Drinkers*, 1978), from which 'The Devil and the Mushroom' is taken.